THE NEWS EVENT

T0244623

The News Event

POPULAR SOVEREIGNTY IN THE
AGE OF DEEP MEDIATIZATION

Francis Cody

University of Chicago Press
Chicago and London

The University of Chicago Press, Chicago 60637
The University of Chicago Press, Ltd., London
© 2023 by The University of Chicago
Published 2023
Printed in the United States of America

32 31 30 29 28 27 26 25 24 23   1 2 3 4 5

ISBN-13: 978-0-226-82473-4 (cloth)
ISBN-13: 978-0-226-82472-7 (paper)
ISBN-13: 978-0-226-82474-1 (e-book)
DOI: https://doi.org/10.7208/chicago/9780226824741.001.0001

Library of Congress Cataloging-in-Publication Data
Names: Cody, Francis, 1976- author.
Title: The news event : popular sovereignty in the age of deep
mediatization / Francis Cody.
Other titles: Popular sovereignty in the age of deep mediatization
Description: Chicago ; London : The University of Chicago Press, 2023. |
Includes bibliographical references and index.
Identifiers: LCCN 2022039070 | ISBN 9780226824734 (cloth) |
ISBN 9780226824727 (paperback) | ISBN 9780226824741 (ebook)
Subjects: LCSH: Mass media—Political aspects—India—Tamil Nadu. |
Digital media—Political aspects—India—Tamil Nadu. |
Journalism—Political aspects—India—Tamil Nadu. |
Tamil Nadu (India)—Politics and government—21st century.
Classification: LCC P95.82.I4 C63 2021 | DDC 079/.5482—dc23/eng/20221014
LC record available at https://lccn.loc.gov/2022039070

Contents

INTRODUCTION

In the Event of News

"They're gonna kill me! They're gonna kill me!" yelled the elderly man in
Tamil as the police dragged him forcefully from his bed. It was the middle
of the night. M. Karunanidhi, one of the most recognizable faces in Indian
politics, was arrested over allegations of corruption in his house in Chennai
at 1:45 a.m. on June 30, 2001. Shaky, flashlight-lit footage of the frail seventy-
eight-year-old patriarch of the Tamil-nationalist movement getting roughed
up and the sounds of his hoarse screaming are etched into Tamil Nadu's collective memory. I was shocked seeing the one-minute news clip on television
that morning. I imagine these images must have affected anyone who happened to watch national news programs in the rest of India that day. Everyone
knew that the Chennai City police were executing the commands of Karunanidhi's bitter rival, the newly reelected chief minister of Tamil Nadu, J. Jayalalithaa. She had been jailed for a month on charges of corruption a few years
earlier, under Karunanidhi's rule. In her estimation, the time for revenge had
arrived. A triumphant Jayalalithaa was pictured in the daily press soon after
the arrest, gifting an elephant to the famous Guruvayur Sri Krishna temple in
gratitude for her party's majority in the state assembly elections.

Jayalalithaa's victory was short lived, however. She did not anticipate that
a young cameraman named Mari from Sun TV News would be at the scene
of the arrest. More importantly, the chief minister appeared to have miscal-
culated how shows of sovereignty work in the then newly emerging media
environment of twenty-four-hour news broadcasts. The footage of police
brutality against the aging leader had been playing on a constant loop on Sun
TV throughout the morning following the "midnight arrest," as it had come

to be known. I was studying Tamil in preparation for dissertation research in the southern city of Madurai at the time. Every household I visited was glued to the screen all day long. Those who didn't have televisions at home gathered in front of the neighborhood tea stalls that did, staring in disbelief. My language classes had been canceled, and stores were shuttered in anticipation of violence across the state. By the afternoon, the repetition of Karunanidhi's arrest sequence was interspersed with scenes of crowds taking to the streets to vent their anger at the vengeful arrogance of the state's new leader. The press, meanwhile, inevitably invoked comparisons with Indira Gandhi's authoritarian declaration of a state of emergency across India twenty-six years earlier.

The television news station that had captured and broadcasted this image of personalized state violence was, in fact, founded just one year earlier by Karunanidhi's own grandnephew. Sun TV News had become the most watched news channel in the state. It was closely associated in everyone's mind with Karunanidhi's political party, the Dravida Munnetra Kazhagam (DMK), or Dravidian Progress Federation, even sharing the party's iconic logo depicting a rising sun. While Jayalalithaa's own party channel, Jaya TV, did its utmost to provide a counterframing of the event as a response to a corrupt political family obstructing justice, they failed to control the public narrative for any but Jayalalithaa's most ardent followers—those who would only come to admire her strength of will more than ever, as the arrest turned into a polarizing political spectacle.

By the evening of July 1, the moving image captured by Sun TV had spread beyond the state of Tamil Nadu to the whole country of India and done its crucial work. Public discontent with Jayalalithaa's actions before television screens and in the streets of Tamil Nadu had refracted into a confrontation with the central Government of India in Delhi. The ruling Bharatiya Janata Party (BJP) government, which was in an alliance with the DMK at the time, forced the governor of Tamil Nadu to resign for lack of independent oversight and sent a delegation from the Home Ministry to Chennai. Charges were then dropped against two DMK ministers, who had also been arrested the following day, after they refused to accept an offer of bail. Karunanidhi remained in judicial custody for five days, also rejecting bail, during which time judges found no evidence against him. In a final effort to rescue her claim to sovereignty under such compromised conditions, Jayalalithaa asserted that it was she who had released Karunanidhi on "purely humanitarian grounds," considering his "advanced age." In the words of an editorial titled "The Midnight Knock that Boomeranged," published in India's newspaper of record, the *Hindu*, "the hunter became the hunted." The chief minister's efforts to assert her image as a powerful leader of the Tamil people had been turned against her in the judo-like combat sport that is political publicity in the age of deep mediatization.

News media represent events happening in the world, but, in the very act of representation they can also provoke a change in the situation. Some well-known examples of news having a significant influence include the *Washington Post*'s reporting on a break-in at the Democratic National Committee office at the Watergate Hotel playing a role in the premature termination of Richard Nixon's presidency, or how a major weapons contract involving corruption at the highest levels of government in India—broken by the *Hindu* and known as the "Bofors Scandal"—did irreparable damage to the reputation of the Congress Party, which had long prided itself as leader of the nation's independence movement under Gandhi and Nehru. Nehru's own grandson, Prime Minister Rajiv Gandhi, was implicated. In a different register, the televisual force of Jayalalithaa's midnight arrest blunder could also be said to have cost her a great deal of political clout, shamed as she was by the national government and eventually rejected by voters in the next assembly elections.

Texts and images can certainly do things under the right conditions. However, to assume that the revelatory powers of news disclosures change the course of history is to obscure crucial aspects of how media produce news events in the public sphere.[1] The performativity of news works in both directions, through acts of circulating information publicly that also invite those represented in the news to shape that very representation in pursuit of particular ends. People regularly perform for the news. (We can surmise that Karunanidhi was screaming, at least in part, for the camera without diminishing the cruelty of the attack.) The popular phrase *media event* points to the fact that we have long recognized conditions in which events are staged in anticipation of recording by news cameras and reporters.[2] Leaks, misinformation, and manufactured crises are common political tactics. And journalism might incite actions from those subjects it represents as well as from consumers of the news. Journalists and institutions of news production—as important as they are for society to objectify itself, to think critically about itself and the state—are deeply conditioned by milieus of capital, technology, and law shaping their contributions to the field of politics. This constantly changing ecology of forces encourages dynamics of performativity and the emergence of feedback loops that are more complicated, and for that reason more interesting, than the model of news as disclosure might suggest—now, in the age of digital media and its network effects, more than ever before.

So, how are news events made? In answering this question, *The News Event* investigates the deep entanglements connecting news media with the world they represent. Drawing from the archive of notable news events in Tamil Nadu, a state that has long led the way in media-saturated politics in India, it seeks to understand reciprocal energies animating relationships between the events being reported in the news and events of news coverage. In doing so, this ethnographic history develops a concept of "the news event" to grasp moments when the news itself can be said to become an event in its own right. I do so because imaginaries of popular sovereignty have been remade through the production and experience of such events. Political sovereignty is thoroughly mediated by the production of news. And subjects invested in the idea of democracy are remarkably reflexive about the role of publicly circulating images and texts in the very constitution of their subjectivity. This book examines the news event as a way to understand the often-fuzzy limits of what is permissible to represent as news in public and with the remarkable consequences that ensue when such thresholds are crossed. The law comes to stand as both a limit and positive condition in this process of event making, where acts of legal and extralegal repression of publication can also become the stuff of news about news makers. Perhaps it is because of the very centrality of mass mediation to the modern political imagination that the media— their technologies of recording and circulation, how they construct reality, how they cause reactions in people and governments, and whether their representations conform to juridical norms—have become an increasingly important topic in the news, opening ethical and political questions about the means, ends, and effects of journalism.

Public concerns about the role of journalism in shaping the political field through acts of representation are old, but they have changed and sharpened over time. Part of the story told in this book is therefore about the transformation of politics in Tamil Nadu over the past few decades of technological upheaval. Twenty years ago, in an age when privately owned cable-news television was still brand-new to India, most reporting in the press on the midnight arrest of Karunanidhi gave as much importance to Sun TV's brutal images of the event (making the arrest the political problem it became for Jayalalithaa) as it did to the legal dimensions of the arrest itself. Television was already an integral part of the story of the event, as it had become difficult to disentangle the motives and effects of media coverage from the broader politics of the event. Sun TV's news editor at the time of Karunanidhi's arrest,

A. S. Panneerselvan, told me he was proud of his team's "sharp, critical journalism," invoking professional distance from the event while admitting that their coverage certainly "resonated with people." Others found fault with the looping footage, calling it a form of party propaganda that played on viewers' emotions while dodging the deeper problem of political corruption. The Chennai police commissioner, for his part, sought an injunction against Sun TV for telecasting "objectionable material," and reporters from the station were harassed by police in the days following the arrest.[3] In response to critics, the editor argued that the Sun TV coverage played a relatively minor role in Jayalalithaa's subsequent misfortunes, while many in the industry and beyond remember the recorded arrest as a new type of media event that forever altered the contours of Tamil politics. Debates on the role of media technologies in representing reality, provoking violence, modulating affect, and mediating politics have only intensified since, even while we are becoming ever more aware of the fact that it was never the case that journalists simply reported about the world "out there" from a safe distance. The rapid layering of new media technologies that has occurred over the last two decades has come to play a defining role in what counts as news. Now, in an age of digital media that raises more profound questions about who or what really controls the circulation of information, distinctions between the event of representation and the events being represented in the news have become more problematic than ever.

The very event-punctuated experience of contemporary life appears internal to the logic of what Ravi Sundaram terms the *circulation engine*: a proliferating digital media sphere that has erased earlier postcolonial distinctions between the world of politics and carefully regulated sites of news production.[4] Compared to India, the integration of practices of news production and commodity rationalities demanding maximum circulation might have taken place earlier elsewhere. But the crisis of confidence in our capacity to distinguish events from their reporting is certainly now global and long term, and it goes beyond even the question of politics. Old questions about how mass mediation shapes our very experience of what is really happening in the world have taken on a new urgency. Reflecting on his earlier thesis on the society of the spectacle, founding member of Situationist International, Guy Debord, for example, argues that the spectacle "integrated itself into reality to the same extent as it was describing it, and that it was reconstructing it as it was describing it. As a result, this reality no longer confronts the integrated spectacle as something alien."[5] Indeed, media theory has a history dating to the 1970s of debating the question of media saturation. For Jean Baudrillard, consumption-based society had "reached that stage at which the commodity is immediately produced as a sign, as sign-value, and signs (culture) as commodities."[6] Paul Virilio, for his part, conceptualized technological convergences in media as "de-realization" in the fashioning of a "synthetic space-time," where the "electronic day" replaces sunlight while obliterating our sense of belonging to a place.[7] These thinkers leave little room for claims to experience that are not always already part of the late capitalist event-making media engine.

It is not only prophets of the postmodern condition who were concerned about the collapse of the constitutive distinctions underpinning political modernity. In fact, the very same thinkers of the public sphere who have argued that news media, and print in particular, acted as a positive condition for society to imagine itself in democratic terms have also theorized the negative dialectic though which commodified media logics subsume possibilities for collective agency first experienced through print.[8] More recently, elaborations of these narratives have come to recognize that news media and associated culture industries serve to deceive people into thinking that they are acting in the world when they are, in fact, consuming it. Theorists of digital capitalism like Jodi Dean, Yann Moulier-Boutang, and Shoshana Zuboff have all argued, in different ways, that these media also act as infrastructure for a regime of exchange value that generates profit through the circulation of information while claiming to enable critical engagement and dialogue on scales previously unthinkable.[9]

And yet, for all of these important critiques, it is clear that imaginations of popular sovereignty are often sustained by some faith in the self-organizing quality of publics that come into being because they are addressed by the news media, even if serving as ideological grease for a capitalist machine that trades in signs. The effects of this faith tying political capacities to media technology are very real, and the tolls of cynicism are very high. We are becoming more and more concerned with the problematic status of media as the habitat within which action is afforded with the rise of new media technologies, and for very good reasons. But our worries are fueled in large part because of the high value we attribute to forms of belonging and action that are enabled only by these very same media. It remains difficult to imagine aspirations for a more democratic life without some theory of how the mass or networked mediation of collective action might make such a world possible.

This book argues that moments of event making—when news becomes the eventful subject of further news—must claim a central place in any such theory of mediation. This process of event making is conceptualized here as more than a disturbance in the normal relationship between events in the world and their representation in the news. The widely distributed capacity of media to report on their own circulation and thereby produce events in the world is a fundamental condition of possibility under which contemporary political life unfolds. It is therefore not only from outside of the capitalist media machine that possibilities for claims to popular sovereignty lie but just as importantly from emergent domains of difference generated within it, however we might theorize the limits of such an apparatus. What McKenzie Wark terms *the kinds of addressable space* produced by the evolution of new media technologies can, in fact, "afford kinds of situations, moments, occupations, or events that were not anticipated in their design and are discovered by accident or experiment."[10] A study of the increasingly chaotic world of news media has much to contribute to our understanding of such affordances inasmuch as they constitute a great deal of our very experience of reality. In more practical terms, we can note that in southern India and elsewhere people have not yet given up on the capacity of news media to represent the world while recognizing that media are very much enmeshed in, even conditioned by, the late capitalist world they represent. Events of political import involving collective will mediated by journalism still occur, and the fact that there are more news channels, papers, and websites now than ever before indicates a continued public investment in the genre.[11]

Media Politics in Tamil India

Tamil Nadu is unusual in the extent to which politics has been entangled with mass media from the very beginnings of democratization. Many of the most important anticolonial nationalist and anticaste newspapers in India were based in Madras (now Chennai), and the Dravidian movement against North Indian and Brahmin domination that has defined politics in Tamil Nadu since the mid-twentieth century would be unthinkable without a robust press, platform oratory broadcast over vast spaces through amplification, and one of the world's largest film industries. M. Karunanidhi, whose arrest is recounted in the opening vignette, built a political career that powerfully illustrates these entanglements. Popularly known as Kalaiñar (Artist), he began his public life by starting a newspaper while still a teenager in the early 1940s, and he burst onto the wider political stage through two media spectacles: (1) in 1952, as a scriptwriter for the classic Tamil-nationalist film *Parasakti*, and (2) through a sensational protest the following year, where the young man lay down on the railroad tracks demanding that the town of Dalmiapuram, so named after the Rajasthani industrialist who had set up a factory there, be called by its Tamil name, Kallakudi. Karunanidhi would go on to become the chief minister of Tamil Nadu five times over a political career stretching across nearly seven decades. He was a quintessential man of the public. His paper, *Murasoli* (Sound of the drum), remains an important organ of the movement. And the "Artist" himself was a great public speaker in addition to being one of the most prolific writers in the modern history of the Tamil language—ranging from high literature to journalism, popular films, and television serials—until he passed away in 2018.

Karunanidhi's party, the DMK, was founded by another talented tactician and wordsmith, C. N. Annadurai, also known as Ariñar (Scholar), the first major leader to definitively break with Gandhian abhorrence of modern technologies of communication and unabashedly embrace mass media as an arena for politics. A series of massively popular hit films written by Karunanidhi, Annadurai, and their followers secured a new hegemony in Tamil politics defined by a Dravidian aesthetic in which the ancient civilizational past of the Tamils was deployed through modern media to interpellate the masses as newly empowered subjects of democracy.[12] As the DMK outflanked the once-dominant Congress Party over the course of the 1950s and 1960s, they dropped earlier secessionist demands for a separate Tamil or Dravidian nation-state, doubling down on regional nationalism based on claims to language and ethnicity within, and against, the Indian state. During this time, every one of their leaders started their own newspapers to push the cause of Tamil non-Brahminism.[13] By the 1980s Karunanidhi's nephew Murasoli Maran had taken over as editor of his uncle's newspaper (which he had named himself after), also launching a number of other papers and popular magazines.[14] And by the 1990s Maran's son Kalanidhi expanded the political family's imprint across media technologies, founding the Sun Media Group, among the first entrants into the world of privately owned television in India, which quickly became one of the most profitable media empires in Asia. Upon winning the state assembly elections in 2006, the DMK government distributed free color television sets to every household below the poverty line, closing the circuit connecting production to consumption while introducing the idea that access to broadcast media now stands among the primary measures of socioeconomic development and well-being. The fact that Maran's other son, Dayanidhi, would become union minister of communications and information technology in Delhi from 2004 to 2007, at the very beginning of India's massive cell phone boom, certainly helped the family and their party establish even greater control over the distribution of information.

It was much earlier, however, with the rise of the DMK star actor M. G. Ramachandran, known as MGR, in the 1960s that the dynamics of media spectacle had already begun to envelop that of the Dravidian ideology that had gained so much political ground through its instrumental use of the media. As an actor and leading member of the DMK, MGR rode to super-stardom through films in which he played a poor laborer, fighting the rich on behalf of the masses, as his own star power grew larger than the charisma of the party with which he was associated.[15] Each film became a claim to representation for MGR, invoking that elusive "direct connection with the people" that forms the rhetorical foundation of populism through his persona on-screen and off. After falling out with Karunanidhi, it was therefore easy for MGR to found his own party in 1972: the Anna Dravida Munnetra Kazhagam (ADMK), later renamed the All India Anna Dravida Munnetra Kazhagam (AIADMK). Continuing to act in films, by the time he became chief minister, in 1977, MGR inhabited a domain of personal sovereignty that far exceeded his office or the very parliamentary state that lent this office authority qua office. The party built through his cinematic charisma and MGR led the state of Tamil Nadu from that point until his death in 1987. After a brief interregnum of DMK rule, his protégé and fellow actor Jayalalithaa—who would later send Karunanidhi to jail—became chief minister of Tamil Nadu in 1991, trading in her own cinematic fame for political power and thus establishing a solid pattern of what the film theorist M. Madhav Prasad has conceptualized as "cine-politics," an imaginary of popular sovereignty in which cinema stars have enjoyed an extraparliamentary power as legitimate leaders of the Tamil people.[16] From that point until her death in 2016, the state of Tamil Nadu was ruled either by the actress-turned-"Amma" (Mother) Jayalalithaa, holder of this executive office a total of five times, or her nemesis, Karunanidhi.

In the absence of an independent Tamil nation-state, both Dravidianist parties have cultivated a mass-mediated public culture founded on an "idea of polity, which is a virtual—sensual, but not abstract—space of the commons," to borrow from Lauren Berlant in a different context, for over half a century within the official structure of Indian federalism.[17] Emulating the DMK's Sun TV model, the AIADMK started Jaya TV in 1999, and the party also boasts a number of popular news and entertainment publications similar to those run by the extended family ruling the DMK. While the Maran family's Sun Media Group had a near monopoly on distribution in the early days of satellite television, the government of Tamil Nadu nationalized access to television through Arasu Cable during a family squabble within the DMK in 2008. This move, initiated by Jayalalithaa and then pursued by Karunanidhi, would later grant Jayalalithaa the power to shut off stations that circulated unfavorable news about the leader and her party.[18] Through aggressive use of crowd violence (discussed in chapter 1) and legal repression (discussed in chapters 2 and 3) to regulate the contours of what can be published or said on television, both parties have pursued politics built through their media empires while forcing any party that tried to break into electoral politics in the state to launch their own television channels, often running at substantial losses. It was only in the 2010s that nonparty news channels began to operate, coupled with the rise of lateral communication technologies (discussed in chapters 4 and 5) that nevertheless had to contend with a deeply politicized field of news production and distribution indelibly shaped by the ethos of Dravidianism.

The concept of "mediatization" is useful to understand how the political field in Tamil Nadu and elsewhere has been shaped by a rapidly changing sociotechnological environment while taking into account the degree to which mass media have also been purposefully developed by parties as an arena for highly aestheticized political representation. Defined for our purposes as the process through which mass and networked mediation exert a specific force on the whole of social life, *mediatization* has certainly taken on extreme qualities in Tamil politics. Parties and leaders played an uncommonly dominant and early role in the production, distribution, and even the consumption of news and other forms of political publicity. And the blending of politics with entertainment in Tamil Nadu would appear to have provided a model for forms of populism that were to develop later in other parts of India. Twenty-first century politics in other regions are equally invested in media without this long history of cine-politics and party ownership.

In national politics the BJP's brand of Hindu nationalism has remade the media sphere and news production in more recent decades, forcing a homogenized vision of India that owes a great deal to the rise of state-controlled televisual media in the 1980s.[19] The politics of *Hindutva* (Hinduness) also circulated widely in the "pirate kingdom" of underground video cassette and then video compact disc circulation.[20] Since this time the BJP has successfully exploded commonly understood distinctions among religious devotion, entertainment, and electoral politics in large part because of the attention the Hindu-nationalist movement has paid to media. What was once seen as a peripheral obscurantism by the secularist establishment that long controlled a media sphere with deep connections to the state now appears completely normalized in the mainstream of news production both in state-controlled media and in the private realm. As neoliberal economics have unfolded further under Narendra Modi's leadership, the BJP's close connections to India's largest corporation, Reliance Industries Limited, have enabled their politics to dictate news coverage across a wide range of television channels and newspapers well beyond immediate state control (see the epilogue) while allowing the industrial giant to quickly assert hegemony in the field of cellular telecommunications.[21] And the rise of "IT wings" in political parties to manage public perceptions or to incite political passions through Twitter, Facebook, and most importantly WhatsApp—again, led by the BJP over the last decade—speaks to an even stronger entanglement with everyday media consumption at a time when the distinction between broadcasting and telecommunications is melting away. There appear to be no limits to politicized media seeping ever deeper into the crevices of daily life.

Media Ecology and the Mediatization of Political Life

Beyond the specifics of Indian politics, the broader arguments about mediation, media, and mediatization developed in this book are both theoretical and historical. At an anthropological level, our media world has always been the condition in which social life unfolds.[22] Media work through "a process of exteriorization"—whereby "technics is the pursuit of life by means other than life" according to the philosopher Bernard Stiegler—whether we are considering cave paintings, written language, photography, film, or the latest social media platform.[23] We might even go further than this relatively anthropological approach to argue that a medium should be defined more basically as "a technology within which a culture grows."[24] This ecological conceptualization informs a great deal of media theory, a body of scholarship that is too often dismissed through the accusation of "technological determinism" made of traditions that fail to center human actors or social context. Perhaps the time has come to let go of these lingering divides inasmuch as few would hold on to a vision of the human as a unitary sovereign subject, and we tend increasingly to think of agency as distributed through media. N. Katherine Hayles has gone so far as to show how cognition itself is distributed among living things and technical media.[25] It would be similarly hard to imagine a "social context" in our age that can be separated from the technological milieu through which it might be experienced or theorized. Hence, my approach is to embrace a theory of media as "enabling environments that provide habitats for diverse forms of life, including other media," such that the environment itself could even be thought of as media.[26]

The historically grounded theoretical claim of mediatization that follows this expansive view of the medium, however, is more specific. How representational traces are concretized and circulate changes over time with the development of new technologies and shifting ecological forces that, in turn, enable the rise of new social imaginaries. Consider the forms of "imagined community" that were mass mediated by the Qur'an, by printed books such as the Bible, or newspapers, for example.[27] Electronic broadcast technologies that layered themselves on print infrastructure afforded another space of intersubjectivity based on simultaneity and the possibility of "real-time" communication over vast expanses. Digital media enable forms of fractal scalability and automation previously unimagined, and their distributed logics of circulation have been said to give rise to a new "network imaginary," and so on.[28] The reflexive incorporation of technological affordances within the domains of experience, intellection, political action, and aesthetic production form the stuff of ethnography that we tend to study and narrate as anthropologists. I am thus specifically invested in questions of imagination and located perspective while adhering to an approach to media that sees the proliferation of technology and the interaction among regimes of circulation as the basic habitat, or the infrastructure of being, within which subjectivity might be said to emerge.[29]

At once a process and a perspective, mediatization speaks to our collective awareness of how things, people, and events in the world are increasingly oriented to mass mediation as an important condition of their very being in the world.[30] It is, in fact, scholars of South Indian anticolonial and ethnic nationalist politics, like Theodore Baskaran, who must be counted among the early theorists of mediatization, showing how popular cinema provided a medium that redefined the political field, enabling the emergence of populist counterpublics in the colonial world.[31] If social life was always mediated, and thereby made possible, by language and other representational forms, as anthropologists have long argued, the concept of mediatization points to the historical dynamic whereby shifting media ecologies give rise to styles of politics suited to specific technologies, institutions, and modes of circulation. Many of the most powerful political movements in a world defined my majoritarian populisms, for example, are specifically equipped to exploit the potentials for events to "go viral" in networked media. In approaching this more global story, then, Tamil Nadu's decades-long tryst with what Paula Chakravartty and Srirupa Roy call "mediatized populism" makes it an apt entry point to better understand how social life organizes itself around these now rapidly changing technologies and the now pervasive sense that the domain of politics is impossible to abstract from more general processes of mass publicity and networked circulation.[32]

Toward an Anthropology of the News Event

Among the most important effects of mediatization is a tendency to warp the relationship between events happening in the world at large and their representation in media genres like the news. For a long time, news was thought of as a medium for rendering, publicizing, and commenting on things happening elsewhere. Drawing on the semiotic distinction between what is said and the act of saying—the *énoncé* as opposed to the *énonciation*, for Benveniste— we might say that what was being narrated as a news event had an existence independent of its narration even if an event of communication was necessary for it to take on a wider public life.[33] Stuart Hall, for example, demonstrated brilliantly how, "a 'raw' historical event cannot, in that form, be transmitted by, say, a television newscast."[34] Undergoing a discursive transformation, he explains, "the event must become a 'story' before it can become a communicative event." But the "raw" historical event communicated in Hall's influential model nevertheless had an ontological status that was theoretically separate from, and anterior to, the communicative event of its transmission. Similarly, when Daniel Dayan and Elihu Katz wrote their influential analysis of "media events," two decades after Hall they could still provide a definition of the event in which it was an "interruption of routine . . . *organized outside of the media*." Such media events, like the Olympics or Anwar el-Sadat's historic journey to Jerusalem, were preplanned and meant to invoke reverence, standing as important rituals outside of the routines of daily life. In contrast to these depictions of events taking place outside of the defining force field of mediatization, the news events that form of empirical core of this book cannot be said to have an existence wholly independent from the event of their coverage in the media.[35]

The "news event" I am concerned with is that very moment when the events of news publication and circulation become difficult, if not impossible, to disentangle from the events being represented in the news. In Stiegler's phenomenological account of technology, *Technics and Time, 2: Disorientation*, this moment when the constitutive opposition between a storyline and what it reports collapses is termed *event-ization*. He explains that with the industrialization of media, which he conceives of as external memory devices, the criteria for what counts as a historical event have been altered to suit the production of surplus value. Under such conditions, "media are not satisfied with 'co-producing' events, but actually integrally produce them, in a veritable inversion by which media recount daily life so forcefully that their 'life story' seems not only to anticipate but ineluctably to precede—to determine—life itself."[36] We can find echoes here of Debord's complaints quoted above about reality no longer confronting media as something external in the integrated spectacle of mediatized circulation. In this conceptualization of the historical event as that which is produced through commodified practices of media recording, we are also led to consider conditions in which images and texts are produced primarily with their capacity to circulate in mind. Indeed, the lament that selling newspapers—or capturing television-watching eyeballs, or web page visits, for that matter—has more to do with information's value in circulation than it does with its capacity to represent the world at large has taken on new dimensions in recent years.

Jodi Dean is a scholar working on the question of mediatized politics who helps to frame the political ramifications of this orientation with the concept of "communicative capitalism," referring to the valuation of texts and images as determined by their capacity to be reproduced, cited, repeated, forwarded—what I will call their "communicability."[37] According to this logic, "media circulate and extend information about an issue or event, amplifying its affects," reaching a tipping point when caught up in in the engines of circulation, such that the event "of feedback and enjoyment itself operates as (and in place of) the political issue or event" that was once a source of information to be amplified.[38] Dean argues that the exchange value of information as determined by circulation measurements has definitively eclipsed action oriented toward reaching understanding in this new kind of capitalism, tending toward a foreclosure of politics. Such a concept helps us focus on the politics of communicability. But the larger theory it is a part of also has its drawbacks insofar as it recapitulates a narrative in which politics was once really about reaching understanding through communication. Perhaps the politics of communicability were already an important feature of earlier forms of print capitalism that we are now more attuned to as a result of our experience of digitalization. Drawing on the concept of communicative capitalism to better understand the feedback loops images and texts are subject to—as news becomes the event and as events become commodities in capitalist circuits of accumulation—this study is interested in forms of politics that happen *within* this political economy.

The intensifying commodification driving technological change has certainly made it more difficult to conceive of politics outside of the domain of circulation that constitutes mass-mediated or network culture, but we need not assume a standardized set of effects to follow from this fact. And this is where, following Stuart Hall, I depart definitively from the narrower claims about determination found in some corners of media studies or less refined varieties of Marxist theory.[39] If newspapers' power to mediate political publicity had certainly massified through "print capitalism's" development of vernacular markets, religious texts and the power of images to affect their addressees radically expanded through commercialization, too, as Kajri Jain's work on divine chromolithographic prints in the market economy of the Indian bazaar demonstrates so beautifully.[40] Mediatized commodification might well be uniform in some of the vernacularizing capitalist logics that drive it and in the very technologies through which it proliferates while affording irreducibly heterogeneous experiences of time, space, and event making for those living under its sway. Such heterogeneity is indeed the condition that enables the very spread of vernacularizing capitalism.[41]

Adopting an ethnographic approach to these arguments about eventization and communicative capitalism, this book is thus interested in how "actors anticipate the conditions of their acts' recordability and act according to the constraints of this industrial façade of time" as an anthropological problem, opening new questions:[42] What kind of actions or events are possible in a world so saturated, where the force of media coverage is thoroughly enmeshed with that on which it reports? Can institutions like the law continue to claim autonomy under such conditions? Can news media themselves claim to be independent observers and reporters of their own effects? And what kinds of politics arise if our actions are so thoroughly conditioned by the fact of their recordability and circulation? There is no end to politics, and embodied representations of "the people" remain as important as ever for claims to popular sovereignty. But the proliferation of social media-enabled crowd protests, for example, cannot be understood within a framework that would rigorously distinguish between the event of networked media circulation and that of crowd politics on "the street" (see chaps. 1 and 5). Where the chapters that follow depart from Stiegler's and Dean's arguments is therefore in their interest in reading these types of actions and events beyond the lens of constraint; the stories below are shared instead with the aim of thinking critically—and concretely through empirical events that are as mediatized as they are "real"—about the new ethical and political questions raised by both the implosion in the order of representation and the corresponding drive to communicability.

Recent anthropological studies of news media demonstrate how much we already know about actors, including journalists and editors, orienting themselves to the recording and circulation of their acts. Amahl Bishara's work, for example, examines how the political weight of US news reporting invites officials of the Palestinian Authority to try to shape the narrative framing of events such as Yasser Arafat's funeral, showing powerfully "that in these events, U.S. media were as much actors as audience, whether or not journalists and editors intended to be so."[43] Among Bishara's most significant arguments is that the power of news media to elicit responses from other actors and to produce events with significant effects for those they report on is profoundly unequal: residents of the United States can afford ignorance of how other societies represent them, while US reporting on Israel and Palestine "affect PA [Palestinian Authority] actions and how Palestinians constitute themselves as a polity."[44] Some actors on the world stage are more keenly aware of how they will be evaluated by exterior standards than others, leading to a heightened concern with how they imagine others are reporting on them. But, in less clearly defined imbalances of representational power, news producers, too, can be concerned about how their coverage will be interpreted as an event in its own right, especially when they are subject to the vicissitudes of deeply impassioned political polarization. In Venezuela, how a journalist reports on urban violence was read as a definitive political stance on Hugo Chávez's style of left populism, leading a strong opposition to embrace news as a stage on which to denounce the state's negligence and unwillingness to combat crime and others to "channel the state" through activist television journalism in support of the regime.[45] In many of these cases, imagined uptake and circulation of media reports and images are perceived by political actors, producers, and consumers of news alike to overdetermine their significance at the cost of what journalism is claiming to represent or tell about the world.

Digitalization intensifies this dynamic, at once undermining the near monopoly professional journalists had on the production of news while augmenting the feedback loop whereby news appears more responsive to the conditions of its own circulation than it is to a world outside of itself. The "screenworkers" featured in Dominic Boyer's study of news making in the digital age, for example, do little if any reporting of their own about the world beyond the screen.[46] Their job is precisely to reframe and disseminate information gathered online, leading to a feeling of agency, as they wind their way through the internet, which is paradoxically determined by the very automaticity of digital media. Zeynep Devrim Gürsel's book on news photography in the early days of digitalization similarly shifts the focus away from how images are captured in "the field" to examine the brokers whose job is to circulate images.[47] In an insightful analysis of staged shows of unity in the wake of attacks on the *Charlie Hebdo* offices in Paris, Gürsel elaborates an important observation: "the act of making an image circulate or the fact that a particular visual is circulating widely has itself become a news item."[48] In the latter case, offensive images in the French newspaper appeared to have triggered the assault on their office, which became a monumental news event in its own right, leading to demonstrations by political leaders that had been designed for attractive news coverage, and so forth.

At one level, this kind of "metanews" feedback loop divests what we tend to think of as the world outside of news representation and circulation of its ontological weight. Acts typically labeled as "terrorist" are effective in this media ecology precisely because they are *of* this ecology and so designed with their own circulation as news in mind. And actors filming themselves committing heinous crimes in public while streaming live on platforms such as Facebook—as done by a racist gunman in Christchurch, New Zealand— take the collapse between the event represented and the event of media representation to a grim logical conclusion. The very success of media in saturating the world of experience now appears as a crisis of representation.[49] At the same time, this world-threatening erasure consistently provokes new occasions for reflexivity about news and its commitment to disseminating what Carl Bernstein of Watergate fame once called "the best obtainable version of the truth" as something separate from its representation in the news.[50] The ongoing crisis of representation in news can even provide occasions for journalists and editors to reclaim a sphere of autonomy for themselves in and against a world that appears irrevocably conditioned by networked technologies of communication coupled with the values of commodified spectacle. The news event therefore plays a double role in this theoretical framework: it is at once afforded by technologies of communication and how shifts in the media environment alter the possibilities for participation in mass politics while, at the same time, the news event provides occasions for public concern about the role media technologies and journalism play in shaping political life.

The Law as a Medium of Publicity

To the degree that it can be drawn, the line dividing the world at large and the world of media representation is as ideological as any project of categorization. As such, the division is subject to contestation and redrawing, but not for that reason unimportant in its effects. In fact much of the value producers and consumers place in the news as something other than simple fantasy or entertainment derives from the distinction itself. News must, in a sense, actively produce an exterior world on which it can report even when reporting is driven by the compulsion toward communicability that characterizes so much of contemporary culture and where circulation might well become the subject of news. But this book is also interested in domains of political and social life that are more resistant than journalism is to being fully subsumed by the logic of circulation for its own sake even as they provide the raw textual materials for such circulation.

If news gathering has always been both a vocation and a business, the law emerges in this study as a particularly explosive site for the production of news events precisely because its foundations are more firmly rooted in a set of principles that cannot be reduced to the economic rationalities of commodification. The law has long claimed for itself a majesty that sits above the fray of commercial life, embodied in the sartorial and architectural regalia of the courts, and not only in its normative judgments. Indeed, scholars drawing on feminist legal theory, like Pratiksha Baxi, have suggested that we move beyond legal doctrine to understand the law's legitimacy and pay attention to the court as a "site of theatre and ritual."[51] Statutes on libel, sedition, and contempt are used to regulate media content and distribution and to maintain the auratic power of legal ritual and the state itself by defining the contours of what can be said and shown in public according to normative commitments that are meant to be independent of market logics. In some important respects, then, like the news media, the law, too, is invested in drawing a distinction between the sphere of autonomous observation and judgment on the one hand and the larger media environment in which it operates on the other.

At the same time, however, this dividing line is constantly breached. Law regulates media, but images of the law also form a great deal of contemporary media content—for example, in a dramatic form on television, in films, and especially in journalism where legal reporting makes up a significant portion of the daily news. Recognizing this fact, critical legal theorists have urged scholarship to attend more rigorously to "the remediation of law from text to digital images, and from the gravitas of text and library—scripture, chambers and court—to the internet and entertainment."[52] That the law is, in fact, known to the public and acts in part through such images tells us about its power in the world beyond the legal brief and the courtroom as well as its vulnerability to the politics of media representation. Judges representing the law are deeply invested in publicity and being shown to act in the public interest, while their discourse and image are subject to vicissitudes of public uptake.

The interplay between these aspects of mediation—how the law shapes media, how the law is depicted in the media, and how these remediations might feed off each other—has recently become subject to serious analysis.[53] Law, as prohibition, can become a major vector of communicability, as William Mazzarella's recent scholarship on censorship has shown.[54] Attempts to repress the circulation of information might well attract attention, spurring new waves of publicity. Courtrooms can easily serve as stages on which not only social norms but also the law itself are debated before a news-consuming public, at once democratizing and vulgarizing the juridical field. The ban on cameras in the courtroom should be read as an index of the danger publicity poses to the majesty of law in this context while heightening the mystery-value of the courtroom space. Claiming a great deal of space in newspapers and on television, legal reporting nevertheless provides raw material for the engines of communicative capitalism, all while being subject to different juridical limits from other forms of journalism in the interest of maintaining the aristocratic aura of legal institutions. Focusing on the areas of defamation (chap. 2), legal reporting and contempt of court (chap. 3), news stories that become eventful precisely because reporters and protagonists flout the law to spectacular effect (chap. 4), and the role of citizen journalism in bringing evidence of state crimes before the court of popular justice (chap. 5), this book takes up the task of investigating the remediations through which journalism and the law define themselves and the very political public sphere they serve to produce.

On Method and the Event

In the years since Veena Das gifted us the concept of the "critical event" to understand how traditional categories of anthropological analysis are transformed when "new modes of action come into being," the discipline has posed difficult questions about "where" and "when" the study of events takes place.[55] One line of inquiry has argued for "microanalysis" and a newly revitalized empiricism. In their quest to capture the eventfulness of life and not only social regularities, researchers are interested in moments of newness, emergence, or creativity, highlighting "human efforts to exceed and escape forms of knowledge and power and to express desires that might be world altering."[56] Ethnography in this vein stays close to the ground of experience and subjectivity in an effort to grasp the very singularity of human beings beyond structural constraints, often celebrating moments of indeterminacy. Following a different methodological entry point—one required to apprehend more widely distributed dynamics of collective event making—the following pages are focused on the conjunctures that enable the scaling and interlocking of events across space and time. In this respect, I follow Yasmeen Arif's proposal to develop the "event as a method" to apprehend the social while focusing on the problematic of the technological and institutional mediation of mass subjectivity.[57] The experiences of journalists remain a central concern in this enterprise, as does the focus on contingency, but the event-making process that is of primary interest "happens" at many sites at once in news production.

Although not all the events discussed below are of national significance, like those analyzed by Das in her earlier work, my research remains true to the project of making an "incision" in institutions—such as the courtroom, law enforcement, and the newsroom—to better understand their mutual implications in the production of events and the mediation of new forms of community. Some events discussed in this book are much more transformational than others. And while a number of represented incidents clearly anticipate further acts of representation, others become events at the moment of their representation in the news and through their circulation in media. Mass circulation can transform its own significance to become an event in its own right when represented as such. Many events represented as "breaking news" appear almost too formulaic to justify the name, and some are only recognized as occasions of real significance after the fact through ripple effects. What these events all have in common is their emergent status as newsworthy ruptures from the everyday background of "that which goes without saying."

At once ubiquitous and extraordinary, public events in the making serve as objects of study that are strangely elusive from an ethnographic perspective.[58] Always the product of imagination and sometimes calculated artifice, events appear as such when they have gelled into something publicly available, even if always partially accessible, having an internal consistency that makes them detachable from their surroundings. In this respect, it might help to think of "event-ization" as a process of becoming akin to what linguistic anthropologists have analyzed as entextualization, whereby emergent foreground-background relations allow a segment of discourse or an image to be experienced as present, singular, and somehow self-sufficient as it circulates across contexts.[59] Events can appear to have a momentum of their own, not captured completely by either the structuring forces that can be said to have enabled them or by the contexts within which they are experienced and interpreted. Following Sundaram's felicitous formulation, "beyond an event's artifactuality, it would be useful to examine how events are part of a generative loop or movement, where practices, objects, and people attach themselves to changing assemblages."[60] The approach developed here is thus interested in the uncertain interplay between singular encounter and structural dynamics, placing contingency before linear causality, while recognizing conflicting and contradictory principles of selection for what counts as a public event. But more significantly, I am interested in process over ontologies that would rigorously separate being from becoming, focusing on the actualization of potentialities for circulation and how circulation feeds back into the moment of actualization.[61]

This method allows for a reading of how events index the more abstract dynamics animating them while at the same time attending to new orientations induced by the experience of disruption. Events produced through acts of representation in news media raise difficult questions about the journalist's role as a knowledge producer in a world of constant flux when journalistic forms of knowledge are fueling that very change. The anthropologist, too, is faced with challenges that come with studying the inherently evanescent, similar at times to the journalists they study, although the academic demands of the discipline require the production of distance and retemporalizations at other times. The ethnographer of news events who wishes to understand their currency while also representing their currency in narrative form is faced with a paradox that gets to the heart of the question of methods in media anthropology. The ethnographer objectifies and analyses subjective experiences of encounters with text images, objects, and narratives circulating across media forms while not claiming to stand wholly apart from the field of circulation we also describe and analyze. This kind of exploration of how media are experienced by other readers and viewers, or by the ethnographers themselves, is a key part of participant observation of media today. And I would furthermore argue that we must all be doing some kind of media anthropology now whether or not media are thematized as an object of inquiry. We should therefore take into consideration lessons from media studies about how an increasingly integrated media environment is the condition in which participant observation of media circulation or any other public event, for that matter, takes place.

In a number of cases analyzed below, I happened to be in Chennai or elsewhere in Tamil Nadu when a news event was taking place, sometimes sitting in the very newsroom or pressroom in the court where eventhood was being produced as such from an otherwise relentless stream of information.

In a number of other cases, I was far away, sometimes at work teaching at my university in Toronto. Still other events and stories analyzed here took place before I had even begun this research. Even when "present," I have relied extensively on what are commonly framed as "secondhand" journalistic accounts, paying particular attention to that moment of event-ization when "media becomes a source of news about its own effects" and where the secondhand representations become the ground on which further accounting takes place.[62] This method entails revisiting events through the traces they left in news texts and images, in court cases and in my interlocutors' memories, and even in field notes I had taken in earlier stretches of research. It has also meant learning how to experience events as they are unfolding through the lens of journalists who are hyperaware of their role in mediating eventhood for wider publics and in enacting that break with the ordinary that gives their representations of the world distinctive value. This method furthermore draws on our experience of contemporary media to pose new questions about older media formats to better understand how they have been involved in the production of news events.

The narrative that emerges as a result of these methodological orientations does not assume the indetermination of the event to be an unqualified good; rather, it attempts to come to terms with how uncertainty and metamorphosis work as fundamental conditions through which power flows. Event making is the lifeblood of communicative capitalism, and event makers are subject to powerful forces that require their very event making to thrive and multiply. Political leaders, especially in recent years, have come to recognize the power of the news event to sustain affective and ideological engagement and even faith in their leadership. Narendra Modi's government, it has been argued, rules through what the well-known Hindi television journalist Ravish Kumar has termed *eventocracy*: substituting impressive mass-mediated displays of mastery over chaos for questions of governance and justice.[63] Espousing very different political visions grounded in regional identity in contrast to Hindu nationalism, leaders in Tamil Nadu have long shown a flair for the drama of event making in their mass-mediated shows of sovereignty. Political actors everywhere take a deep interest in how news coverage of events becomes the object of further publicity that can either suit or contradict their efforts to project power. The instability of the news event thus emerges as a source of both strength and potential vulnerability for those seeking to manage its effects. What has become clear, however, is that the draw of wagering on the public event appears to be boundless, bringing together a wide range of protagonists, including the self-declared "daredevil" journalists, proud media business owners, charismatic television anchors, outlaws, judges, political aspirants, and accidental activists who people this account.

Overview of the Book

As should be clear by this point, I do not take the tendency of news to become an event in its own right to be a completely new phenomenon caused by digital technology. Television had already exploited what Mary Ann Doane argued was the "significance of the media event, where the referent becomes indissociable from the medium."[64] Indeed, the "midnight arrest" of Karunanidhi recounted above was an analog broadcast television event, and we will see how print media have also been invested in the event-making potential of news. This monograph is therefore designed to investigate these dynamics in the longish *durée*, cutting across media formats and technologies as it traverses at least two decades of news events (2000–2020). The longer time period covered is also a result of my having witnessed profound changes in news reporting, technology, and media circulation over the course of my many years of research on a project that began life as an ethnography of regimes of circulation in India's booming newspaper market.[65] The book's architecture has a very rough chronological dimension, although some chapters move back and forth in time. It is generally intended to help us come to terms with the intensification of processes through which news becomes an event over the longer term than a study focused primarily on digitalization would. As such, it seeks to provide a conceptual vocabulary and method to define a robust position between overblown claims that everything has changed as a result of technological upheaval and the equally predictable tendency in anthropology to stress structural continuities of social form or an essentially human creativity in the face of mechanized artifice.

The book begins by reframing what appear to be rather straightforward struggles over representations of political leaders in the news. It then moves into the domain of the law as an important institutional medium through which news events are produced for public consumption, and it ends with new types of political contestations enabled by the digitalization of the public sphere. Chapter 1, "Populist Publics," thus examines the daily and weekly press by posing questions about mediatization and crowd theory that are more commonly asked of digital media. It interrogates the long-standing opposition drawn in liberal theory between reading publics and the crowd violence that is generally taken to characterize the politics of "the street" in an effort to reframe the public sphere as a zone of deeply embodied contestation. The chapter draws on a history of politicizing newspapers in the Dravidian movement and focuses on three events of crowd attacks on newspaper offices in response to negative portrayals of political leaders: Chief Minister J. Jayalalithaa, the DMK's M. K. Azhagiri, and the Dalit leader Thol. Thirumavalavan. "Populist Publics" argues that dynamics of mutual recognition and reflexive displays of violence characterize the blurry line between crowds and publics more than the politics of self-abstraction that even critics of classical theories of the public sphere take to be foundational.

Chapter 2, "Defamation Machine," focuses more squarely on the juridical field to ask how accusations of defamation made by political leaders and the criminalization of journalism might serve to fuel the very engine of print capitalism while providing greater exposure (positive and negative) for both the politician and the news organization involved. In a world in which political leaders' claims to sovereignty are experienced through commodity images, the gendered body becomes potent grounds on which to delineate and contest the limits of what can be said or represented in public by provocative media. The government led by former cinema star J. Jayalalithaa was especially aggressive in pursuing legal action against the English-language *Hindu* as well as the Tamil political magazine *Nakkeeran*. Focusing on these two kinds of print publication that are otherwise opposed in their styles of representation, the chapter examines how the frequent use of criminal defamation charges against journalists serves to conflate the persona of the political leader with the people and state they represent.

Our examination of the law as a vector of public event making continues in chapter 3, "Law at Large," where ethnography of legal reporting at the Madras High Court shows how judges are also deeply invested in their public image, not completely unlike political leaders. Beginning with a famous and widely quoted judgment in favor of the Tamil novelist Perumal Murugan's right to free expression, it then follows two cases that became major media events and the career of Justice C. S. Karnan, who was arrested for "scandalizing" the court through accusations of casteism. The analysis demonstrates how public affect and opinion loop back into the texts of High Court judgments. The chapter argues that when legal authority is routed through the mediation of normative news-consuming publics and not only in legal procedure, judicial sovereignty is vulnerable because it demands from the very media of publicity a forum for displaying its power that can easily be withheld.

Chapters 4 ("Celebrity Outlaws") and 5 ("Short Circuits"), as well as an epilogue ("Environmental Engineering"), bring the question of media technology closer to the foreground. Moving from lawkeepers to lawbreakers, "Celebrity Outlaws" examines how Veerappan, India's most famous bandit, became closely connected to a journalist, Nakkeeran Gopal, who became a celebrity himself over the course of the 1990s because of his relationship with the outlaw. The logic of mutual publicity animating their interactions is juxtaposed to a more recent mediatized outlaw, the leader of a social media–based vigilante group who murdered a young Dalit man thought to be romantically involved with a woman from his caste. Claiming celebrity through viral audio files he released, the caste vigilante was eventually interviewed on news television while still running from the police, raising serious concerns about the limits of what is permissible on "live" TV. Overall, the chapter tracks encounters between forms of mass publicity providing a basis of celebrity for the outlaw and emerging networked publics engaged in multilateral communication that has now been electrified through digital media. New avenues to publicity for the celebrity outlaw pose new ethical dilemmas for journalism.

"Short Circuits" takes up recent debates on the left about the space-time of deep digitalization from a different perspective: to think specifically about the explosive energies and new forms of public contestation unleashed through the "short-circuiting" of traditional forms of representation. Drawing on the ethnographic archive of protests that erupted over the course of Tamil Nadu's season of discontent following the death of the popular leader J. Jayalalithaa, it interrogates how short-circuiting occurs through the introduction of techno-political "switchpoints" with the potential to divert the flow of social energies, reconfiguring the possibilities of how popular sovereignty is imagined in the process. Agitations against a copper plant in Thoothukudi, a mass uprising against the ban on a bull-wrestling sport called jallikattu, and rural antihydrocarbon environmentalism shared some methods of leaderless mobilization. Focusing in particular on WhatsApp, the chapter shows how the digital circulation of popular documentation of acts of violence against the citizenry during protests led to even greater disaffection with established structures of representation and an intensification of techno-political processes of short-circuiting.

The epilogue examines how the increasingly decentralized character of news media circulation is nevertheless subject to political projects of reengineering. In building new media environments to allow for particular types of events to resonate, political power is adapting to changing technologies of representation and circulation. Hindu-nationalist forces have emerged at the forefront of these strategies of networking advantageous events so as to modulate the contours of the media ecology in Tamil Nadu. At the same time, journalism now begins from the premise that high-velocity nonprofessional media representations produced through cheap and widely available digital technology are already involved in shaping the story that must be represented as news, raising new and difficult questions about the empirical basis of journalistic claims on the truth.

CHAPTER ONE

Populist Publics

Coimbatore City, June 8, 2018. The widely watched Tamil news channel Puthiya Thalaimurai (New generation) was telecasting a debate show when a heated exchange of words quickly turned into a fistfight. Reflecting on a continuous spate of protest movements that had taken place across Tamil Nadu, the question on the table was whether these were actually representative of "the people," or whether crowds were instruments used by cynical political parties in their attempts to capture state power. Part way into the program, the acclaimed film director Ameer was speaking critically about the ruling parties, especially the Hindu-nationalist BJP (Bharatiya Janata Party), whose state leader was also at the roundtable. He argued that today's so-called antisocial elements become tomorrow's leaders and that violent state repression of protest was fueling the problem. In the end, he said, violence begets violence, comparing recent protests to communal tension in Coimbatore a few years back. Interpreting his comments as an affront—referring to the murder of a member of the Hindu Munnani (a religious nationalist group) that had led to retaliation—some men rose from their seats and rushed toward the stage in a display of outrage. Taping stopped while mayhem erupted in the college auditorium where the show was being filmed. Ameer was eventually whisked away by another participant in the program. Local Hindu Munnani supporters threw stones at their car as the two sped away from the venue.

Following a policy of delayed telecast in anticipation of a problem like this, Puthiya Thalaimurai had edited the comment Ameer made as well as the attack on his person, deleting them from the show people saw on their television sets. But everyone read about the violence the following day in the newspaper. At first just another news item, this event took on a second life a few days later when police proceeded to file charges. They did so not against those who attacked Ameer, however. Police framed criminal charges against the film director himself, the political leader who helped him, the Puthiya Thalaimurai television channel, and Karthigaichelvan, the well-known news anchor who had hosted and moderated the debate. All four parties were charged with "promoting enmity between different groups on ground of religion" and "intent to incite one community against another."[1] According to the police and the government of Tamil Nadu, it was the news channel, the journalist, and the provocative debaters who had caused the violence, not those who attacked the stage.

It has become clear for some time that classical theories of the public sphere are both utopic and disembodied. They do not engage adequately with either the spatiality of discourse circulation, despite the metaphor of a sphere that has grounded English translations of *Öffentlichkeit*, or with the materiality of the body in the production of a mass-mediated subject of politics. Of those authors writing about the public sphere, Michael Warner argues most persuasively that what he terms the "utopias of self-abstraction" animating liberal understandings of democratic publicity are not merely contingent; rather, they lie at the very core of a minoritizing logic of exclusion.[2] This distinctively modern form of power has relied on an ideology that privileges silent, replicable, private acts of reading enabling the unrestricted circulation of texts among strangers. Indeterminacy of address in this vision of democracy is misrecognized as universality, and people who cannot imagine themselves as unmarked by race, gender, or sexuality—those who are excessively embodied, as it were—are relegated to inhabit particular identities. In the liberal model, according to Warner, only unmarked publics can transpose their agency as citizens to the generality of the state through the logic of self-abstraction.[3] By means of this analysis, he argues against the default liberalism in earlier descriptions of subaltern counterpublics, like Nancy Fraser's insofar as minoritized groups appear in these accounts to work through a disembodied rational deliberation that resembles the very dominant publics they are contesting.[4]

I would like to begin by noting that the powers of self-abstraction and minoritization proper to liberalism set the terms of North American debates on the public sphere and even what has sometimes been termed the *post-public sphere*. The primacy of liberal orientations lurks also within Warner's own analysis. In his essay on the mass public and the mass subject, he argues that the major political movements of the late twentieth century "presuppose the bourgeois public sphere as background" within which concerns with personal identity are politicized.[5] Similar assumptions about the public sphere are elaborated in his later, insightful work on counterpublics inasmuch as the subaltern appears, in his words, "as an almost inverted image" of the dominant male, white, bourgeois public premised on self-abstraction.[6] Such analyses of the ideology that allows some people to speak for humanity in general through a politics of disembodiment are important insofar as they represent an immanent critique of liberalism.[7] But the liberal model tends to predetermine our understanding of alternatives. And it can do so precisely by creating the appearance of "almost inverted images" of itself through the figure of excessively embodied others. The conundrum is familiar from orientalist discourse: whether theorizing counterpublics or other dominant spheres of publicity, we are stuck with either failed aspirations to replication of the classical model or an alterity that is defined in largely predetermined ways. This problem is an effect of liberalism's relative hegemony in the very field of publicity these scholars were both describing and addressing.

A concept of publics, construed as political subjects that know themselves and act by means of mass mediated or networked communication, remains as essential now as it ever was.[8] How, then, might we work toward a more capacious understanding of publics than has been allowed for in scholarly traditions that assume self-abstraction as the primary logic through which publics enact power? What frameworks might we develop to understand the embodied publicity at play in news events such as the one described above, where physical force, critical debate, mass-mediated images, and instrumentalized law enforcement are so thoroughly imbricated? What if such events where not thought of as an anomaly, and how might analysis of the news event itself help us understand the formation of political publics? This chapter begins to answer these questions through a focus on events where acts of representation in the news incite public action against news producers through performances of violence that become the subject of further news. It does so by developing strains of postcolonial political thought that think democracy from a perspective where those who enjoy the self-image of occupying the socially unmarked anonymity of abstract citizenship sit at odds with muscular claims to a popular sovereignty over which they have little control. As practices of democracy expand, deepen, and transform into new forms of majoritarianism in the process, the liberal minorities of India have been increasingly challenged by political actors more at home in vernacular languages than they are in English, more involved in setting the terms of political debate, and more likely to win elections.[9] In fact, the history of the political press in Tamil Nadu, recounted in some detail below, can be read as one of the replacement of a rather Brahminical anticolonial liberalism, often produced in the English language for a relatively elite readership, by a non-Brahmin, Tamil language and social movement-based journalism, more at home in the rough-and-tumble world of street politics than in the parlors and clubs of high society.[10] Political mobilization around community and collective identity continues to deepen a political society that defines itself against received narratives of civil society.[11] In the opening vignette above, for example, we can see how the world of news publicity has been shaped by collective, embodied demonstrations of political power. Puthiya Thalaimurai had, in fact, sought to bring journalistic ideals of objectivity and impartiality usually associated with the foreign press to popular news in Tamil only to find that there is limited room for these aspirations in a media world so thoroughly defined by the politics of community interest.

Some might point to the "live" nature of the television broadcast that encourages the formation of more visually oriented, affectively saturated, and embodied political publics. Mary Ann Doane, for example, has shown how television formats the experience of catastrophic events in ways that are particular to this medium that thrives on crisis.[12] Theorists of digital network culture like Tiziana Terranova go further to argue that the *"power of affection* of images, as such"* constitutes the new domain of the political in the contemporary public sphere.[13] We will reopen the question of technological transformations and politics later in this book, but my aim in this chapter is to sketch a deeper history and broader sociology of Tamil news media politics to begin the work of understanding how displays of physical force can act as news events *across* media technologies. The affective power of images has a past that we should recognize as such. It often spurs political debate, and this power is not limited to new media or television. This is where a political theory that seeks to understand the massification of popular sovereignty must also become a theory of media that resists narratives in which sober reading publics oriented toward mutual understanding mediated through print are replaced by the passions of the crowd because of the introduction of new technologies of circulation.

In fact a theory of publics as understood through the production of news events over the longer term would do well to begin with a critical analysis of the very distinction between reading publics and crowds—the former central to theories of "self-abstraction" in the formation of the public sphere through print media and the latter associated with physical collectivities of people particularly prone to violence more than reason. Crowd-like behavior, or what is often thought of as "mob mentality," has been associated with face-to-face gatherings, embodied affect, and also with the dangers of new technologies, as in the television broadcast depicted above. Digital media studies have been especially important in returning our attention to aspects of social contagion that first emerged in crowd theory.[14] A turn to the news media in Tamil Nadu, however, raises questions about a world of democratic politics in which physical force and a very embodied publicity have been deeply intertwined with the printed word for some time. What Habermas once dismissed as "pressure from the street" animates the mass-mediated public sphere of print journalism and readership in ways that disturb both his model and other immanent critiques of liberalism. In this specific sense, this chapter shares William Mazzarella's aim to focus on the "mutual imbrication of the categories Habermas wants to separate" in addition to the very act of separation as a key strategy of ideology.[15] This chapter, as well as chapter 5, will, however, have much more to say about crowds as political actors in their own right as they are self-consciously remediated through mass publicity and not primarily as figures of thought. The critique of the figure of the crowd has raised important questions for how we might rethink the place of mass affect, representation, and collective action in democratic strategy beyond liberalism without assuming a sharp distinction between readers and crowds. Whereas much fine scholarship on publics in India starts with what is commonly thought of as the most affectively saturated medium of cinema, and this chapter began with a fistfight fueled by the power of television cameras, we will spend the remainder of this chapter with that classical medium of "rational" public formation: the newspaper.

Politics in Tamil Nadu's Print Capitalism

Unlike traditions of journalism that have sought to maintain ideals of objectivity or neutrality in the production of news, the South Indian press, both Tamil language and English, has long worn politics on its sleeves. Newspapers flourished first as engines of anticolonial nationalism and later as the media of politics in the spread of Tamil nationalism, often reflecting and encouraging protests in the streets. Democratic politics were mediated by the press while political oratory played a decisive role in greatly expanding what began as a restricted claim for self-rule by 1918–1919 with the rise of the labor and home rule movements.[16] Well before cinema came to play a strong role in Tamil politics from the 1950s on, the daily press was closely tied to social and political movements. Over the course of the twentieth century the print market itself took on the character of mass media, catalyzing energies across castes and classes.

Many would point to the prominent Indian nationalist leader of colonial Madras, G. Subramania Iyer, as the founder of modern South Indian journalism. One of a group of Brahmin students and school masters known as the "Triplicane Six," Subramania Iyer helped found the *Hindu* in 1878 as a weekly paper to support the campaign to appoint T. Muttuswamy Iyer as the first "native" judge to sit on the bench of the Madras High Court.[17] In its opinion pieces, India's first daily evening paper, the English-operated *Madras Mail* (1868–1961), shuddered at the thought of an Indian sitting in judgment of whites, and the newly founded paper's mission was not only to counter the colonialist press but more broadly to expand the very scope of whose voice would count as constituting "public opinion."[18]

The *Hindu* turned into a daily evening paper in 1889, and it would go on to become the most important English paper in the Indian-nationalist movement. It was sold in 1905 to a barrister named Kasturi Ranga Iyengar, and the paper has remained within the control of his family since the initial sale. Dubbed the "Old Lady of Mount Road" by Jawarhalal Nehru, the paper is referred to more commonly now as the "Maha Vishnu of Mount Road," the latter sobriquet noting the paper's Vaishnavite Brahmin family of owners and editors in the somewhat derisive popular idiom of the non-Brahmin politics that would come to dominate in the years following independence. Not content with publishing in English, G. Subramania Iyer would also go on to found the first Tamil paper owned by Indians, *Swadesamitran* (1882–1985).[19] Also purchased by Kasturi Ranga Iyengar in 1915, the Tamil paper counted the revolutionary nationalist poet Subramania Bharati among its important editors in this period. Whereas the Tamil paper was flooded with competition and eventually closed, the *Hindu* remains as India's most respected paper across political affiliations, read by every journalist working in Tamil or English, and it is the best example of liberal opinion.

It was in the 1930s that new players in journalism would challenge the largely Brahmin-owned press. Originally from Bihar, Ramnath Goenka, of the Marwari trading community, had been sent to Madras as a jute dealer only to buy shares in and then take over the *Indian Express* in 1936, a paper that had been started a few years earlier by the great nationalist and anti-caste activist P. Varadarajulu Naidu.[20] In addition, Goenka backed *Dinamani* (1934–present), which rapidly overtook *Swadesamitran* as the most popular

Tamil daily, eventually earning him the title of the "Indian Citizen Kane."[21] Also affiliated with the Indian National Congress until the 1970s, Goenka had shut his presses in support of Gandhi's Quit India movement, and he ran as a Congress candidate in the first elections in 1952. He finally won a seat in parliament in 1971 as a congressman only to become one the of the fiercest critics of Indira Gandhi's declaration of emergency, described in greater detail in the next chapter, and instrumental in the election of V. P. Singh as Prime Minister against Congress later in his life.

As Dravidianist social reform formalized itself in political parties—first as the DMK in 1949 and later the AIADMK (All India Anna Dravida Munnetra Kazhagam) in 1972—the daily press would take strong positions for or against the non-Brahminism that had become the main currency of politics by the 1960s and 1970s. The early DMK was a profoundly literate party, for example, and nearly every leader of the movement had started their own newspaper by the 1950s attacking upper-caste privilege and promoting pride in the Tamil language. Among these, Karunanithi started *Murasoli* in 1942 when he was only eighteen years old, and he wrote in the party organ until just before his death three-quarters of a century later, having forced his competitors in the party to shut their presses. But it was the daily *Dinathanthi*—started in the same year by a relatively disadvantaged caste member, a Nadar English-trained lawyer by the name of S. P. Adithan—that is credited with being the first to spread a newspaper reading habit among the working classes, both urban and rural.[22] Using language to be read aloud and new methods of distribution, *Dinathanthi* was able to massify the newspaper over the course of the mid-twentieth century, reshape Tamil itself, and bring the daily to the center of everyday politics in this turbulent era. At the time of its launching, the paper was resolutely Tamil nationalist. Adithan was among those jailed for his participation in the anti-Hindi agitations, and he formed his own political party named Nām Tamilar (We Tamils) to demand a separate ethnic homeland state that would stretch across the Palk Straits from southern India to northern Sri Lanka before eventually joining the DMK as speaker of the legislative assembly when the party first won power in 1967.[23]

Dinathanthi is not alone in this field. *Dinamalar*, which would soon rise in opposition to Dravidianism, was started in 1951 by a Brahmin industrialist named T. V. Ramasubbaiyar as part of a demand to merge the Tamil-speaking region of southern Travancore with what was then Madras State, helping form what we now know as the state of Tamil Nadu. Consistently writing against the DMK and what its owner termed "rowdy trouble makers," *Dinamalar* has especially targeted the new middle classes of urban Tamil Nadu. It has often acted as the most vocal media critic of state-level Dravidianist governments, in accordance with general middle-class upper-caste antipathies toward the welfare state and caste-based reservation, and has been sympathetic to Hindu-nationalist causes. The paper now publishes the most widely viewed Tamil-language website in the world. The last major daily that must be mentioned in the context of Dravidianist politics, also discussed below, is *Dinakaran*, which was started by Adithan's son-in-law, K. P. Kandasamy, when the former split with the DMK in 1977. While the owner also went on to serve in the legislative assembly for the DMK, the paper was long considered to be a DMK party mouthpiece. It was bought by Karunanidhi's grand-nephew, Kalanidhi Maran's Sun Media Group in 2005, and rose then from being a small paper to become a major player in its own right. Even more so than the Hindi press, which has received more scholarly attention, the Tamil mass press has been integrated into the system of regional party politics from the beginning of its mass appeal.[24]

After the Emergency, in the 1980s, 1990s, and into the first decade of the twenty-first century, two important and interconnected processes begin to unfold in the press: First, a looser relationship developed between newspapers and formal politics and the blossoming of critical news magazines precisely as political parties began to show interest in the new medium of cable television. Second, this is also the time when market logics tended to exert a stronger pull on publishing, one that only accelerated as the liberalization of the Indian economy expanded. Among the most industrialized states, with a high literacy rate by Indian standards, Tamil Nadu was one of the leaders of a tremendous explosion in regional-language newspaper reading and production during this time. According to the National Readership Survey, for example, the Tamil-language daily *Dinathanthi* was the most widely read paper in all of India in the year 2000, when fewer than 6 percent of Indians spoke the language. In many respects, *Dinathanthi*'s rise to prominence over the second half of the twentieth century is emblematic of the sort of historical changes described in Robin Jeffrey's important book *India's Newspaper Revolution*, which describes how between 1976 and 1996 the total circulation of daily newspapers in India increased from 9.3 million to 40.2 million.[25] The rapid expansion of the daily press only increased in the 2000s. Between 2005 and 2009 the number of daily newspapers in India increased by 44 percent, and during this period India overtook China to become the leader in paid-for daily circulation, with 110 million copies sold every day. More recent expansion of the market has happened in Hindi, with southern languages reaching a plateau. Once the domain of an educational elite, newspaper reading of some sort or another has become an everyday habit for a range of people across a wide swath of the country.

In addition to a lively daily press, the Tamil-language weekly magazines have played a very strong role in deepening reading habits across genders and classes through the twentieth and twenty-first centuries, publishing a wide variety of genres from serialized stories and autobiographies to political gossip columns and longer-form investigative journalism. It is, in fact, the weeklies and biweeklies, like *Ananda Vikatan* (1926–present), that have just as often provoked political leaders and their followers to the punitive actions described in this chapter and the next. Whereas many began with more literary ambitions, the popular right-wing satirical fortnightly *Thuglak* (1970–present), long under the editorship of the actor and script writer Cho. Ramaswamy, who was known for his razor-sharp wit, had paved the way for a more political weekly press. Even more than the dailies, it was the magazine format that evolved most rapidly in the 1980s with the general expansion of the field of journalism. A new genre of muckraking tabloid journalism emerged in this period, allowing for sharper political commentary than was permitted in dailies. The Vikatan group started *Junior Vikatan* (1985–present), popularly known as "JuVi," which remains a top-selling biweekly focusing on crime, politics, and the overlap between the two. This period also saw the rise first of *Tarasu* (1985–present), and then *Nakkeeran* (1988–present), both of which took some of the more aggressive elements of the type of masculine political gossip found in teashops and brought them into print for all to read. *Nakkeeran* has made a particularly important place for itself in the Tamil political sphere (described in more detail later in this chapter, the next, and in chapter 4).

For the moment, I want to emphasize not only the size of the Tamil newspaper reading public but also the diversity of transmission patterns, journalistic styles, and perspectives among papers. The major papers are associated with particular social classes, with some still closely tied to the working-class world of the street and others successfully projecting a more middle-class domesticity, but they have also cultivated different regimes of circulation.[26] *Dinathanthi* developed a distinctive mode of transmission by becoming the iconic paper associated with reading aloud and discussing politics at teashops and barbershops, a world then mediatized by *Nakkeeran*. *Dinathanthi*'s headlines are formatted and written for the purpose of reading aloud, building on older orientations to the recitation of texts in common spaces. It continues to be associated with working-class masculinity precisely because of its spatial politics of circulation more than its main news content. *Dinamalar*, on the other hand, recognized earlier than other Tamil-language dailies that the future of the vernacular press in India is closely tied to the rise of the new middle classes in major metros and in second- and third-tier cities, expanding the readership associated with weeklies. By cultivating a readership that includes women and younger generations through its special weekly supplements, this paper has come to be associated not only with domestic space, and hence home subscription, but also with a readership that has greater spending power in general. By the 2010s *Dinamalar* could claim that about 80 percent of its sales are through subscription to homes, following the business model already established by English-language papers. While its competitor *Dinathanthi* can still claim the highest advertising prices (because they have the largest readership), the latter paper has nevertheless tried to rebrand itself by launching its own television channel and by including a Tamil version of the *Economic Times* within its broadsheet in an effort to represent itself as product that is consumed across class barriers.

Indian anticolonial nationalism, Tamil Nadu's strong non-Brahmin movement, and subsequent ethnolinguistic mobilization provided the political context in which newspapers began as means of disseminating political ideology. Once daily print started to prove its economic value as a commodity, however, the pull of selling copy has reflected a massified politics fused to caste and class-based consumption habits since at least the 1980s. Ideology has often taken a back seat to market-driven decisions. The once radically anticolonial paper *Swadesamithran* found it difficult to massify and sustain itself in the postindependence era in part because it failed to appeal to an increasingly self-conscious non-Brahmin community. Market pressures have oftentimes conditioned the political stances papers have been willing to take. Adithan, the first editor of *Dinathanthi*, is said to have sent his workers to collect scrap paper to be recycled during the Second World War just so he could disseminate the news among the working classes of southern Tamil Nadu and push for a Tamil-nationalist, non-Brahmin agenda. But the paper is now commonly perceived as making itself close to whichever political party is in power for fear that criticism will invite reprisal. *Dinamalar*, while promoting Hindu nationalism and more often aligning with the AIADMK than with its bitter enemy, the DMK, nevertheless remains a critical paper among the majors while supporting a broadly neoliberal economic agenda. And the policy at the DMK-associated *Dinakaran* is best described in the words Maran used when instructing its chief editor: "Just don't be an *anti*-DMK paper!" Even under Maran's ownership the opinion pages of this paper would host a number of pieces by Karunanidhi himself.

Sitting in his office in that great bastion on Mount Road and celebrating the fact that readers in Tamil Nadu know whose interests are being projected as news, the *Hindu*'s reader's editor and onetime editor at Sun TV, A. S. Panneerselvan, explained to me, "Media has been part of the political structure from the beginning. Everyone knows that *Alai Osai* was an AIADMK paper, that Goenka was a Congress candidate, Adithan's son-in-law started *Dinakaran*, and they read it through that filter. . . . What is truly much more dangerous is those who claim to be neutral!" Each newspaper has taken up a particular niche in the political ecology of the state, and each newspaper has, in its own way, tried to develop its brand in other media. Papers are now invested in internet-based video dissemination in addition to cable television channels, and they remain a highly visible part of public culture across the state, from the smallest village to homes in midsized cities to the streets of Chennai. Tamil dailies and magazines have the capacity to make and break political reputations, and they quite frequently provoke those involved as cadre members in party politics to take to the streets themselves in defense of their leaders. It is to these phenomena of crowd violence, party politics, and their imbrication with capitalism that we now turn.

Political Crowds, the Printed Word, and the News Event

The politics of twentieth-century mass mobilization in India have proven to be an important vantage point from which to consider the production of publicity from the perspective of those who are not privileged enough to inhabit the disembodied voice of reason. Scholars of subaltern studies, for example, long emphasized the degree to which Indian nationalism had to articulate its demands through a language of kinship, insurrection, and mass affect because the very category of public opinion was limited to whites and elites in the colonial world.[27] Research on South India has examined how mobilization around language brought new segments of society into the fold of politics for the first time through fiery oratory, poetry, and mass spectacle.[28] Work on Dalit emancipation explores the paradoxes of entering into the field of political recognition through tropes of victimhood, violence, and embodiment.[29] These studies have, for the most part, emphasized the democratizing role of what is sometimes called the "plebianization" of politics even as they show new forms of domination that are produced through this democratization. Another line of scholarship has focused on the darker side of massification and tendencies toward majoritarian violence.[30] Although few of these scholarly projects are framed as a study of media per se, taken as a whole, this body of research nevertheless helps us understand the increasingly tense interface between technologies and different circulatory regimes of mass mediation, allowing what might have once been considered local events to take on large-scale significance and national politics to be localized through actions on the street.

Recent political theory compliments aspects of this research when arguing that the questions raised by mass affect for our understanding of democracy can shed light on the production of political subjectivity more broadly. It is in this context that interest has revived in the work of earlier thinkers about the crowd, like Gustave Le Bon, Elias Canetti, Sigmund Freud, and Gabriel Tarde.[31] What many of these early studies of crowds have in common is a sense that the forms of mass mediation characteristic of industrial society have intersected with modes of collective social life that do not correspond to the coolly cultivated stranger sociability attributed to reading publics. Mass society has not been able to transcend the fact of embodiment, as it were, and the place where bodies and mass mediation meet was theorized as a zone of both danger and possibility. Although they are generally thought of as distinct from publics, crowds have stood as the sign of democracy's limits as well as its potential.[32] The crowd appears as a sort of necessary supplement to theories of the political public in many narratives.

For example, Tarde defines a public as "a group of men who do not come in contact with each other—they are all scattered across a territory reading the same newspaper—and in this bond lie their simultaneous conviction—without seeing the others."[33] So far, we have an early iteration of common sense about the literate public sphere and imagined community. Tarde opposes reading publics who are virtually connected to the crowd (*la foule*), which "has something animal about it" because it is produced by physical contact. Then, he allows for an interesting possibility: "Admittedly, it often happens, that an overexcited public produces fanatical crowds. . . . In a sense a public could also be defined as a potential crowd. But this fall from public to crowd, though extremely dangerous, is fairly rare."[34] The intersection of mass media with physical groups of people is hazardous because the forms of petty violence that are characteristic of communal life and attributed to the crowd can be amplified, massified, and directed from above. In a sense, Tarde is anticipating the politics of mass embodiment proper to totalitarianism. Indeed, crowds have often been derided insofar as they are signs of less than democratic regimes of political legitimacy precisely because they lack the self-regulating agentive capacities of reading publics.

But what if crowds and reading publics are but two different aspects of the same political field? That media act as triggers or as a broadly enabling condition of mass-political action in the streets is a fairly well-known story. Particular media productions provoke crowd responses, often through politics of outrage that are commonly viewed as being manipulated by unscrupulous politicians. The use of crowd violence in response to media productions—especially controversial films by the Hindu right, for example—has been well documented and has become a rather systematized part of this movement's political tactics.[35] We will return to questions of instrumentality and political agency below, but here I would like to emphasize the extent to which the physical structure of media outlets and the bodies of journalists are increasingly acting as the targets of crowd violence. It is not only cinemas but also newspaper offices that are subject to crowd violence. Individual journalists have also been targeted for retribution, as has been well documented by the First (1966–1974) and Second (1979–1984) Press Council Reports.[36] Nikhil Wagle and the Marathi daily *Mahanagar* that he owned and edited, for example, were repeatedly attacked by the Shiv Sena in Mumbai from the early 1990s into the 2000s, playing a role in shaping national perceptions of the nativist party.[37] While the deployment of public political violence appears to have intensified in recent years across India—perhaps in response to the new proliferation of images afforded by television and other newer media, as in the case of the Puthiya Thalaimurai melee—there is an older story to be told about party politics and aggression against the press in Tamil Nadu.

Members of the DMK played a central role in the much-broader student movement involved in the anti-Hindi agitation that led to riots in Madras in 1965, but it is less widely remembered and perhaps ironic that this most press-oriented, literary, and rationalist of Tamil parties was also the first to be publicly associated with the use of physical force against the press in particular. The latter crowd actions had already begun in the early 1970s under the leadership of the great journalist and screenplay author Karunanidhi shortly after the death of party founder Annadurai. Ostensible incongruities aside, this fact illustrates the porous quality of the divide between reading publics and crowds already anticipated by Tarde. It furthermore throws into question any easy equation between obscurantist fascism and party-inspired crowd violence against news organs even if the strategy of using violence against journalists has become deadlier as it has been used more frequently by the Hindu right in recent times.

As we delve into this relationship, it is important to bear in mind the difference between ordinary protests on the street in front of publishers' offices—when copies of the offending paper might be defaced, for example—and more violent attacks on buildings and people. So, for instance, in 1972, DMK-affiliated crowds demonstrated passionately before the *Ananda Vikatan* offices, burning copies of the magazine, which they claimed had defamed their leader. An apology demanded of the editor was duly published in what some believe to be a text produced in anticipation of more serious violence. But in 1975, DMK cadres went on to attack the weekly *Kumudam*'s office, and the police were found by the Sarkaria Commission that inquired into the incident to have not arrested anyone involved, even when the DMK-led government illegally seized copies of the offending issue of the magazine.[38] Velur Narayanan's *Alai Osai* office was similarly attacked and employees injured. The Press Council found that the attack was clearly "meant as a measure of punishment for the attitude which the paper had adopted both in its news and editorial columns" in lending support to striking workers at Simpson and Company who were confronting the DMK-led government. In all of these cases taken up by the Sarkaria Commission of Inquiry and by the Press Council, however, neither body was ever able to pin acts of violence on Karunanidhi himself but only to the atmosphere of aggression toward these press houses created in the party and by the party newspaper, *Murasoli*.

Retribution against news institutions would intensify under the AIADMK, especially when Jayalalithaa was chief minister, becoming one element in a broader onslaught against freedom of the press. Apart from a spate of criminal defamation cases (analyzed in the next chapter), aggression shifted from the occasional violence against property to frequent attacks on journalists. For example, two scribes from the weekly *Tharasu* were killed in their office by a gang of men from the AIAMDK in 1991; *Nakkeeran* recorded a series of attacks against its reporters across the state at this time; and a Sun TV cameraperson was famously roughed up by a crowd at the elaborate wedding Jayalalithaa held for her adopted son in 1995. A range of attacks on the press culminated in 2001 with another attack on a Sun TV cameraperson leading to large protests held by journalists that were widely attacked by both police and party members and sympathizers.[39] While each of these assaults was carried out in different circumstances and even victims of these acts were sometimes unsure about what was commanded from above in the party structure, it is clear that violence has become a medium of expression of sorts, one that has been used by many others but that became closely identified with the leadership style of Jayalalithaa.

In the years since the establishment of this new norm of performative violence in Tamil Nadu since the early 2000s, a public reflexivity has developed about the fact that these events of violence are furthermore remediated and massified through the press, television, the internet, and social media like WhatsApp. Certain propensities for retribution, beyond Jayalalithaa's reputation, were well known and even exploited, making the distinction between trigger and target increasingly more complicated than it might appear to be at the outset. Attacks on media outlets become media events in their own right, creating a feedback loop of the sort described and theorized in the introduction to this book.

This is where a concept of "the news event" as that point of entanglement connecting events of representation in the news and the event of news representation can help us understand the political logics at play in this very embodied public sphere. Journalists and editors are often aware that the news they run might provoke reactions on the street and can be quite frank about the publicity such attacks might give them. Those in the news business know that violence has the potential to sell copy, even when that violence is directed at them. The news event is, after all, also a commodity. And in this respect, the vernacularizing drive of print capitalism might be linked to an overarching process where the exchange value of information as determined by circulation exerts great force on editorial decision-making. The news event is also an occasion for political maneuvering, a weapon to be used by a newspaper against enemies. Attackers themselves are also quite aware of these economic compulsions and political potentials, just as they are conscious of the fact that they are performing before an audience on the street where action is unfolding, in teashops on other streets, in people's living rooms as they read the paper or watch cable television, and now on people's smartphones, wherever they are.

Dialectics of Violence and Print Mediation

With this history and these phenomena in mind, we are now in a position to return to some of the questions raised by crowd theorists and their more recent interpreters from a different perspective in an effort to rethink the public sphere through an incorporation of crowd violence *within* the sphere of mediation and as generative of news events. It is in this context that we can then read the studies of mass politics mentioned above with a new focus on issues of mass mediation and the forms of political reflexivity that are at play when performing before a mediated public. Where crowd violence is so deeply connected with the politics of the daily press, how might we begin to think differently about the capacity of print capitalism to condition crowd actions and vice versa? How might crowds and readers coexist in a more structured relationship based on mutual recognition? Allow me to share three more news events in some greater detail that might help us explore these questions.

EVENT ONE: ROWDYISM ON DISPLAY

In May of 2007, the daily paper *Dinakaran* printed the results of a survey they had conducted in association with the Neilson Corporation asking who was the "likely political heir" to replace then chief minister, M. Karunanidhi, as the head of his DMK Party when he was no longer able to lead. The poll was titled "Makkal Manasu" (The people's hearts), indicating that this was not simply an objective question about likely succession but one about who had the people's support. Karunanidhi was already eighty-two years old at the time, and it was assumed that one of his sons would take over the party leadership. *Dinakaran*, which was closely tied to the DMK published the results of their poll showing the younger M. K. Stalin, former mayor of Chennai, leading in public opinion by a large margin with 70 percent support. His older brother, M. K. Azhagiri, who is based in the southern city of Madurai and known more for his dealings in pirate videos and violent crime than for his political acumen, received only two percent of the vote. Another two percent of respondents supported Stalin and Azhagiri's half sister, Kanimozhi, and the rest remained undecided.[40]

On the day the poll was published, a group of protesters led by the mayor of Madurai began a series of street protests by burning copies of the newspaper and blocking traffic in front of the *Dinakaran* office. Some had already begun to throw stones at the office building when a group of Azhagiri loyalists, led by the infamous muscleman and gangster known as "Attack Pandi," pulled up in an SUV. They attacked the office with stones and metal and wooden clubs, and they threw twenty crudely made petroleum bombs. The office exploded in a raging fire, killing two computer engineers and one security guard. By all accounts, the Madurai police simply stood by while the violence was unfolding. Two hundred people were initially charged in the protests, twenty-five people were eventually arrested for rioting, and two were specifically arrested for the death of the three workers. Trials ended in 2009 with the acquittal of all the accused when every one of the witnesses turned hostile, presumably responding to threats from Attack Pandi's men.[41]

This attack was to have wider significance, illustrating what Stanley Tambiah terms the *transvaluation* of a relatively local event of violence as it gets taken up in the media ecology.[42] In order to understand the stakes involved, it is important to know that *Dinakaran* had recently been purchased from Adithan's grandson, K. P. K. Kumaran, by Kalanidhi Maran, owner the Sun

Media Network, among Asia's most profitable media companies at the time. The paper was being rebranded even though it retained its old name. Kalanidhi Maran is also the great-nephew of Karunanidhi himself as well as the brother of Dayanithi Maran, who was union minister for communications and information technology in Delhi as result of the DMK's strength in the 2004 elections. That a rift between the Maran family and the Karunanidhi family, including Azhagiri, had been brewing for some months was well known to everyone. But the survey and the violent reprisals that ensued seemed to have sparked a starker breakdown of party discipline as factions that once operated behind closed doors now led to open attacks in newspapers and deaths on the streets of Madurai. Within a few days, Dayanithi Maran was asked to step down from his post as national minister even as he was being investigated for corruption in the telecom industry through a Malaysian cell phone company. Dayanithi was replaced as telecom minister by A. Raja, who would eventually become a primary suspect in the 2G-spectrum scam, among the biggest cases of corruption in Indian history at that point in time.

Meanwhile, under Kalanidhi Maran's ownership, the price of a single issue of *Dinakaran* fell from three rupees to one, and the paper crept up to become the second most widely read daily in Tamil in 2006. After the publicity provided by the Madurai attack, the paper had shed its connections to the Karunanidhi family, which had gone on to start their television channel, Kalaigner TV to rival the Marans' Sun TV. By 2010 *Dinakaran* had surpassed the top Tamil paper in sales to become one of the most widely read newspapers in India, with a net circulation of over 1.2 million (though *Dinathanthi* retains a higher total readership). It now appears that as minister, Dayanithi is also alleged to have supplied his brother Kalanidhi with over three hundred free high-speed cable phone connections. If the allegation holds true, the Sun Media Network that owns *Dinakaran* was partially subsidized by the state through this transfer that enabled Sun to broadcast around Asia using government lines. Dayanidhi Maran was officially charged with corruption in October 2013 by the Central Bureau of Investigation for the phone line transfers. Even so, he was still offered a DMK seat in the 2014 elections. Maran lost that election before being reelected in 2009 and 2019, and the *Dinakaran* paper continues to prosper.

EVENT TWO: HATE AND THE DOUBLE CONSCIOUSNESS OF SUBALTERN PUBLICITY

The next story I would like to share is also about the public image of an important political leader, but it concerns social actors who are very differently situated in the field of caste politics. In January of 2008, only a few months after the Madurai attack, party cadres of the Dalit Viduthalai Ciruthaigal Katchi (VCK; Liberation Panther Party) attacked the offices of the third largest Tamil newspaper, *Dinamalar*, then located on Mount Road in Chennai. They did so in response to an article critical of their leader, among the most important Dalit politicians in South India, Thol. Thirumavalavan. Many in the media consider the article to be an example of writing that borders on hate speech in light of the disadvantaged caste backgrounds of the VCK leader and those he represents. Around twenty men attacked the *Dinamalar* office on Mount Road in Chennai by throwing glass bottles and wooden logs. Two security guards suffered injuries to the head, and there was substantial property damage at the entrance to the office. A senior VCK party official appears to have warned the heavily fortified office ahead of time that they should expect street protests because of the article they had run, but *Dinamalar* only appealed for police protection after the attack. Two party activists were arrested.[43]

The full import of this event can only be understood if we recall and take into account that *Dinamalar* is owned and run by a Brahmin family with political leanings toward the Hindu right. They have frequently criticized Dalit political leaders, among other groups, and have been accused of hate speech before.[44] The problem of being associated with excessive violence is one that has followed the VCK from the time they developed as a party from the Dalit Panthers movement. As Hugo Gorringe shows in his research on the movement, under Thirumavalavan's leadership Dalit politics has often felt the need to respond to caste domination through displays of force, but the party is also very aware that it is subject to upper-caste stereotypes about Dalits when it shows physical force on the streets.[45] The show of strength in responding to the newspaper article was an extension of this logic into the mass-mediated world, and the activists who took part in the attack must have been acutely aware of the risks of being stereotyped in this fashion. In this case—as in other media events in which stigmatized communities act with a form of DuBoisian "double consciousness" that come with knowing one will be measured by the values of dominating communities—the gamble of acting for oneself while being watched by others is fraught with risk.[46] *Dinamalar* played its role and made much of the attack in its pages to further criticize Dalit politics in a circulation of images of violence provoked, in a sense, by the paper itself. Later that year they would go on to publish the Danish cartoon depicting the Prophet Mohammad, originally published in *Jyllands-Posten*, leading to a similar display of popular anger at their office in the city of Salem. The following year the news editor at *Dinamalar* would eventually be arrested in a defamation case for running a scandalous article implicating many well-known Tamil film actors in a prostitution ring.

As in the first attack, where Azhagiri had to signal his strength to a Madurai DMK public at the expense of his less than stellar national image, in this case VCK activists had to protect the image of their leader while knowing that their own image might be further defamed through upper-caste media coverage of the event. But they were in a position of much less local strength than those supporting the DMK leader. The editors also knew they were playing a risky game. As one former editor at *Dinamalar*, who now works for another paper, put it, invoking a powerful ethical image from the *Ramayana*, the *Dinamalar* family like to walk right on the "Lakshman Rekha," the line between safety and potentially dangerous results, never explicitly intending to provoke violence but knowing that there might well be consequences of their work. The *Dinamalar* newspaper moved offices to a more easily securitized building in the years following these attacks. One of the current editors candidly told me that they take possible repercussions, legal or otherwise, into account when running critical articles and that economic recompense is also sometimes at stake when running a potentially inflammatory article. But there is always a deniability that remains plausible to some.[47]

EVENT THREE: HEARSAY GASTROPOLITICS

Finally, in early 2012, the offices of the biweekly *Nakkeeran* were attacked by a large crowd made up of members and supporters of the AIADMK party. The leader in scandal-provoking investigative journalism ran an article claiming that the AIADMK leader, J. Jayalalithaa, then chief minister of Tamil Nadu, ate beef. As soon as the story hit the stands, a group of party workers rushed to the *Nakkeeran* office on Jani Jahan Khan Road in Chennai, causing significant damage after assaulting the security guard. Like in the Madurai event, and unlike the VCK attack described above, the police appear to have been present but not to have interfered. Not only was the newspaper office subject to damage, any and all stands carrying that week's edition were subject to attacks across the city.

The office was already well fortified, and the editor of *Nakkeeran*, R. R. Gopal, vividly narrated to me the story of how he barely escaped with his life. Always happy to regale listeners with stories of his fantastic exploits, of which we will hear much more in following chapters, he explained to me that he had long gotten into the habit of hiring security guards who sported the same style of bushy handlebar mustache for which he was known in order to confuse potential attackers. Those who broke into this office that day had trouble finding the real "Nakkeeran Gopal" as he is known, and fought with his security guards while threatening to take the editor's life. After hiding for a few hours while his office was being ransacked, Gopal slipped out through the back and made his way to safety by jumping into an auto-rickshaw that was waiting for him behind the building. "I've become an expert at escape, whether its cops or crowds," he boasted to me while chuckling and grinning through his trademark facial hair. This was but one incident in a career of what had become known as "daredevil" journalism. Gopal would then appear in the papers the following day demanding police protection from the AIADMK crowds who were after him and who had also attacked newsstands selling the article.

Presenting quoted speech attributed to the chief minister coupled with a caricatured image, *Nakkeeran* printed, "I am a beef eating *mami*," using a term for "aunty" from the Brahmin dialect of Tamil. The article claimed that Jayalalithaa used to serve and eat beef with her then lover and mentor, the former cinema superstar and wildly popular chief minister for ten years (1977–87), M. G. Ramachandran (MGR), who was also the founder of the AIADMK party. Jayalalithaa was indeed a Brahmin who was rumored at the time of the article to be increasingly under the influence of Brahmin and Hindu-nationalist advisers, chief among them Cho. Ramaswamy, who published the conservative rival weekly *Tughlak*. She had also recently dramatically broken up with Sasikala, her longtime friend and confidant, kicking her out of her house in the Poes Garden neighborhood in Chennai. This lent further credence to public impressions Jayalalithaa was being advised by a new circle, the "Mylapore Mafia" (referring to the Brahmin neighborhood in South Chennai) who were intent on steering her away for the Dravidian-nationalist politics her party was established by MGR to pursue.[48]

Jayalalithaa, the leader of a state where the Dravidianist non-Brahmin movement continues to be a hegemonic field within which all political actors must contend, was thus subject to a cheeky poke in the form of a mock defense of her "non-Brahmin" gastropolitics. This was, once again, a self-conscious choice on the part of the editor, knowing that there were likely to be violent repercussions. In 1997 Jayalalithaa had already slapped a ten million rupee lawsuit against Gopal for printing what he claimed to be secret letters that she had sent to MGR. The court ordered Gopal never to print defamatory material about Jayalalithaa again without giving her a chance to respond in the pages of *Nakkeeran*. It was because he had defied this prior order that Gopal and his associate editor at the time, A. Kamaraj, eventually had to apologize in public for the article about beef eating.

This weekly, unlike the dailies I have so far described, really does live on such provocations as much as its reporting of more standard news items. Although Gopal and his reporters had been attacked many times—which he has documented meticulously in a book called *Challenge* (1999) and a series of books called *Yuththam* (War; 2012)—this attempt on his life eventually caused him to move. While his house remains in Royapettai where the office and press once stood, when I visited Nakkeeran Gopal to interview him in 2017, he had shifted both the office and press to a new, hidden, and even more securely walled location in the industrial estates surrounding Chennai. He has made a name for himself as a master of the kind of combative and intimate relationship with political crowds, especially with the AIADMK, that others in the field of investigative journalism imitate intermittently.

Instrumentality and Mediation in Popular Politics

It has long been common to understand attacks like these through narratives in which crowds are thought to be used by powerful political leaders to quell criticism. This is a story where political power represents itself *before* the people who lie under its sovereignty.[49] Many see both crowds and the media that animate them into action largely in terms of instrumental representation serving another purpose. The positive dialectic of mass mediation as an experience of collective agency through self-abstraction, characteristic of the public sphere when it is free from coercion and not directed from above, is entirely lacking here. What Habermas, in his later refinements of public sphere theory, conceptualizes as the importance of "communicative power" and its "dispersing effect" in generating popular sovereignty alongside administrative procedure leaves little room for violence itself as a communicative act.[50] It is indeed hard to reconcile the communicative power of such events with a politics of deliberative democracy. The framing of crowd violence as a deviation from democratic norms is often coupled with the assumption that the crowds involved in displays of force would not have even read the newspaper article in question, and that they are acting on behalf of someone else's interests. There is something to the spectacular nature of these events that lends credence to such interpretations. But I think they are based on faulty assumptions about readership and political knowledge. These analyses are ultimately unable to explain how this sort of mediatized drama over representation works to produce real political effect, and the actors involved are not granted the kinds of reflexivity that are usually attributed to reading publics.

Several political theorists have tried to find and way out of this discourse on crowds and other subaltern forms of political life through a more serious consideration of the role of the popular in modern democracies. In the study of India, we have often turned to Partha Chatterjee, who conceptualizes a populist "politics of governed" where political action articulates aspirations among those who are excluded from participating in the main organs of civil society or the public sphere because their modes of social action and communication have no place there.[51] Subjects are shaped by the strategies of a governmentality that takes an instrumental approach to populations, and they participate in a political society through idioms of community and kinship, not the abstract principles of national citizenship.

One of the difficulties with this formulation is a certain ambiguity about whether "the governed" and their corresponding "political society" is a demographic category referring to types of people or whether this is rather a modality of political action.[52] This problem is cleared up, however, in Ernesto Laclau's formulation of populism as a widely shared social logic where, he argues, the libidinal excess of crowds in populist movements can help illuminate the workings of any form of democratic mass politics to the degree that any mass-political movement operates through modes of rhetoric and semiotic indeterminacy that are often pejoratively attributed to populism.[53] Populist reason, in Laclau's account, amounts to the political as such insofar as it breaks with fantasies of total revolution whereby society is completely reconciled to itself on the one hand and with forms of developmentalism that reduce politics to administration on the other. "The people" are indeed a necessary if underdetermined subject for nonliberal democracies if we are to take some of the claims of contemporary populists seriously, and for liberal ones as well, if we are to move beyond the individualist act of voting as the primary sign of political decision-making.[54] But neither Chatterjee nor Laclau have seriously considered the role of mass mediation and remediation of the people and community apart from apparatuses of the state. This is a problem with political theories that tend to abstract the question of politics from that of technologies of representation and media of contestation.

"Populism puts pressure on the liberal settlement by dreaming of a direct and immediate presencing of the substance of the people and, as such, a reassertion, a mattering forth of the collective flesh," as Mazzarella writes. But it does so through claims to immediate connections between people, leader, and land that are in fact enabled by complex interactions with technologies of mass and networked mediation.[55] And it is not only the media worlds afforded by an internet that appears to confirm biases and stoke the passions that serve this function, as the three events depicted above show us. The press has long served a similar function, even if the sensory modalities of political engagement are changing along with regimes of circulation. One of the virtues of both Habermas's and Anderson's theories of the modern social imaginary was, in fact, to consider the centrality of print-text circulation and its imbrication with capitalist social forms to the formation of mass-political subjects. This is a centrality I would like to extend beyond print capitalism and across media forms to "communicative capitalism" in general—that regime of exchange value that generates profit through the circulation of information—in the analysis of publicity and imaginaries of popular sovereignty that unfolds in this book.

If critics of populist mobilization tend to view crowd action through the lens of cynical instrumentality, and the populist response is to claim a direct connection between leader and crowd, my analysis pursues the problem of mediation as both a political economic and sociotechnical process in some depth. And if we now add a concept of the news event as that moment where political consciousness and affect crystallize around concrete representations of the political leader that circulate on a mass scale, we can begin to better appreciate the work of mediation in the very experience of immediacy. The processes of "presencing" the people narrated in the events above involve an unfavorable print media representation of their leader, a crowd response, and further remediation of that crowd response across media forms, including print. The collective embodiment of peoplehood, here, throws into question the intuition that there is something virtual about a reading public as opposed to the actual crowd on the street. It would appear that the crowd in the street acts also as a virtual presence, or at least a potential entailment of decisions taken by editors and journalists back at their offices: embodied people and physical structures that are themselves subject to consequences of representing a political leader in poor light. The news event as a complex moment of mediation is thus crucial to understanding how such a "mattering forth" of the collectivity takes place. Following Karen Strassler's powerful work on photography, I would also add the "image-event" as a critical site through which political subjectivity is forged (see also chap. 5).[56]

Forms of Political Knowledge

The time has come to rethink the public sphere from a perspective that assumes the libidinal, corporeal, and poetic ties of kin and community as a

FIGURE 1.1. Image of the DMK leader M. K. Stalin printed on the front windshield of an auto-rickshaw in Chennai. Photograph by the author.

starting point in politics, not as a set of constraints on critical debate. This means decentering unmarked stranger sociability as the primary means through which popular sovereignty is enacted in accounts of political modernity. The problem with which we began this chapter, for example, is the very ideological border that is maintained between the empty stranger/citizen of the public sphere and the marked, embodied subject. The latter is a subject of democratic politics that may well have captured important elements of state power through the forms of scaling up or down enabled by mass mediation but not through the forms of self-abstraction that have been commonly associated with public sphere formation. The deified politicians, their families, and their crowds ultimately win democratic elections in large part through a politics of mediatization and news events that are produced and framed for political advantage. But this is a formation of publics that coalesces around political leaders and the people as embodiments of the abstract principles of popular sovereignty. The very concept of popular sovereignty is, of necessity, a rather open-ended field of contestation but one that can be configured quite differently from the utopias of self-abstraction animating some normative models.

This is a political process that also throws into question the binary set up by the theory of representation whereby a democracy works insofar as representatives transparently represent the will of those they would represent. Such a theory of representation completely misses the reciprocity involved in the constitution of mass-mediated political subjects. Nor can it account for the possibility of a will to be represented. Mediation is a two-way process in which "the represented depends on the very representative for the constitution of his or her identity."[57] Or, in the words of VCK leader Thirumavalavan, "We must both mold the movement according to the people and mobilise the people behind the movement."[58] There is a deep sense in which "the people" don't exist as such without the movement, and it is for this reason that classical theory is fundamentally unable to explain how working-class South Indians come to be so invested in these political leaders and how they are being represented in the press. Crowd violence is often orchestrated, to be sure, as I think it was in the attack on *Dinakaran* in Madurai. But the attribution of a complete lack of agency is at the root of common metaphors like "puppets," or Tarde's image of the "animal," and can only be based on the logical inverse of liberal democracy such that the followers simply obey the will of the leader.

The key point that must be brought to the center of a theory of popular sovereignty and publicity concerns the forms of political reflexivity surrounding mediated representation and the potentials of remediation that are generated through processes of attending to media as constitutive of people making. Here I am not only talking about the forms of reflexivity discussed by Warner, of strangers acting in concert through textual circulation in secular time, but I am also arguing that being an actor in such a populist public requires performing displays of passionate participation before an interested and oftentimes intimate audience, either face-to-face or mass mediated, and one can easily lead to the other, stretching the normative limits of citizenship and throwing them into question. The participants in the drama, we might call it, all display an awareness of the power of representation and mass mediation, not as a universalization of disembodied voice but more as a mass-mediated and deeply embodied battle ground organized along community sensibilities that may be at cross purposes.

There is an acute awareness on the part of all participants and those they represent—editors, journalists, political leaders, and those who represent the power of political leaders on the street—of the fact that these bodies on the street will be further mediatized and recontextualized in the course of mass uptake. Everyone is aware of participating in a news event, and with this comes the knowledge of the fact that the outcome cannot be determined by any one player. The production of populist publicity through news events is a game of chance. In this sense, Judith Butler's attention to the vulnerability and dispossession of bodies in forms of public protest that depend on the mass uptake of others is critical.[59] What should be added or emphasized, however, is that bodies taking to the street are *already oriented as such* to the fact of mass mediation as a constitutive part of their very action on the street. Media act as infrastructure for street politics. Awareness of this fact, that bodies are always already mediated, as it were, has become part of a public common sense. I would argue the political leaders of parties like the DMK and AIADMK, also the Shiv Sena, pioneered this media expertise as an elementary aspect of political knowledge over the late twentieth century in response to a changing media environment. Other examples of such political expertise at play in populist mediations have come from the anticorruption movement, especially Arvind Kejriwal's Aam Admi Party and the BJP under Modi. All of these formations can be justifiably criticized for their majoritarian tendencies, and they must be. The current Hindu nationalist fixation on degrading the Muslim body, for example, has no counterpart in decidedly more ecumenical world of Dravidianist politics. But the mediatization of combative political action on the street is doubtless now a defining feature of politics across ideological formations.

Conclusion: Normativity, Empirics, Theory

It is difficult to draw a strong normative theory out of the observations and arguments offered here about limits of self-abstraction and the profoundly mediated quality of crowd action. This is not to leave the question of norms aside in an appeal to greater empirical rigor. Hate speech leading to retribution in profoundly unequal games of mutual defamation appears to proliferate. And the exertion of force by more powerful political actors coupled with capitalist logics demanding maximum circulation have certainly eroded important democratic claims made by subaltern actors in this quickly changing media environment. But to the extent that political theory's engagement with questions of mass democracy has been framed by a set of norms broadly derived from liberal thought, it has frequently served to render unfamiliar worlds of mediatized politics as immature and lacking in universal norms. The ethical normativity of political thought is consistently transposed in this fashion into the empirical realm of norm and historical deviation. In media studies there has been a related and consistent bifurcation of intellectual labor characterized by a tendency to focus on concrete technologies in the high theory emanating from Euro-American centers on the one hand and empirical studies of the global South relegated to "discrepant histories of use, interesting for their variety but illuminating nothing essential in all the range of their forms, on the other hand."[60]

There is no question of grasping the empirical phenomenon of popular mobilization, in India or elsewhere, in itself, shorn of theoretical presupposition. That said, there is no reason to restrict our understanding of politics to a tradition solely derived from Greco-Roman conceptions of the polis. Powerful insights into questions of politics, justice, and ethics can certainly be derived from ethnographic and historical analyses coupled with a careful reading of Indian-language texts, both ancient and modern.[61] But the search for an overly coherent vernacular model of politics would likely suffer from problems of ahistoricity that obscure the very real contest between current conceptions of the political and all too readily ignore the globalized forms of mass and networked mediation that lie at the center of contemporary political action. The work of critical "contemporanizations" of non-European conceptions of the technological and the political has only recently begun in earnest.[62] Rather than building an airtight model, we must focus on vernacular idioms that engage with a range of traditions and intertexts, where republican notions of popular sovereignty and subaltern critiques of caste, mediated by numerical imaginations of community, might easily be grafted onto discourses on just kingship that are by now irrevocably linked to the question of economic development. Such a politics continues to be experienced and understood by most in the form of newspaper articles, satellite television news programs, and digital imagery circulating though WhatsApp that bleed almost seamlessly into images of leaders on posters and painted city walls and on to street action and speeches blasted over loudspeakers that saturate the sensorium.

And so, we must foreground aspects of reflexive mediation and embodied action in popular politics that dominant strains of political theory had all along sought to contain. These foci entail a rethinking altogether of democracy in the age of deep mediatization. If such a move requires a loosening of normative ideals such that we retain a commitment to popular sovereignty without holding on to the utopic dimensions of self-abstraction specific to a provincial claim to universalism, we must search anew for a language of massification that does not presume a world of disembodied strangers. In such a world of large-scale intimacy, where politics was perhaps never disenchanted, attention to these forms of reflexivity about embodied publicity in the making of modern politics has the advantage, at the very least, of keeping the question of struggle over the very terms of participation in democracy at the center of our theory.

CHAPTER TWO

Defamation Machine

"I've got to go to court on Monday. I'm a criminal, didn't you know?" Mani chuckled gently as he explained why he wouldn't be able to have a follow-up meeting with me that day. A seasoned freelance journalist who had recently teamed up with a new political news magazine I was following, he was proud of the fact that he might well have attracted one of the first criminal defamation charges for an online publication. Mani's article on the rumored ill health of the chief minister, J. Jayalalithaa, was published on the English-language rediff.com website, wherein he also noted that media were afraid to discuss the matter in public for fear of retribution. The sting came soon enough for Mani in the form of papers issued by the public prosecutor's office. Fighting the defamation case against the Government of Tamil Nadu meant attending hearings once a month, thereby losing a day of work that was always much needed for a freelancer like himself. Mani knew the drill. He had done it before.

Making light of his legal woes for a moment, Mani was in fact worried. Not so much for himself; these cases almost never lead to conviction. But like most journalists I talked to at the time, he was deeply concerned about the state of affairs in Tamil Nadu, where a thin-skinned political leader could use the justice system without restraint against hundreds of scribes like him in an effort to intimidate them into either forced praise or silence. Mani perked up when I told him that I had already read about the criminal defamation case against him and his colleagues at rediff.com in the *Times of India*. "At least someone noticed!" His eyes lit up behind the thick lenses of his glasses.

Politics in which reputation is paramount excite dreams of iconoclasm, which might, in turn, be framed as acts of defamation, libel, slander, or even sedition. This chapter is about such dreams of breaching the aura surrounding political leaders and the legal means used by those in power to fend off the attack. It is also about how these instruments, those who wield them, and journalists who are targeted by the law all become the objects of further publicity. Over the course of my research, more criminal defamation cases had been filed against journalists and leaders in Tamil Nadu than in any other state in India. In fact the widespread use of criminal defamation law to settle political scores in Tamil Nadu and elsewhere led the Supreme Court to revisit the vital question of whether or not to retain such a law in the Indian Penal Code. Many, including judges, have criticized its abuse and noted the "chilling effect" extensive use of the law might have on free speech in general and journalism in particular. Nevertheless, in May of 2016 the court ended its proceedings with a decision in favor of upholding the validity of this legacy of British rule. The related colonial-era charge of sedition is also regularly used in Tamil Nadu and elsewhere as a means of harassing those who are simply critical of the government or political leaders, often blurring the distinction between defamation as a crime against a person and sedition as a crime against the state. The Supreme Court has often taken a liberal stance in limiting effective use through important precedents in the past, but it is only beginning to question the basic validity of the law of sedition itself.

Whereas the debates on defamation and sedition have been conducted mostly in the realm of normative legal theory—where the argument for decriminalization is well reasoned—this chapter adopts a different, more sociological approach.[1] It analyzes a broad set of relationships that has developed between news media, party politics, and the legal system to examine the field of political contestation that has resulted from the law's application in efforts to quell dissent. To merely note that this triangle is itself mediated by questions of political economy would be a truism. My more specific wager is that accusations of defamation made by political leaders and the criminalization of critical journalism might serve to fuel the very engine of print capitalism while providing greater exposure for both the politician and the news organization involved. While someone like Mani had relatively little to gain from his encounter other than some notoriety among local journalists, more lucrative forms of publicity are oftentimes made out of attempts at censorship. Furthermore, I hope to show that this process must be understood in relation to a world in which political leaders' claims to sovereignty are in fact experienced and contested through the poetics of commodity images. A leader's reputation, an otherwise abstract quality, is radically dependent on tangible signs of leadership, and an investigation of defamation thus entails a study of fame itself. Political power is deeply invested in questions of media representation, including images of the state as well as the leader's body, and those in power have often resorted to both legal and extralegal means to shape the contours of that representation in efforts to project their fame.

Taken together, these logics have made for relationships between news media, political leadership, and the law that are both agonistic and interdependent. Rapidly proliferating digital media of production and dissemination have made attempts to manage the political image more difficult. This is a problem regarding recent changes in the nature of political publicity addressed later in the chapter and more squarely in the final two chapters of this book. This chapter follows from our previous examination of crowd violence to argue that paying attention to these relations of mutual recognition can unlock some of the deeper dynamics animating the political public sphere in contemporary Tamil Nadu, where the medium of defamation law has also acted in a substantial manner to consolidate the personality of political leaders as the grounds of a sovereignty that exceeds even that of the state. If the previous chapter had gone some distance in distinguishing the ethos of the liberal English press from that of the a more affectively charged Tamil vernacular, the present one will bring the "split public" of news media described by Arvind Rajagopal into a single frame in an effort to understand less easily seen processes connecting strains of journalism that might otherwise appear to inhabit completely separate worlds.[2] In order to get at the logics underpinning this complex field, let us move next to a story where abuse of criminal defamation law is fairly straightforward—such that accusations of wrongdoing can be turned back on the accuser with relative ease—before moving on to murkier waters.

Of Rubble and Reputation

On the evening of June 28, 2014, an eleven-story building, still under construction, collapsed in the Chennai suburb of Moulivakkam. Sixty-one people died as a result, the majority of them construction workers from across southern and eastern India. The following morning, on Sunday, newspaper and satellite television headlines were full of details, both heroic and horrific, about efforts to rescue those who were trapped under the rubble. It was on Monday morning that sharper questions started to arise about the causes of the collapse. On that day the Tamil daily *Dinamalar* ran with its typical one-word headline, "Tragedy!" But this was followed by two more accusatory subheadlines introducing the front-page story.[3] The first noted that two different government orders had been issued to ease normal safety regulations for the building, and the second reported that the chief minister, J. Jayalalithaa, said that the government planning agency responsible for approving and monitoring such constructions, the Chennai Metropolitan Development Authority (CMDA), had done nothing wrong. The article in *Dinamalar* used specific evidence obtained from a government report to indicate that officials from the CMDA must have known about and excused infractions in the building process. When talking to reporters and editors from the newspaper later that week, I learned that they had obtained a leaked email from within the secretariat where they gleaned the details that gave the article its heavy evidentiary weight.

Although nearly everyone suspects large-scale corruption in the construction industry, discussing this among friends, or even strangers on the street, is very different from printing incriminating evidence that points back to the state's involvement in one of Tamil Nadu's most widely read daily newspapers. The following day, M. L. Jegan, the Chennai City public prosecutor, filed a complaint of defamation, citing section 499 of the Indian Penal Code before the principal sessions court on behalf of then Chief Minister J. Jayalalithaa, accusing the paper of "malicious intention" to harm the reputation of the chief minister. The chief minister's office in Tamil Nadu often uses criminal defamation suits to restrict the domain of the publishable. But such direct confrontation with Jayalalithaa was somewhat unusual for *Dinamalar* at that time. The paper had long supported her party, the AIADMK (All India Anna Dravida Munnetra Kazhagam), from the days when party founder and superstar actor M. G. Ramachandran fought with the DMK (Dravida Munnetra Kazhagam) to form his own party. Indeed, *Dinamalar* and Jayalalithaa shared a common opponent in the person of M. Karunanidhi, who is said to have shut off electrical power to the newspaper in retaliation for a negative article in the 1970s and who started the practice of withdrawing government advertisements from *Dinamalar* for their criticisms, thereby depriving them of a major source of revenue.

Relations had already soured before the Moulivakkam report, however, and it was time for the paper to assert a new degree of independence through critical journalism. This scoop was also too good to give up. Other papers had not seen the leaked email. While many accusations of defamation are never noted in a newspaper that finds itself in the position of defendant, this time *Dinamalar* took a different route. This paper, which frequently reports on the real-world effects of its own journalism, published a front-page article the day after the case had been filed about the filing of the case itself. The headline and article provided a great deal of publicity for themselves as leaders of critical journalism through a defense of their original story about Maulivakkam and a refutation of the charges of defamation in a single text.[4] Although never directly accusing the chief minister of any wrongdoing, *Dinamalar* did stick to its accusations of irregularity in the planning process, citing government documents.

Feedback and the Gender of Political Fame

In the short narratives above we can see simple instances of how an attempt to block publicity can become the very stuff of publicity itself. Censorship becomes news. We might term this the "absorptive" capacity of news media as it remediates a legal system that regulates news media while also providing it with much of its content. By pointing to remediation, I take the law as a media system as well; it is a system that can absorb attempts by the press to police advocates and judges through public scrutiny while also relying on news media to render its power in public form. Apart from attempts to block the flow of information through threats of contempt or defamation, judges actively use the media as a stage for social commentary when giving judgments, a topic taken up in greater detail in the following chapter. Each media system—law and news—plays a role in both normalizing the other as a distinct domain while periodically staging events of interpenetration that are framed as breaches of the norm that has otherwise been achieved.

Censorship becomes an interesting entry point into this dynamic of eventing and normalizing not only in dramatic cases of defamation or sedition but also in more mundane invocations of contempt of court that are used to control news coverage in ways that rarely provoke comment in the news media itself. When a publisher or editor *does* decide to make a news event of such an intervention, the results are unpredictable. Accusations of defamation are not only means of silencing the press—although they are that, too, and often effective—the force of defamation charges just as often exceeds the proximate aim of censorship. Such a display of power is itself "a gamble on publicity," to borrow an apt phrase from William Mazzarella and Raminder Kaur.[5] All of the parties involved have a sense of the stakes, but none knows the outcome ahead of time.

What legal historians have seen as the problems of amplification or magnification—where the publicity provided by the accusation of defamation leads to greater scrutiny of the faults attributed to the plaintiff and greater renown for the defendant—appear to be old ones.[6] The Maharaj Libel Case of 1862 is a well-documented example of this dynamic in colonial India, where a defamation suit brought against the Bombay-based Gujarati newspaper *Satya Prakash* led to intense public concern about sexual practices among devotees of the Pushti Marg sect.[7] But something somewhat different is happening in more recent times such that amplification and magnification, processes of publicity that were foundational to the rise of a critical press since the early nineteenth century, have turned into a positive feedback loop of sorts not wholly unlike that produced through violence. In this process not only the accuser but the press, too, can claim new notoriety when it is put on trial. In the words of the senior advocate and legal scholar, Rajeev Dhavan, "the press has been able to make symbolic and other gains by making social and political capital out of court cases. . . . The trial process becomes a vehicle for transforming restraints into possibilities." Amplification and magnification extending to the press are not only collateral effects of critical journalism but can become sought-after ends in themselves, avenues of possibility providing grist for the mill of print capitalism. Some in the press reflexively court defamation cases or other legal reprisals in search of publicity as a means of putting both their journal and their political target in the spotlight.[8] Norms of civil address in the press and other news media have changed rather rapidly since the late 1980s as a result of this feedback loop that encourages the production of constant scandal and controversy. A quick glance at the political Twittersphere, as it expands thirty years later, reveals this feedback loop and the search for sensationalism to have overtaken many other rhetorical aspects of communication.

Without indulging in undue nostalgia for an age of idealist journalism, we can nevertheless note that in a world where the critical function of news publicity has come to bleed almost seamlessly into its commodity value, the kind of secrets that are unveiled in the name of public scrutiny of government authority are often of the same quality as those that are at the heart of the culture industry.[9] Both share in the logics of commodity imagery, public personality, and even celebrity reputation. This melding of critique and the commodification of scandal takes on a gigantic quality in a place like Tamil Nadu, where many of the characters involved were in fact film celebrities, their entry into formal parliamentary politics proceeding from the "cine-political event" in the terminology of film theorist M. Madhav Prasad, to which we will return.[10] The aestheticized personalization of politics had intensified greatly when Jayalalithaa emerged as the first woman to shift from the screen to the political stage in the 1980s, becoming both adulated and vilified more than any man before her. Her rise to dominance in the pantheon of Tamil politics over the following decades thus marked a change but also a certain clarification of dynamics that had developed before. To the degree that genre distinctions between political leaders and celebrities have been more generally blurred for decades in Tamil Nadu, a study of logics of political publicity in this state has much to tell us about more recent trends elsewhere. Before resuming our analysis of how political leaders and the press engage in battles through the dialectics of legal restraint and positive publicity, let us first get some clarity on the legal media involved and a little history of their uses.

Laws and Practices of Defamation

Along with other aspects of tort law in colonial contexts, defamation was criminalized in article 499 of the Indian Penal Code drafted in 1860 such that it exists today as both a criminal and a civil offense. As noted above, the Supreme Court recently ended extensive deliberations on whether this article is constitutional. Other charges that have been used in a similar fashion include obscenity and sedition in sections 292 and 124A of the penal code. The former has formed the basis for laws that extend well into the realm usually associated with defamation, and the latter has also been used to silence political opposition. Sedition has, in fact, been theorized in the literature as a form of "defamation against the state" and can have a similar field of application if not a similar status in legal theory.

What marks independent India's significant departure from the restrictions of the colonial penal regime is article 19(1) subclause "a" that gives the constitutional right to free speech modeled partly on the First Amendment of the US Constitution. But as Gautam Bhatia and Lawrence Liang both note, this was immediately curtailed in subclause "b." which goes on to allow "any law relating to libel, slander, defamation, contempt of court or any matter which offends against decency or morality or which undermines the security of the state or tends to overthrow the state."[11] The restrictions were further amended in 1951 with the addition of the word *reasonable* before the restrictions, in addition to language about friendly relations with foreign states and "public order." Another restriction concerning speech that might threaten the "sovereignty and integrity of India" was imposed in 1963 in part as a reaction to DMK demands for a separate nation-state of Dravidastan in what is now South India.[12] In conjunction with the original subclause and amendments, the other major constitutional protection that comes into play to restrict the original freedom of expression is article 21, the frequently invoked "protection of life and personal liberty" that is alleged to have been violated when accusations of defamation are made. There are therefore rather clear conflicts between colonial-era penal regulations and the spirit of free expression granted in the constitution as well as potential contradictions within the text of the constitution itself.

In the realm of postcolonial legal theory in India, the landmark Supreme Court ruling, *Romesh Thapar v. The State of Madras* (1950) remains an important precedent upholding the journal *Cross Roads*'s right to publish leftist literature against the charge of sedition and establishing freedom of the press as a foundation of democracy. From the lawmakers' side of the story, the archive tells us that after the original Press (Objectionable Matters) Act from 1951 was taken off the national books in 1956, leading to the establishment of the Press Council of India to self-regulate, it was K. Kamaraj's Congress government in Madras that passed a new state-level amendment to the Penal Code and Code of Procedure in 1960. This law made "scurrilous or grossly indecent writings intended for blackmail" punishable with imprisonment or fine. I have found few political uses of this law that included the same exemptions protecting speech or writing about public persons found in article 499 on criminal defamation. According to senior journalists I have talked with, the practice of policing the press through criminal defamation using the older penal code was, in fact, initiated by Karunanidhi, especially during his second tenure as chief minister beginning in 1971, but on a limited scale. This was a period that is remembered by many as one of political ferment and the rise of a more forceful, sometimes violent form of populist mobilization against those seen as enemies in the press discussed in the previous chapter.

The Emergency declared by Indira Gandhi from 1975 to 1977 marks a turning point both in Tamil Nadu and across India, with article 19 of the constitution no longer in effect. The DMK protests against restrictions on speech eventually led the prime minister to dissolve the state government and impose an executive president's rule, during which many were imprisoned under extremely violent conditions. Few news publications in Madras defied national censorship and its legal armor other than the *Indian Express*, run by Ramnath Goenka; its Tamil daily *Dinamani*; Cho. Ramaswamy's satirical weekly *Tughlak*; and the DMK mouthpiece *Murasoli*. All four journals published acts of protest that are remembered as remarkable acts of bravery in journalistic lore. For example, the *Indian Express* published empty columns in the opinion pages in a symbolic act of resistance, and *Tughlak* was printed with pitch-black cover pages. *Murasoli* published cartoons likening Mrs. Gandhi to Hitler in an obvious affront to the prime minister, and it also published front-page headlines in bold type about how "Okra Is a Healthy Food!" in a more subtle act of satire pointing to the inane topics that journalists were allowed to report on at the time. Both the AIADMK and the CPI supported the prime minister's program.

M. G. Ramachandran (MGR), when he was chief minister of Tamil Nadu (1977–1987) extended emergency logic through an "anti-scurrilous writing" ordinance in 1981, widely used against dissent and originally issued as a government order against a DMK evening paper called *Ethiroli*.[13] The paper had carried a report on the then health minister accepting a Premier Padmini car in exchange for allotting a medical college seat, and its editor Arcot Veerasamy was sent to jail for twenty days for this reporting.[14] Like a similar law that Rajiv Gandhi later tried to bring into the central legal framework, the law in Tamil Nadu borrowed the language of "scurrilous writing" to alter the parameters of laws on obscenity and decency, effectively blending these infractions with defamation. Infraction was made a cognizable and nonbailable offense, enabling police to arrest and jail a suspect without warrant.[15] The draconian act was repealed in 1984 after a series of protests but not before it was extensively used against political opposition.[16] MGR, who was extremely ill with kidney failure and related complications through the final three years of his life, was almost legendary in his obsession with secrecy surrounding reporting on his bodily condition.[17] Doctors who spoke, and papers that wrote, about the chief minister, who was proud of his famous physical prowess, faced both legal and bodily attack.

Another case from this period is that of the legislative assembly asserting breach of privilege and sentencing S. Balasubramanian, editor of the popular weekly *Ananda Vikatan*, to rigorous imprisonment for three months in 1987 for a cartoon he published depicting government ministers and members of the legislative assembly as pickpockets and robbers. This was a rather simple case of parody that was seen as too plausible by many in the assembly, and the editor eventually won an appeal in the Madras High Court, where he was awarded a thousand-rupee "notional compensation" for his wrongful arrest. Balasubramanian famously kept the two five-hundred-rupee notes and a photocopy of the check in a frame sitting above his head behind his desk as a trophy celebrating his triumph over the assembly.

When it comes to the use of defamation law as a means of controlling news media, however, every senior journalist interviewed over the course of this research agrees that it was during Jayalalithaa's first tenure as chief minister that a new level of combat became the norm. Between 1991 and 1993,

180 criminal defamation cases were filed on behalf of the government against journalists and political leaders. She withdrew all the cases on December 30, 1993, in a dramatic act of sovereignty premised on the exhibition value of official pardon. But the political use of such cases continued with remarkable regularity, although spiking at times for reasons I will return to in the conclusion. Shortly after Jayalalithaa returned to office in 2011, for example, the public prosecutor filed a criminal case against the Chennai edition of the *Times of India* for reporting on the high number of road accidents in the state, accusing them of being defamatory against the image of the then chief minister because it gave the impression that she was not concerned with the safety of the people traveling on roads.[18] *Ananda Vikadan* was accused of defamation for an article they ran summarizing the AIADMK's performance in government over the course of its term. And reporting on the alleged failures of the government during the massive Chennai floods of December 2015 attracted yet another round of cases against the *Times of India* and *Dinamalar*. By the time of Jayalalithaa's death in late 2016, the government of Tamil Nadu had filed over two hundred cases of criminal defamation against the media and political leaders since she came into office in 2011, more than in any other state.

In these cases, as in the story about the Maulivakkam building collapse described before, the government went to the courts in an effort to protect the image of their role as governors. That is, the newspaper articles that attracted the charges of defamation were about official actions of the state even if the tacit assumption underpinning both the articles as well as their contestation in court was that the reputation of the chief minister is very closely connected to the image of the state government, and perhaps even isomorphic. In these cases Jayalalithaa might be seen as recapitulating earlier efforts on the part of her mentor, MGR, who is alleged to have used his harsher state-level law to quash stories about schoolchildren becoming ill after eating food provided by his midday meal scheme.

All such allegations of defamation were filed in the name of the chief minister, retroactively blurring the line between criticism of the government and attacks on the person of the chief minister. These cases all follow some of the logic of branding as an exercise in name recognition and reputation inasmuch as the publication of a fault in the product of government care reflects back on the more intangible properties of the sign that would stand for the very essence of care for the poor, namely, the persons of MGR and Jayalalithaa, respectively. This is where personal reputation and government work bleed into one another, and the very accusations of defamation serve to further solidify this connection. As a result of these cases, the Supreme Court of India eventually took the unusual step in 2015 of advising the government of Tamil Nadu to stop taking criticism of governance as personal insult.[19]

Negative reports on issues of law, order, and development are important triggers for defamation cases, but they are not the only ones. A great many allegations of defamation are more directly concerned with the very person of the chief minister. These cases turn on the accusation of untrue and, more importantly, "maliciously motivated" depictions of that person as known through tangible images of personhood, not only through their good works as governors. It is precisely the question of using instruments of the state, like the public prosecutor's office that executes criminal defamation cases, to pursue personal ends that the Supreme Court noted in its deliberations on the future of this law. To the degree that political power is invested in a person who also claims to stand for the government but whose broader claims to sovereignty in the popular imagination are relatively separable from the state, the state apparatus becomes a mere instrument in support of extraparliamentary politics.

Political leaders are not the only ones invested in this system. The press can derive value from it as well even if the logic of a celebrity's right to reputation stands as the grounds for attacks through defamation law or related accusations. The news media, too, have been invested in the heightened aura that has surrounded political leaders, and they seek to mold the political image well beyond questions of state-level governance. Is it here that we can return to the dynamic I sketched before, of amplification turned into feedback insofar as print capitalism thrives on the uncovering the veiled faults of celebrity political leaders, focusing in particular on their bodies.

Two Ends of the Journalistic Spectrum

The integration of critical political journalism and celebrity exposé is most obvious in Tamil weekly and biweekly political journals. These are the muckraking journals that have promoted investigative reporting and also developed the genre of the political gossip column, where the attribution of sources of information is purposefully vague in keeping with the logics of gossip and rumor. Many journalists would insist, for very good reasons, that these magazines do not abide by the same high standards of evidence that the leading English-language newspapers do. But all sorts of journalists are nevertheless connected by the fact of having been charged with defamation. In the words of a senior *Times of India* editor in Chennai who sought to distinguish himself from biweekly tabloids, "we are a serious paper, totally different from them. It's only the defamation law that we have in common." Let us, then, begin this part of the analysis with an example from a newspaper that is generally very cautious when reporting on the state government to develop a sense of the larger field of contestation that has been opened by laws restricting the press before moving on to more extreme cases.

A LEGAL ASSAULT ON LIBERAL REPORTING AND OPINION

The Chennai-based English-language daily, the *Hindu*, India's paper of record, is no sensation-driven tabloid. Many consider it to be rather dry compared to other papers if also more reasonable and responsible to the facts. But this august standard-bearer of liberalism was not only repeatedly accused of criminal defamation by Jayalalithaa, it was also charged with the more serious offense of breach of legislative privilege in 2003. Responding to a critical editorial titled "Rising Intolerance," which had accused the Jayala-lithaa administration of "contempt for the democratic spirit," the legislative assembly charged the *Hindu* with a serious criminal offense that could land the well-known family that publishes, owns, and edits the paper in jail. The privileges committee of the assembly went on to make the same charge against S. Selvam, editor of the DMK's *Murasoli*, for simply reprinting in Tamil what the *Hindu* had published in English. In the words of the committee, both papers were guilty of publishing "indecent phrases . . . motivated by a desire to diminish the goodwill and fame that the Government enjoys."[20] That *Murasoli* had been charged with the same offense illustrates the extent to which it was the simple fact of publication and not that of authorship that constituted the breach according to the committee. This attack on the mere citation of an earlier text illustrates the leaky nature of authorial intent as it is construed by those who would accuse the press of defamation.

While employing the language of "fame" and "goodwill" in its denunciation, in keeping with the logic of defamation, at a strictly legal level the legislative assembly had effectively accused these papers of inhibiting the right of the member of a legislature to speak to the house without the fear of being sued for slander. This is the freedom of expression for lawmakers that legislative privilege is meant to secure. Here, paradoxically, a legal safeguard against defamation became the grounds on which to accuse the press of libel. In this respect, the assembly was greatly extending the law protecting their speech to the point of treating the press as an obstacle to democracy, as this body had done earlier against *Ananda Vikatan*, illustrating how legal media meant to preserve free speech can be turned around to be used as instruments to threaten the press.

As a result of the motion passed by the assembly's privileges committee on November 7, within half an hour Chennai police descended on the houses of publisher S. Rangarajan, editor N. Ravi, executive editor Malini Parthasarathy, associate editor and chief of the Tamil Nadu bureau V. Jayanth, and special correspondent Radha Venkatesan, in an attempt to arrest them and send them to jail for fifteen days. These journalists, who were accused of limiting the freedom of expression of lawmakers, had been warned about their imminent arrest from friendly sources, and some had already left town for Bangalore, where several of them were meant to attend an event celebrating 125 years of the *Hindu*, in any case. They had narrowly escaped arrest when they were briefly stopped by the Tamil Nadu police on their way, and they were eventually housed in Karnataka chief minister S. M. Krishna's house, giving an indication of the kind of political connections the *Hindu* had cultivated over the years. Krishna was scheduled to speak at the celebratory event. Meanwhile, another of the accused, N. Ram, editor in chief, was back at the office in Chennai that night when the police came twice, the first time without proper paperwork to conduct searches and arrests, the second time surrounded by the cameras and microphones of local media.

Many years later, I had the opportunity to discuss these events with Ram, who remembers that day vividly. He had invited me to his office on the third floor of the classic art deco building on Mount Road. Walking by the giant statue of his grandfather, Kasturi Ranga Iyengar, I was directed by an assistant to Ram's interior office, which was lined with books and memorabilia of a life spent at the epicenter of Indian journalism. Sitting together on a large leather couch, the renowned journalist and champion of the free press walked me through the story.

"I was driving in my car to work going up the beach road when right in front of Queen Mary College I received a call from Bala at *Vikatan*. He told me, 'a source says it will come up today in the assembly.'" It was his friend S. Balasubramanian who had himself faced jail time for the very same charge that had been leveled by MGR's government fifteen years earlier who had warned him. Ram thought that the charge of contempt would be raised in the assembly only so that Jayalalithaa could show herself to be a magnanimous sovereign in excusing them. "But the pardon never happened! Then, at the office I got a call from Dayanidhi Maran [DMK leader] who told me they were on their way. The police. By the time they arrived, our entire union was outside protesting." The police made their way past the protesting journalists and staff inside the beautiful building without a warrant. Ram explained to me that the commissioner, Vijay Kumar, was in fact a very "decent person," and when asked for a warrant he relented. The police came back with an arrest warrant the second time, when they searched the premises for the accused.

Ram was in the news editor's office when the police returned, surrounded by journalists and by news cameras. He personally walked around the whole of the *Hindu*'s massive office complex with them to assure them that he was alone among those accused of criminal publication. He made it a show of sorts, he told me, to look under tables, behind doors, and so forth, turning the search itself into an event, all in front of the press.

> Rangarajan [the publisher] was still in Chennai but luckily not in the office that day. They really wanted to catch him and humiliate him, and Ravi [Ram's brother and the editor] was also among the accused, but he went to Bangalore with Murali [Ram's other brother]. So, we made the police search into an event to show the injustice of it. I had already gotten a message from the Madras High Court offering anticipatory bail but decided to stay here. Today if it happened it would have been different, I wouldn't have been offered even that. It was a very serious search.

Narrating the details of the buildup to the motion in the privileges committee and the arrests, Ram noted that while the *Hindu* had been subject to legal harassment before, this was unprecedented. He used the contrasting example of the decency of the Congress government after he personally worked to break the Bofors corruption scandal that would cost them greatly with the pettiness of the AIADMK's state government at the time. The early 2000s was an era of increased assaults on journalists, such as the party worker and police attacks on journalists protesting violence against the press in 2001. The *Hindu* was itself preparing a report on freedom of the press for the upcoming Supreme Court hearings on the topic.

The following day's front-page news in the *Hindu* was spectacular. The capacity of news media to metabolize positive publicity out of censorship was on full display. Most impressive was the powerful photograph of Ram sitting at his desk confronting two police officers. Above this image read the headline, "T.N. Assembly Sentences *The Hindu* Editor, 4 Others for 'Breach of Privilege': High Drama as Police Descend on Newspaper Office without Warrant." In a large column, next to the photo on the front page, the paper responded with a resounding criticism of the abuse of legislative privilege in a stinging editorial titled "A Crude and Unconstitutional Misadventure."[21] Another small box of text on the front page noted that Ram was on the phone with Prime Minister Atal Bihari Vajpayee that very night. At the bottom of the page was an article detailing the search and Ram's arrest, explaining how when the police walked him out of the office, the crowd "mobbed them, shouting slogans, 'Down with police high-handedness,' 'Down with Jayala-lithaa' and 'Long live the press.' Pacifying the crowd, Mr. Ram said: 'The authors of this outrageous misadventure will pay heavily for this.'" This, too, was accompanied by a photo of Ram being escorted by police through the crowd followed by a wall of television and still-photo cameras. Looking back over the years, when I was interviewing him, Ram admitted that the edito-rial might have been a little "overcooked," in his words. But those were very trying times, and he was keen to make a strong statement for freedom of the press, a cause with which he has long been associated.

Here, as had happened before, the chief minister's gamble with the public-ity produced by the attempt to censor the paper appeared to have backfired in certain respects. Within three days the Supreme Court had stayed the arrest of all the accused, and the chief minister's reputation for excessive use of force to silence her critics only grew among a certain reading public. The Hindu's accusations of intolerance where confirmed for its English-language readership, while it is also probable that the chief minister garnered addi-tional respect from her own largely Tamil-speaking constituency among the poor for her show of force in defense of her reputation.[22] As noted in the previous chapter, such spectacular acts against the press are in fact perform-ing simultaneously for very different publics and serve to delineate the very oppositions that emerge among these fragments of public uptake.

For the moment, I would like to step back from the event of the arrest and how it was turned into further publicity, amplifying the sense of injus-tice journalists felt at the time, to dwell on the language that was used in the offending reports and opinion piece leading to the charge of contempt in the first place. I do so not to mitigate the violence of this crackdown on expres-sion but to understand the reasoning though which the newspaper's words were interpreted to have tarnished the "fame and goodwill" attached to the chief minister as office and person. It appears that the privileges committee was disturbed in particular by how the Hindu had been reporting on speeches given by Jayalalithaa in the legislative assembly. The paper had characterized the chief minister's behavior as an "unrestrained attack on the opposition." They had described Jayalalithaa's speeches as "diatribes" filled with "sting-ing abuse" delivered in a "high-pitched voice" in which she "fumed" while chastising the opposition party. While these descriptions were taken from a series of reports on the legislative assembly, the paper had used language normally reserved for theater or concert reviews to criticize the chief minister's performance.

It was the tight focus on Jayalalithaa's uncontrolled bodily demeanor, and in this case her voice, that provoked retaliation from the committee that was controlled by the AIADMK. In its response to the motion, the *Hindu*'s opinion piece expresses surprise that a mere list of "innocuous, if unflattering" words describing the chief minister's bodily demeanor should be taken as offensive as opposed to what the paper saw as the much more serious and, in their words, "well-reasoned" arguments against her politics, especially her use of defamation. Citing British parliamentary practices and contrasting it with India, the opinion piece that triggered the assault notes that "The House of Commons on whose practice the privileges of legislatures are still based does not allow privilege issues to be raised over reports of proceedings unless they relate to proceedings behind closed doors or expunged portions of any speech."[23] This focus on the body and its performance in the assembly is significant for our analysis of the logics underpinning contestations about the political image, where reason has been pitched against excessive emotion and embodied action. Jayalalithaa was too "animated" in her performance as chief minister.[24] These verbal images of the body gain importance especially in light of a gender politics where the news media treat women who occupy the space of publicity with general aggression. Indeed, the chief minister's adoption of the fictive kin identity of "Amma," coupled with her trademark cloak-like sari covering her whole body, must be seen as moves to counter the otherwise negatively sexualized aura of feminine publicity in a marked departure from her earlier image as an attractive film star.[25]

The response offered by the newspaper pointing to abuse of defamation is also noteworthy and helps focus our attention on a sort of impasse that emerged in the competition to define the public aura surrounding the gendered political body. Charges of illiberalism couple easily with aesthetic evaluations of political leadership that presume different standards of civil publicity between men and women. The blunt legal response offered by the Jayalalithaa government only served to fuel accusations of intolerance or "crudeness" and to provide material for claims to journalistic heroism. This was a scene that replayed itself over and over again with startling regularity across the journalistic spectrum, as different as the *Hindu* is from many Tamil publications at the levels of objectivity and broader journalistic ethics. As we now shift our attention to look at papers more deeply interested in fueling

FIGURE 2.1. Mural of J. Jayalalithaa being admired by an adoring follower in Madurai. Photograph by the author.

the feedback loop of exposure, legal attack, and public condemnation around the unauthorized circulation of the political body, verbal or pictorial, we can see a wider field of political contestation emerge. Sober English dailies and more wild Tamil political magazines can inhabit different positions within the same domain that has been opened through the medium of defamation law.

A TRICKSTER'S TRADE IN MALEDICTION

To understand the broader nature of investments in the cycle of arrest, legal intervention, and publicity and what this all means for the political body, it is useful to move beyond individual cases and turn to the whole career of "Nakkeeran" Gopal, the enfant terrible of Tamil journalism whom we met briefly in the last chapter. As a young man from Aruppukkottai in the deep south, shaped by the energetic iconoclasm of the Dravidian movement, R. Rajagopal moved to the capital city of Madras first in a failed rubber business venture and second to begin his career in journalism. He worked for MGR's journal *Thaay,* and then as a layout artist for the Tamil political gossip weekly *Tharasu* in the mid-1980s. This was a moment when the weekly press was exploding around India in the aftermath of the Emergency and with a general opening of the economy. It was from his job as an artist and then junior reporter at *Tharasu* that Gopal decided to start his own magazine in 1988.

Already figuring himself as a kind of modern-day *āsura*—an opponent of the gods in Hindu mythology—Gopal named his journal *Nakkeeran* after the great medieval Tamil poet who is said to have had confrontations with Lord Shiva himself by pointing out the flaws in the great god's poetry. He had bought the right to publish under this name from a friendly senior colleague who gave it to him for a nominal price because of how well it suited the fiery young man. "Nakkeeran" Gopal's new biweekly followed in *Tharasu*'s footsteps and eventually overtook it in sales through what he calls "dare-devil journalism," publishing the details of violent criminality with connections to the state and exposing corruption and other official misdeeds. Although initially a rival of *Tharasu*'s, having eaten into its share of the political news weekly market, *Nakkeeran* ended up making a name for itself reporting on a defamation case that the Jayalalithaa government had filed against the older publication during her first year as chief minister in 1991, leading to the first of many arrests for Nakkeeran Gopal. Gopal is, in fact, the person most English-language-daily journalists would point to as a specific example of how different they are from the world of Tamil weeklies and biweeklies.

When I met with the infamous journalist in his fortified office in the industrial outskirts of Chennai—where he had moved because of the numerous attempts on his life in his earlier, more central Royapettah location—he invited me in, past a modernist Chinese-style gate and an armed security guard who also sported the same trademark handlebar mustache. Gopal walked me past an outdoor fish tank into his reception foyer for lemon tea. We sat on a couch under a wall that had been completely covered with a giant photograph of Gopal standing before the news cameras after being released from one of his arrests. After explaining the picture and learning who I was and why I wanted to interview him, Gopal declared that he is basically a visual artist:

> I learned what I needed to at *Tharasu*, designing the covers and doing the layout. How to catch people's eyes, to tell a story. One of the important breaks we got at *Nakkeeran* was a photo! One of my *tambi*s [little brother, the term he uses for employees] heard that Jayalalithaa was in Ooty with Sasikala, and we managed to get a copy of a picture they had posed for together at a professional photography studio. We just paid the photographer. It was the first picture to be published of the two of them together.

The surreptitious, intimate print of the most powerful woman in Tamil politics on vacation at a hill station with her companion, whom many believed to be her lover (in part because of *Nakkeeran*'s reporting), was but one of many images that would define the journal. Only a few years later, *Nakkeeran* would go on to print the image of then Chief Minister Jayalalithaa on the cover of the magazine dressed in a Hitler costume and mustache, with the headline "A Hitler Is Here!," harkening back to *Murasoli*'s cartoons of Mrs. Gandhi during the Emergency.

But the words printed in *Nakkeeran* have been just as forceful, leading to countless encounters with the police.[26] The journal came to incorporate a new written feature in which the editor answered questions sent by readers based on gossip he had picked up from the street. This section of the journal is named "Māvali Bathilkal" (Mavali's answers), after the *āsura* King Mahabali, whose greatness made the gods envious, and the genre was picked up by other journals. In Gopal's telling of the story, they had no phone in the beginning. "We had an arrangement with a nearby tea shop and would pay a certain amount for every call we received. We had a boy to collect the messages from the shop and convey them to us every hour." The image of the teashop, where political debates are thrashed out in a semipublic, uncensored, markedly masculine domain, is noteworthy. It is the teashop ethos that Gopal brought into the printed pages of his magazine along with a willingness to make himself part of the news as a journalist—what some detractors consider a lust for publicity characteristic of "yellow journalism." But Gopal is clearly happy with his reputation for stirring things up. As he was quick to point out to me, even those who look down on the style of his journalism respect the deep network of loyal reporters who provide fodder for his journal's widely read columns.

The list of Gopal's tussles with the laws of defamation is colorful and very long. Apart from outrageous magazine covers, many of his feature articles are clearly meant to provoke publicity through sales-generating friction with authority. For instance, Gopal secured his place as a primary protagonist in wars over the limits of free speech in India when he tried to publish the autobiography of "Auto Shankar," the auto-rickshaw driver turned serial killer who terrorized Chennai in the late 1980s. Auto Shankar had left a diary, serialized in *Nakkeeran*, that gave a number of details explaining government officials' collaboration with the notorious gang leader. While many references to public figures are veiled in euphemism, the autobiography did go so far as to name a member of the legislative assembly who was a former speaker of the house as a partner in crime, in addition to the deputy superintendent of police, who is alleged to have helped Shankar set up his network of brothels in the city.[27] "That was when I got a call from the cops informing me that *auto varum* ["an auto is coming," a euphemism meaning that a hit had been put out on his life]. I went u.g. [underground] for two months. It was the first of many times. I had to take my family."

In a court case filed by the government to stop the publication of Auto Shankar's writings that went all the way to the Supreme Court of India, the bench cited US Supreme Court precedents to argue that it would be unconstitutional "to impose a prior restraint upon publication of material defamatory of the State or of the officials."[28] The frequently citied judgment in Gopal's favor, *R. Rajagopal v. State of Tamil Nadu* remains an important reference point in free speech law to this day, with its argument that defamation is an offense that can only be taken up by the law after the fact of publication. Gopal has been hailed by Supreme Court justices and journalists alike as a champion of free expression as a result of this and other rulings.

But it is with Gopal's relationship in the late 1990s and early 2000s with the forest bandit and sandalwood smuggler Veerappan (described in detail in chapter 4) that the magazine shot to national fame. Gopal was eventually arrested and jailed for terrorism under the draconian Prevention of Terrorism Act for his connections to the wanted outlaw, and it was during this time that the battle between Nakkeeran Gopal and Jayalalithaa took on epic proportions. While *Nakkeeran*'s editor was imprisoned and continuing after his release, the journal published a series of articles critical of the chief minister, often focusing on Jayalalithaa's relationship with her live-in companion Sasikala. *Nekkeeran* had, for example, published an article based on secret sources detailing how they slept in the same bed, which was later used as evidence in a defamation case against him. Both the chief minister and her friend filed a civil claim for twenty million rupees in damages for defamation against Gopal and his associate editor, A. Kamaraj, in response to a series of such articles. While the case was working its way through the legal system, the court also granted the plaintiffs an injunction against *Nakkeeran* publishing any inflammatory material about Jayalalithaa without her prior approval. While the civil claim remained unresolved at the time of Jayalalithaa's passing and continued to be used against Gopal when he pushed the limits of image making, along with extensive use of criminal defamation cases, the injunction was found by the Madras High Court to amount to the very form of prior restraint that *R. Rajagopal v. State of Tamil Nadu* had established as unconstitutional.[29] The prior restraint on publishing first imposed by the court was dropped in 2006. At our meeting in 2017, Gopal boasted that he was currently fighting over two hundred cases in various courts at the time, including at least fifteen defamation cases filed by the Tamil Nadu government and others by private parties. There are also well over 250 First Information Reports against him that are still being investigated, and his journal has spent tens of millions of rupees between 2001 and 2010 on legal battles.[30] These numbers are a source of satisfaction for him of a job well done.

While we were discussing these figures, Gopal asked his personal assistant, who also acts as one of his lawyers, to make photocopies for me of two other important documents. Smiling as he handed the first set of stapled pages to me, Gopal told me to look inside. It was the AIADMK party's election manifesto for the 2001 general assembly elections, with Jayalalithaa's face on the cover. On the seventh page was a section the lawyer had highlighted in yellow marker. Following a few lines accusing the ruling DMK government of corruption, it reads, "Further Karunanidhi's Government also indulged in unlawful activities by encouraging Nakkeeran Gopal, who was himself involved in criminal cases." This is perhaps the first time a journalist had been named in an election manifesto, and it stands as a landmark in his story of becoming a political force through journalism. "People think I'm a DMK man, but I'm not. My guru was Chinnakuthoosi, who taught me about truth in journalism. It was from him that learned social responsibility, and it is Chinnakuthoosi that I follow, not the party. Read what I've written about them!" Gopal pointed to the freshly garlanded picture of his guru, who had passed away some years earlier, hanging on the wall next to another giant fish tank behind his desk in the main office upstairs. The renowned archatheist writer R. Thyagarajan, better known as Chinnakuthoosi (Small needle), had written regularly first for the Kamaraj's Congress's *Navasakti*, switching in the 1980s to report for the DMK's journals, starting with *Ethiroli*, and then moving on to Karunanidhi's own *Murasoli*. Chinnakuthoosi had served as a leading Dravidianist intellectual and a mentor for many aspiring young journalists in the movement who would come to visit him in his simple flat in Triplicane until he finally moved in under Gopal's care for the last years of his life. "Chinnakuthoosi refused hand-outs, so he wrote articles for me in exchange for my taking care of him," Gopal reminisced, looking fondly at the framed picture.

The second document that had been photocopied and handed to me was clearly a legal petition from the year 2000, typed in the ubiquitous courier style font of electric typewriters of the time. The first paragraph read like many such petitions before the court I had read before:

This application is by the plaintiff under Order XIV, Rule 8 of the Original
Side Rules read with Order XXXIX Rule 1 C.P.C., restraining the respondent
and her agents from publishing in any media anything defamatory against
the applicant/plaintiff in any manner again or by way of repeating any of
the false and defamatory statement [*sic*] made by the respondent against the
applicant/plaintiff in her press release dated 14.8.2000 and published in
"Dinamalar" and "Dinakaran" on 15.8.2000 or similar or further statements.

When I looked down at the second paragraph I read that the "plaintiff is
the Editor of Nakkheeran Publications" and quickly understood that this
was his attempt to turn the legal tables, as it were. Gopal filed a defamation
case against Jayalalithaa! The document goes on to quote the offending press
release that had been published in major dailies accusing Gopal of being a
"blackmail guy" who only used his connections to criminals to extract money
from politicians based on false claims. A journalist who had become so famous
and controversial as to elicit what he alleges to be defamatory statements by
one of the most powerful leaders in India has indeed made his political mark
in public.

Returning to Gopal's own legal troubles, an examination of the allegedly
libelous articles cited in the Madras High Court and Chennai Public Prosecutor's cases against Gopal shows, once again, the degree to which the stuff
of offense was focused on the plaintiff, Jayalalithaa's body. For example, the
only passage from an article that is explicitly quoted in the injunction case
judgment dates from the May 20, 2003, issue, and it compares the lack of
alliances between the chief minister's political party with the willingness of
several illnesses to make themselves at home in her body, and it goes on to
make claims about huge numbers of pills she has to take.[31] The article even
claimed that her companion Sasikala was plying the chief minister with "certain other things," even that she was solely responsible for administering the
medicine. The advocate representing the plaintiffs maintains that this was a
thinly veiled reference to alcohol and that this article amounts to nothing less
that "character assassination." Many friends had gossiped with me at the time
that Jayalalithaa was rumored to be addicted to painkillers. Many in Tamil
Nadu continue to suspect that Sasikala was perhaps administering toxic sub-
stances to Jayalalithaa and that this might have had something to do with her
death. The arguments made on behalf of the plaintiffs in these cases focus on
the degree to which this reporting on the chief minister and her friend were
attacks on their reputations, and because they touched so deeply on their
personal lives they were defamatory as such.

Despite the civil suit and the large number of criminal defamation cases against him, Gopal appeared as motivated as ever to draw his opponents into battle until Jayalalithaa's final months in Apollo Hospital. In 2012 *Nakkeeran* courted violence against their offices and even newsstands when they printed an article in which they claim that Jayalalithaa used to cook and eat beef with MGR.[32] Because of the unresolved civil case, after officially complaining about the physical attacks on his paper, *Nakkeeran* nevertheless had to publish an apology for the offending article or face a charge of contempt of court. The *Hindu* was also charged with defamation at the time for reporting on and quoting from the *Nakkeeran* article.

In August of 2015 the magazine was charged with criminal defamation for printing rumors that where spreading wildly on WhatsApp and other social media at the time about the chief minister's ill health, suggesting that she might at any moment be taken to Singapore or the United States for treatment of a large number of illnesses.[33] The section called "Dialysis Garden Report" (punning on her home neighborhood of Poes Garden) was written in rumor format, drawing on a widespread genre in Tamil political reporting, that attributed the source of all this talk about the details of her health problems and even her weight to social media, using the epistemically uncertain quotative suffix -*ām* (it seems). This article, which "impeaches the reputation of the 'Chief Minister'" in the words of the petition filed in the Chennai Sessions Court, was printed at a time when Jayalalithaa had not been seen in public for ten days shortly after being reelected in a by-election after her arrest and after failing to show up for a number of scheduled events. Chennai was rife with talk that she had indeed left the country to seek treatment for her many problems. Such reporting walking the line between calumny and investigation continued, first around the slow and mismanaged government response to the terrible floods that ravaged Chennai and Cuddalore in December of 2015, and then once again around the chief minister's health during the state assembly elections. Each of these reports attracted a criminal defamation case.

Nakkeeran Gopal's nemesis, with whom he shared an intimate yet very public vendetta, died shortly after starting her fifth term in office in December of 2016. The magazine continued to attract controversy during Jayalalithaa's three months in hospital before her passing and has been especially truculent in pursuing the many conspiracies surrounding her death. In yet another event that would rally journalists in defense of free speech, Gopal was jailed for reporting on a sex scandal that implicated the governor if Tamil Nadu, who used a law similar to the privilege motion claiming that he could not fulfill his duties because of what was written about him in *Nakkeeran*. As he was signing various books he was gifting to me on my way out of his compound, Gopal was still talking about the succession battle then under way as Sasikala, calling herself Chinnamma (Aunty, or "Little mother"), and members of her family were trying to take over the party. *Nakkeeran* had also published much about a daughter Jayalalithaa is rumored to have given birth to but never acknowledged, thereby adding their own masala to a story with many angles. Gopal appears happy to continue stoking the flames of publicity at the limits of legitimacy into this new round of political and legal combat. But I couldn't help but wonder whether he did not also miss his favorite target, at least a little. As much for her willingness to respond through legal counterattack as for her larger-than-life iconographic imagery, which continues to loom across Tamil Nadu.

Conclusion: Powers and Vulnerabilities of the Image-Text

How are we to understand this fixation on the gendered body and its capacity to provoke legal action in the form of defamation cases or other legal attacks on publication? What is the relationship between person and governance? Can political leaders assert "moral rights" over their public image as some in the film industry have begun to claim? As I had begun to argue above, the legal accusation of defamation itself serves to draw the connection between governance in an official capacity and the question of personal reputation. Or rather questions of government are easily subsumed in this manner under the category of a political personhood that is profoundly gendered. Defamation charges appear to have become a weapon by which political leaders assert a personal right to publicity. Taken as a whole, however, the press is not only a victim of attacks on free speech by overzealous politicians who cannot tell the difference between public office and private life. News media have appeared eager to develop this relationship between person and governance, and they blurred the lines further insofar as depictions of the leader's bodily demeanor or bodily condition found such prominence in reporting on issues of state that are supposed to be of public concern. Journalism, too, is invested in personalizing the political, especially in the case of *Nakkeeran* and its imitators. If Georges Bataille could argue that "prohibition gives to what it proscribes a meaning that in itself the prohibited action never had," we find in these later cases of defamation a scenario where the "meaning" of the prohibited action is hard to imagine without anticipation of the imminent act of legal prohibition.[34] The law as prohibition thus also becomes a stage for public personalization.

This particular constellation braids together political, legal, and even technological domains of life. Taking these domains in turn in this concluding analysis, it becomes clear that this constellation has emerged under the overarching logic of commoditization in general and branding under conditions of communicative capitalism in particular. Let us begin with the *political*. Taking into account the type of bodies that are subject to this type of scrutiny, we must note that not all political leaders are subject to the same varieties of personal attack. As more astute readers of the press would have observed, the elderly wheelchair-bound Karunanidhi, who was one of the leading voices echoing *Nakkeeran* demanding that the chief minister reveal details of her health, never seemed to attract the same kind of attention even as he met regularly with journalists and others in ways Jayalalithaa refused to. I have already noted that patriarchal delineations of the public sphere play a very strong role in attracting provocative aggression from the press. But if we are to widen the historical scope of analysis beyond Jayalalithaa's conflicts that we have concentrated on, we must recognize the critical role played by her mentor—and, more critically, her fellow *cinema star* and *actor*—MGR in developing the dynamic of legal attack in defense of positive publicity and bodily image that his protégé inherited and elaborated.

Loved for his beauty, strength, and legendary kindness, MGR was the first great leader to inhabit a domain of personal sovereignty in the Tamil imagination that far exceeded his office or the very parliamentary state structure that lend this office authority qua office, like Jayalalithaa after him and other celebrity leaders who have mass followings. Far from a political body that is transparently at one with the state, as described by Claude Lefort in his memorable essay on totalitarianism, what we can discern among actors turned political leaders is a body around which the aspirations of a people might well be magnetized but one that also has a great deal of independence from the state as a widely circulating commodity image.[35] This is the basis of the "shadow structure of political representation," an extra parliamentary authority or "phantom sovereignty" that theorists of southern film like M. Madhava Prasad, Rajan Krishnan, and S. V. Srinivas have written about with regard to cine-political leaders.[36] The "people," whose own sovereignty is constituted through transactions with the star image in this form of populism, experience the state as the most important among several vehicles through which political power is experienced. The value of the film star leader is an intangible essence that breathes life into particular works, the most obvious being welfare schemes targeting particular populations. Like the classic Marxian commodity fetish, a whole set of social and political relations condense in the tangible form of an overdetermined body. And it is where the image touches ground, taking material form that the power of this social totality is felt. This is also the moment where the political image is most vulnerable.

The image of the cinema star turned chief minister operates much like a commercial brand, which is also defined in financial terms like the legal definition of reputation—as an "intangible asset." Unacceptable citation of the tangible brand image, a possibility that built into its material form as an image, causes damage to this metaphysical asset.[37] In the case of Jayalalithaa, she was, of course, a brand even before entering into politics. Her brandedness was cultivated further, although its qualities certainly changed with the shift toward brand "Amma," which became a registered trademark associated with a range of commodities beyond those available in the well-known affordable eateries that opened in her name, including cement, salt, pharmaceuticals, and water all branded by the government of Tamil Nadu under the "Amma" label. The fate of this brand with the demise of the body to which it was substantially connected is a topic for another analysis, but here we can note that, like the unauthorized use of a material sign pointing back to a trademarked product, depictions of the political body that fell out of bounds were subject to legal sanction as an attack on reputation. The weapon of defamation, one that can be turned back onto those who wield it, must be interpreted in light of this particular populist logic of political representation if we are to understand its proliferation in recent decades.

Turning now to the *legal* structures that contribute to this dynamic, we must begin with the crucial fact that journalists are almost never jailed for criminal defamation. "The process is the punishment," as those in the worlds of journalism and law like to say.[38] Those who have spent time in jail have been charged with other offenses, including sedition, which amounts to an allegation of defaming the state itself. This is because the simple charge of criminal defamation is a bailable offense with a negligible conviction rate.[39] The dull but persistent force of defamation charges rides more on the indignity of journalists having to produce themselves before the Chennai Sessions Court, waiting for long hours with others who have been accused of crimes, than it does on fear of incarceration or even the money involved in fighting such a case. In fact for papers like *Nakkeeran*, the costs of fighting legal battles, although staggering at times when involved in a civil case, might be seen as a form of advertising expenditure insofar that these cases generate positive publicity for the journal in part through the journal's representatives' numerous appearances in court. In response to the political body's illicit exposure and citation in the news media, it is the journalist's or opposition leader's body that stands exposed before the court. But even this can be turned around. For example, responding to an allegation of criminal defamation in the run up to the assembly elections of 2016, Karunanidhi decided to appear himself and produce his frail, aging body before the court and the mass media when he was excused from doing so in order to make a point about abuse of defamation.

Although outdated laws that lend themselves to abuse are distributed across the penal code—ranging from defamation and sedition to the criminalization of alternative sexualities in the notorious article 377 (which was struck down)—legal reasoning has often tended toward a liberal orientation to free expression when cases are tested against constitutional principles. In fact the language of landmark free speech cases—such as *R. Rajagopal v. State of Tamil Nadu* (1994) or *Shreya Singhal v. Union of India* (2015)—has invoked the "chilling effect" as a harm to democratic discourse and reiterated the medium neutrality of the rights to freedom of expression upheld in article 19(1)(a) of the constitution. Judges at both the High Court and Supreme Court levels frequently cite the groundbreaking United States Supreme Court precedent *Sullivan v. The New York Times* (1964) opinion advocating wide "breathing room" for the press when writing about public figures in particular, making "actual malice" motivating a complete disregard for the facts the standard by which cases of defamation must be judged. This is why, in the cases discussed above, the allegation is repeatedly made that a newspaper published with the "malicious intention" of damaging the reputation of the chief minister, while the frequent invocations of "goodwill" and "fame" are indicative of the kind of reputation that is at stake and the forms of vulnerability to which it is subject.

However, it is not only the media dynamic of feedback loops around the political image that encourages blurring of the personal-private and the public-official domains of life. We have already seen the degree to which political and gender logics lead to a dominance of the personal-public dimension. But Indian law is also ambiguous on the question of public servants. On the one hand it maintains the press's special right to scrutinize public officials in the second exception to the law of criminal defamation, section 499 of the Indian Penal Code, stating "It is not defamation to express in a good faith any opinion whatever respecting the conduct of a public servant in the discharge of his public functions, or respecting his character, so far as his character appears in that conduct, and no further." But this protection is counterbalanced by section 199(2) in The Code of Criminal Procedure from 1973, which makes breach of any such criminal law a "cognizable" offense before the Court of Session upon a complaint in writing made by the public prosecutor if the person involved is a public servant of high office. So, the more recent criminal code makes it much easier to book someone for writing about a political leader than it is for another category of person. Furthermore, it is the specific language of section 499 that protects the person of a public servant insofar as that character does not appear in public conduct that make issues of the personal body such potent grounds for accusations of defamation. These are the essential legal contradictions that allow so many of these cases to be filed, posing a legal threat without a corresponding number of convictions.

Finally, I will conclude with the argument that the *technological* domain of social life plays a critical role in affording the proliferation of both image politics and attempts to shape the image through legal means. What we witness in Tamil cine-politics and associated populist leadership styles is not some simple continuation of a logic of kingship, as it has been analyzed in culturalist terms, even if the vocabulary of popular sovereignty in South India and elsewhere often draws on tropes of royalty, or even divinity. First of all, the forms of hierarchical intimacy that connect leaders and their people are radically reliant on the modes of massification, circulation, and distance that contemporary media forms enable. This whole package is animated by the commodity image such that, to the degree that leaders can sustain a sense of the virtual or spectral in the more aesthetic or expressive pole of their representative functions, acting as a fictive mother or big brother to the Tamil people, the auratic or ritual dimension of political leadership is sustained and even enhanced by technologies of image reproduction, including the newspaper. Indeed, the careers of both Karunanidhi and Jayalalithaa, like Anna and MGR, were substantially built through the media of cinema and newspapers as well as oratory at the public rally analyzed so powerfully by Barney Bate.[40]

The dominant political aesthetic these leaders cultivated is tuned to resonate through these very media, and these are the media forms that appear most sensitive to charges of defamation. Television, for example, rarely draws allegations of defamation, although this is also in part because the Government of Tamil Nadu has had a monopoly on the distribution of satellite television since 2011 through the public-sector undertaking known as Arasu Cable TV Corporation.[41] Some recent films have drawn the ire of the political class, demanding that allegedly defamatory scenes be cut, but political speeches by opposition leaders and printed scandal appear to irk leaders and draw them into legal battle more than any other media. The speeches themselves are often known through their being reported in the print media. Apart from the historical connection between the press and the Tamil political aesthetic is a deeper sense that printed words and images have a degree of permanency, allowing them to be citied and recirculated, along with a feeling that they carry perhaps a greater legitimacy by virtue of appearing in print. While some would argue that English carries even more weight (along with imagined circulation beyond the Tamil world) and therefore attracts greater scrutiny, the number of cases shows that both language media, so long as they are in print, are equally liable to legal reprisal.

In recent years, however, images that had been honed through print culture, party-owned television stations, and public street art now make up much of the content of a digital infrastructure that has introduced new forms of contingency and vulnerability into the mix of image politics. Web-based publications already posed new challenges, as Mani's article on Jayalalithaa's health had in the opening vignette. The spurt of defamation cases the government of Tamil Nadu was pursuing in Jayalalithaa's last years also had something to do with a feeling of vertigo in the face of social media like WhatsApp, where the questions of publication and the attribution of authorship are quite tricky and the means of dissemination uncontrollable. Who was responsible for the rumors about the chief minister's health circulating wildly through people's smart mobile phones on these media? You can slap a case on a registered publisher and you can attack a newsstand, but what do you do about your unauthorized image or rumors about your health that are being circuited through such media? The once protected form of oral rumor that long served the disenfranchised has been digitally reanimated and appears more potent and uncontrollable than ever. Cases of defamation and even sedition, along with the threats of violence that can back them up, appear as a grasping for straws in an era of decentralized circulation. The latter phenomenon was also exemplified in the sedition charges meted out against the leftist folk singer Kovan, whose songs mocking Jayalalithaa's dependence on revenues from liquor taxation at the expense of the poor went viral on social media.

With the passing of Jayalalithaa, whose image was at the center of the dynamic that encouraged a proliferation of celebrity-style journalism and a correspondingly high number of legal reprisals, the emergence of new configurations, no longer tied to the world of cinema that has for so long energized Tamil politics, will be examined in greater detail in chapters 4 and 5. In conclusion to this chapter, we may simply note the emergence of an age where, if we follow recent analyses of finance capitalism, we might by extension argue that discursive techniques of risk management around the propriety of the political image are giving way to a politics of uncertainty. If the leaders of mass politics in Tamil Nadu and elsewhere are appearing more and more ghostlike, it is not only the recent deaths of two towering figures that make it so. Their spectral quality has more to do with the logic of a shadow sovereignty over a territory the parameters of which, indeed, the very qualities of which, are increasingly difficult to discern. The changing world of media that enabled the creation of the once novel political form of the celebrity mass-political leader with the power to transcend both state and cinema might well now sound its death knell. Just as the law struggles to keep pace with new decentralized networks of mediation that further fragment aspects of personhood, digital media's new power to shape the cinematic image opens new questions about the fate of the political and its relationship to popular sovereignty in Tamil Nadu and elsewhere.

CHAPTER THREE
Law at Large

It began with fictionalized sex and ended with a resurrection. In between, the Tamil novelist Perumal Murugan declared himself dead as a writer. His award-winning novel *Māthorubāgan* had already been published for years and translated into English as *One Part Woman* when some Hindu-nationalist and caste-affiliated groups objected violently to the book. This tale of a child-less couple's difficult search for the social recognition that comes only with progeny draws on deeply researched oral lore and it is set during the colonial period. *Māthorubāgan*—a local name for Lord Siva as half man and half woman—drew the ire of some readers because it depicts consensual, extra-marital, and intercaste sexual relations that were known to have once taken place on the eighteenth day of the festival of the Arthenareeswarar Temple in Thiruchengode. In the book, the loving wife reluctantly takes part in this celebration where the gods mingled with humans for one night in hopes of ending her isolation by giving birth to a *sāmi kodutha pillai* (god given child), the name given to those conceived in this manner. But memories of the ritually sanctioned mésalliances enabling these divine blessings are now largely ignored or purposefully repressed in a contemporary imagination more focused on the problem of women's chastity in maintaining religious and caste boundaries.

The author Perumal Murugan hails from the western part of Tamil country known as Kongu Nadu, where the story is set. The rough, dry landscape of this region is brought to life vividly in the prose of *Māthorubāgan* as it is in all of his books. Apart from his established fame in literary circles, the author was also a Tamil professor and critic of caste hierarchy as well as abuses in the factory-style poultry farms that now dominate the landscape. Perumal Murugan's novel thus provided the pretext for an orchestrated campaign of pious outrage against him and his book on the grounds that he had tarnished the reputation of women belonging to the dominant Gounder, or Kongu Vellalar, caste. Gounder associations organized book burnings and threatened the author and his family with the aid of the Hindu Munnani, a religious nationalist group keen to strengthen their presence in a region where they saw political opportunity. Fearing a "law and order problem," a local district revenue officer took the unusual step of forcing Perumal Murugan to sign an official document promising to withdraw the book even after he had already issued an apology and agreed to remove offending passages. Already a major news event in India, people were even more shocked by what came next: the distraught author wrote a message on his Facebook page declaring his demise as a writer, who "is no god, so will not rise from the dead." This was followed by the declaration that "hereafter only the humble teacher P. Murugan will live." His post went on to ask that his publishers no longer sell any of his books and that he be left alone. This violent assault on creativity was covered across the globe, in the *New York Times*, the *Guardian*, and countless other news outlets as a sign of growing intolerance in India.

Life was returned to Perumal Murugan, however unexpectedly, through the magical words of a judge. Responding to a criminal case against the author that was brought to the Madras High Court, Chief Justice Sanjay Kaul wrote a 150-page judgment that many consider to be a piece of literature in its own right.[1] In defending Perumal Murugan's creative expression and chastising the administration for its failure to protect the constitution, the judgment begins by delving into censorship from the days of *Lady Chatterley's Lover*. After going through the specific merits of the case before the court and dismissing any crime that is alleged to have occurred, the judgment then moves back into the domain of broader sociohistorical commentary, noting the "rising phenomenon of extrajudicial, casteist and religious forces dictating the creativity of authors and writers." The judgment also contrasts contemporary popular morality with the more flexible norms of sex outside of wedlock in the classical Indian religious traditions, which "truly reflect the liberal ethos, uncorrupted by the Victorian English philosophy, which came to dominate post the British invasion of India." This lengthy and erudite meditation on art, sex, and religion then ends with the most quotable piece of legal prose in recent memory. The final line of the judgment exhorts in bold letters, "Let the author be resurrected to what he is best at. Write." It was reproduced in all news media the following day and quickly prompted a public reply from a grateful Perumal Murugan, who wrote that the judge's words had given him great happiness, comforting "a heart that had shrunk itself and had wilted. I am trying to prop up myself holding on to the light of the last lines of the judgment." The author's name had become part of the free speech movement in India.

A few days later, I was in a taxi driving with Mani, the freelance journalist who was generously introducing me to his colleagues in Chennai, when he received a call from Perumal Murugan on his mobile phone. The two had never met before. Mani's face lit up. He was delighted to hear that the great author had read his analysis of the judgment published in a Tamil news magazine and that he would very much like to meet. Canceling other plans for the afternoon, we headed to the Chennai Press Club, a building that sits under the elevated commuter train tracks abutting shanties that had been set up along the Buckingham Canal and around the corner from the decaying grandeur of the Nawab of Arcot's Chepauk Palace. We were waiting in front of the club when Perumal Murugan pulled up on a scooter, shook our hands with a gracious smile, and sat down outside on the plastic chairs with us. The self-effacing author began by thanking Mani for the wonderful reading of this important work of judicial prose, one of the few nuanced pieces of legal journalism to have been published in Tamil, he noted. While the literary community had rallied around Murugan when he was being threatened by religious and caste organizations, by the time the judgment in his favor had been reached, he explained that fewer people in Tamil Nadu were interested. Attention had moved on to other things even if there was a great deal of writing in the English-language press about it.

Listening to Murugan discuss his plight, his family's move from Kongu Nadu to work at Presidency College in Chennai as a result of threats, and his subsequent relief, I was struck with the manner in which the words of the judge from a faraway place had folded themselves into his life, changing the field of possibilities. He had been made anew through these words, but he appeared to be still unsure about what his newfound freedom meant. Chatting with us over a cup of tea, Murugan repeatedly emphasized how important it was that the specific content of the judgment be known in Tamil Nadu, where threats against artists and intellectuals had risen in recent years. It was not important for his literary career, which had, perhaps unsurprisingly, already reached new heights in the English-speaking world as a result of the ban and his much-publicized social media death. But the judge's words laying out his rights to artistic expression and resurrection as a writer would be crucial in the larger struggle against political repression and censorship in

Tamil Nadu and so had to work their way back into the vernacular through good Tamil journalism. This was something Mani was especially sensitive to given his own confrontations with the government defamation machine under Jayalalithaa. The two bonded on these grounds and agreed to meet again soon before we all went our separate ways.

The story of Perumal Murugan, his death as a writer, and his resurrection through the words of Chief Justice Kaul presents the law in the image of a benevolent authority, sitting above the narrow-mindedness of those who refuse to grant creativity its space of free play or who fail to understand the truly "liberal ethos" of Indian religions before colonialism. In sharp contrast to the instrumentalized abuse of legal statutes and institutions documented in the previous chapter on defamation, the law appears transcendent here. Judges themselves might be thought to epitomize the ethics of enlightened distance that are required for the law to apply impartially to all. And yet the social force of the Perumal Murugan judgment made itself felt through publicly circulating parts of the text that have no legal binding. The frequently quoted extracts consist wholly of what those in the legal professions would call *obiter dicta*, things said by way of argument, as opposed to the *ratio decidendi*, the reason for the decision that sets a compulsory standard for other courts to follow within a jurisdiction. What freed the author to write was not simply a decision in a criminal case but more importantly Justice Kaul speaking to the world by means of a legal judgment that was itself already deeply enmeshed in the world it was addressing. Returning to Perumal Murugan's conversation with Mani, we can see how the public life of law is sustained not only by the judgment itself, which relatively few will read, but also by the way in which the law is invoked, portrayed, and narrativized in print journalism and on television.[2] When "jurisprudence steps off its elitist pedestal," to borrow an evocative figuration from Peter Goodrich, it enters the domain of the popular, ethical, and political imagination.[3] The law is addressed to and frequently cited in the world at large well beyond the obligatory chain of the *ratio decidendi* in arguing cases, to support or contest various ethical and political projects, exerting force in and mediated by wider social fields defined by dynamics of mass publicity.[4]

Thinking with and beyond Weber's well-known argument about inherent incongruities between the substance of popular justice and the rationalized form of legal procedure, this chapter extends our analysis of this broader force of law by examining judicial address and its mediation by news-consuming publics. While the Indian higher judiciary aspires to a self-image as a unified power sitting above a deeply fractured postcolonial society, the news media, in particular, have ensured that the law's tentacles spread deeply into the recesses of everyday life and considerations of justice through the circulation of its discourse. Adopting a stance that addresses the public from afar, judicial discourse employs "a rhetoric of autonomy, neutrality, and universality" delineating a juridical field that nevertheless seeks to intervene in the society from which it stands aloof as an idealized set of representations and norms.[5] In considering the role of the court as a political actor, then, my interest is in the tension at play between the ethics and aesthetics of distance required to maintain this institution's appearance of majesty and impartiality on the one hand and the pull of public address and narrative from which the judiciary draws its language and exerts its broader force well beyond the letter of the law on the other.

In a brilliant anthropological reading of what Veena Das once called the "semiotic excess" of judicial discourse beyond the narrow confines of the immediate decision, for example, she demonstrates how judgments can serve as a gambit for establishing a juridical-state monopoly, not only on legitimate violence but on authorizing legitimate forms of collective identity, memory, and behavior.[6] She demonstrates how judicial observation in the historic Shah Bano judgment regarding a Muslim woman's right to maintenance after divorce served to reduce the complex issues involved around questions of family, religion, and gender to a simple formula accusing communal "fundamentalists" of threatening national integration through a rhetoric of impartiality. This chapter argues, in line with Das's reasoning, that casual observations and commentaries in judicial discourse often serve to bolster the paternal power that characterizes many aspects of the postcolonial state as it is cited across contexts, focusing in particular on women's sexuality. In this respect, it also continues to develop explorations of the narrative quality of judicial discourse opened by legal scholars like Robert Cover and Upendra Baxi, who focused on legal language's dialectical relationship to wider normative horizons to account for both its creativity and its power.[7] As another scholar working in this tradition, Kalyani Ramnath argues, it is through the narrative qualities of discourse other than the *ratio decidendi* that "judgments often are a testament to [the court's] involvement in the everyday public and private lives."[8]

Extending these insights into the narrative and event-making quality of the law, I ask how the very mediation of judicial discourse by publics that constitutes the court's authority in society at large beyond the strict letter of the law also opens the judiciary to vulnerabilities on the very same grounds of mass publicity. To the degree that judges are concerned with maintaining their image of distance that is both "ascetic and aristocratic," they are indeed radically dependent on a form of public recognition that must be assiduously maintained.[9] Not unlike the political leaders discussed in the last chapter, judges, too, are deeply concerned with maintaining their reputations and prestige. In the words of senior lawyer and scholar Rajeev Dhavan, "the majesty of the law is very much bound up in how it is perceived. . . . If this is taken away, the law and its custodians will be de-mythologized. Their mask would disappear. Court proceedings would be like any other meeting—and all the less convincing for being so."[10] The law as embodied in the judiciary must appear to stand above the mundane world if it is to maintain is "mystical foundation."[11] This is a symbolic order that is furthermore subject to the vagaries of a sometimes-raucous news media, eliciting accusations of contempt of court when breached. In this respect, the law of contempt that criminalizes "scandalizing a judge" before the public is to the judiciary what criminal defamation is to political leaders. And the law can similarly blur the line between the reputation of a particular judge and broader concerns about the prestige of the court and of the law itself.

Judges must take into account quite seriously the wider effects and uptake of their arguments in such a context, as their counterparts in the field of mass politics clearly do. As the former Delhi High Court Justice A. P. Shah once remarked when I told him about my research, "I know many judges who can't have their morning coffee without first reading about themselves in the newspaper." How this reading feeds back into their judgments and observations is a worthwhile question to ask. Such a study of judicial reflections on publicity in the more intimate sphere would wield great insight into the dynamics of calculation and maneuver in legal performativity, but it is beyond the scope of this chapter. What follows is a set of interpretations of public records in the form of higher-court judgments and news media representations read through the lens of those legal reporters who did the work of mediating the law for public consumption and interpretation.

Distributions of Law

A prominent statue stands in the center of the graceful Indo-Saracenic buildings that make up the Madras High Court complex. It depicts the law giver and model judge, Manu Needhi Cholan, popularly known as Ellālan, or "Ruler of the Boundary." Sculpted from dark stone in the neo-Dravidian style of the late twentieth century, the statue stakes claim to a Tamil vision of justice amid its colonial-era institutional surroundings. Unlike his Roman counterpart Justitia, who is found in many courts with her eyes blindfolded holding a scale in one hand and a sword in the other, this great Chola king's eyes are large and wide open. He carries a scepter. The legend depicted by the sculpture has it that the king kept a giant bell for anyone to ring and be heard to report an injustice. One day, a cow rang the bell, demanding action against the king's only son, the Prince Veedhivandagan, who was said to have crushed the cow's calf under the wheel of his chariot. Upon hearing the cow's complaint, the sovereign demanded that his own heir be put to death in the very same manner. The prince's body is thus shown at the base of the sculpture being crushed under a chariot wheel, opposite another wheel that sits on the dead calf.

Manu Needhi's parable of justice differs from the abstract principle of distanced impartiality imagined in the form of sightless Justitia. His justice is transcendent because it spares no one, including royal kin. But it is also profoundly entangled with what is seen and heard in the world. This administration of law draws ethical force precisely from the recognition that princes and cows are otherwise differentially placed in the hierarchical order of things. The functions of lawmaker and law preserver are not clearly delineated here, as the sovereign Manu Needhi rules on behalf of all people and animals, not blindly or according to a procedure set from without. In proceedings at the Madras High Court, where I would regularly spend time with reporters, justice was certainly not always as equitable as the legend of Manu Needhi would demand. His image nevertheless provides an apt entry point into some of the conflicting tensions at play in the often-dramatic cases that are decided in this complex, where worldly considerations of representing and safeguarding the diverse populace of Tamil Nadu vie with more abstract claims made on behalf of the universal principles of law. As in other higher courts in India, this bench of over fifty justices carries a great deal of political weight as agents of what is often termed an "activist judiciary." I had seen the statue before beginning my work on journalism and written about the story it depicts in some earlier work I had done on petitioning. It began to take on new meaning, however, when I realized just how much events at the Madras High Court dominated the news cycle—and how political this judiciary can be, acting as sovereigns at times.

Having decided to delve more deeply into the world of legal journalism, I had asked a reporter named Wilson I knew from the *Dinakaran* newspaper to take me with him on his beat in the summer of 2015. This dynamic journalist of Christian background from southern Tamil Nadu happily agreed. In addition to covering the court, he also writes the paper's daily political gossip column in which he ventriloquizes popular street talk through an uncle figure named "Peter Mama." I would meet him at one o'clock in the afternoon every day in front of the court's main gate, facing the busy, old, and dusty neighborhood of Georgetown, where artisan and merchant communities lived under colonial segregation. Wilson would explain to the security guards who I was and then escort me to the air-conditioned press room. There, I caught up with cases that were to be argued that day. I then accompanied Wilson or one of the other reporters on their rounds through labyrinthine corridors of connected buildings, walking past scribes hunched over old typewriters set on the veranda walkways and rooms full of folded stacks of paper on which tens of thousands of petitions had been recorded, as they talked to doormen, assistants, and other employees of the court, looking for a scoop. We would drop into one of the grand courtrooms on occasion to hear a case being argued or an important judgment being read aloud before an assembled crowd of interested onlookers and journalists. Just as often, however, the news came from a photocopied version of an affidavit or judgment that was handed out to journalists by advocates or by judges' assistants in the press room. Petitions before the court and judgments were increasingly shared via WhatsApp through the many journalists' groups that had formed on what was then still a new medium. (But nothing beats legwork for a journalist. Following Wilson around, I realized that the material he used to write his column was gleaned through conversations with people working at the court, his advocate friends, and with the old man who ran the tea stall across the street from the court, where he would smoke cigarettes.)

Legal reporters who spent their afternoons in the High Court were of two types. Those working for print media, all of whom were men, would often send the basics of their reporting to their main office via a USB stick that was plugged into their laptops, enabling them to email through cellular data networks. They would then head back to the office at around 5 p.m. or so for editorial meetings to take part in the decision about what would go into the paper the following day, after which they would type up a more fulsome report on the office computer. Television journalists, on the other hand, could be young men or women. They were more beholden to the "live" quality of their medium. Those in television would return to the office with their notes on the day's events and then sit at a desktop computer with a screenwriter to quickly prepare a text to be read aloud in real-time by the news anchor in the studio across the hall at the seven o'clock news. Or, if it was a highly anticipated judgment, the television journalists would be ready to go to their outside broadcasting vans, sitting on the road next to the main gate of the court grounds, to give a live report on camera.

Sometimes cases that appeared on the surface to be of little public interest turned out to have wide-ranging consequences, as in the first case discussed below, in which case visuals would have to be provided in a more improvised fashion. Even when the outside broadcasting van was not on site, a camera-person from the television channel was usually there to provide visuals that could then be broadcast from the main studio. Video and photojournalists were allowed onto the court grounds outside. If one of the advocates or participants in a high-profile case wanted to speak directly to the public, a make-shift press conference would be held outside on the court grounds, where the speaker would be surrounded by microphones and cameras belonging to the many news stations covering the court. As in many court systems, there is no direct recording allowed of events that take place in the courtroom. What the public comes to know about decisions and how they experience the cases that are argued in the Madras High Court are therefore highly dependent on such professionally mediated written, aural, and visual news coverage.

EXPANSIVE JURISDICTION AND SPECTACLES OF DEFIANCE

One judgment that everyone was discussing when I began this round of fieldwork was handed down by Justice N. Kirubakaran.[12] At first glance, it appeared on the docket as a humdrum case about a traffic accident. The Madras High Court judge was responding to a simple claim for damages in a motorcycle collision when he surprised the press and wider publics alike by issuing a sweeping order requiring every motorcycle and scooter rider in the state to wear a safety helmet. While such a law was already on the books, it had never been enforced. The judgment proved to be a very newsworthy example of "judicial activism." It begins by quoting a Tamil proverb and then continuing to provide a context for its unusual reach.

> "*Tharmam Thalai Kākkum*" (dharma will protect your head) goes the saying in Tamil. Whether "*Dharma*" would save a life or not, wearing of helmet would definitely do so, by acting as a protective headgear. It is really disheartening to note that a number of precious lives are lost due to non-wearing of protective headgear, namely, helmet, as mandated under Section 129 of the Motor Vehicles, Act, 1988. The pathetic position is that in spite of the enabling statute and a number of judgments rendered by the Honourable Supreme Court

as well as various High Courts including ours, neither the authorities' act as per the statute nor follow the directions issued in this regard.

The legislative assembly had not responded to a rapid rise in deaths and injuries resulting from motor accidents or to prior judgments from the appellate courts. In addition, law enforcement appeared completely uninterested in the act that was in place. And so, in a case concerning individual compensation, the court intervened to pursue a much-broader project we might associate with what Foucault termed "security," or the governmental management of populations, citing as a specific reason for action the fact that an average of seventeen people died every day on the roads in Tamil Nadu. After the emotive introductory paragraphs, the judgment then runs through a slew of statistics on road accidents and deaths due to head injury before shifting register to recognize the somewhat unusual nature of its purview by invoking the constitution, and through it, the people's sovereign rights.

> This court has every responsibility to safeguard the rights including the right to live as enshrined in Article 21 of the Constitution of India as this Court is the guardian of fundamental rights of the citizens. When our fellow citizens are being killed in the road accidents, this Court has to travel beyond its jurisdiction to pass novel and unconventional orders in the interest of the society.

The judgment demanded strict enforcement of the law, with much more severe penalties than the original act provided for, by July first, just three weeks after the order was issued. It furthermore required the installation of CCTV cameras on national highways to ensure compliance and explicitly asked that news media play their part in providing governmental publicity to raise awareness of the law among drivers and passengers of two-wheeled vehicles. No journalists were there in the courtroom to cover the proceedings because they were of little interest as listed, so it was the printed judgment itself that made the news.

Justice Kirubakaran, known as "the newsmaker judge," had already developed a reputation for his deep interest in matters biopolitical.[13] Just a year before the helmet case, in what he observed to be a "quick rise in divorce petitions due to impotency and frigidity" before the court, the judge advocated medical testing to be conducted before marriage, leading to debates among sexologists on television news shows about whether these were conditions for which there could be accurate screening. If always caring for the general health of society, Justice Kirubakaran was equally outspoken in his pursuit of sovereign justice. In deciding a high-profile case in which a child had been raped, for example, he lamented the limits placed on the court in punishing offenders. Echoing demands that had emerged in the popular press following the internationally covered Delhi gang rape case of 2012, the judge argued in passing that "castration for child rapists would fetch magical results in preventing child abuse." While based on dubious premises, all of this talk makes for great newspaper copy and television reports, of course. I have been told that the judge even invited journalists into his quarters to give quotes and ensure they report on his judgments the way he would like. Many of my legal journalist interlocutors at the court held a high opinion of the judge beyond the good material he gave them, seeing him as "forthright and honest" even if his comments and judgments might have struck them as somewhat over-zealous at times.

Most people in Tamil Nadu appeared to agree with the spirit of the helmet order. Apart from middle-class car owners who were likely to be more safety minded in any case, almost everyone I knew at the time had lost someone or knew someone who had been severely injured as a result of a motorcycle accident. Although some were annoyed to have to wear these heavy padded fiberglass shells in the oppressive summer heat and humidity or worried that their hair growth would be affected, they, too, complied for fear of being fined heavily and even having their vehicles impounded. A series of questions were raised about whether women riding "pillion" on the back of motor-cycles would also be required to wear helmets, and similar queries filled the press in the weeks leading up to enforcement day. When the order came into effect, people were certainly a little surprised at how rigorously enforce-ment was pursued, with the *Dinamalar* newspaper, for example, exclaiming "1.40 Lakhs People!" as a headline about the number who had been caught by police for infringement two weeks later. The usually lackadaisical police department defied expectations, making the order a more significant event that it otherwise would have been.

There was one group that objected wildly to this aggressive assertion of governmental power by the judiciary, however: the advocates of the Madras High Court itself. I could tell from my early interactions with lawyers that tensions had already been simmering on the court grounds. One advocate, for example, would come by the press room to distribute beef biriyani to everyone for lunch, demanding the right to eat beef in the court canteen and claiming that the court was run in a Hindu-chauvinist manner. He had even put up a large banner on the court grounds, quickly removed, deriding the judges while demanding that Tamil be used as an official language in the court in addition to English. I later learned that it was Justice Kirubakaran, in particular, who had earned the ire of the Madras High Court Advocates Association by requiring lawyers registered to argue cases before the court to show their certificates proving that they had no cases pending against them before enrolling. When I met the association's president, Paul Kanagaraj, and his colleagues on the court grounds during this period, he said that "advocates were not being treated well" by some judges. It appears that the helmet ruling, perhaps surprisingly to those not already in the know, served as the proverbial last straw leading to large-scale insubordination.

It started most spectacularly in the Madurai branch of the court, which serves the southern districts of the state. Advocates of the Madras High Court there refused to respect the helmet order, organizing a motorcycle rally flaunting their bare heads to make their discontent known. Some then went to far as pull the helmets off the heads of other motorcycle drivers who were following the law in the vicinity of the court. Newspaper readers and television news audiences were especially surprised by the lawyers' uncivil behavior when they burned helmets in a bonfire on the High Court grounds and assaulted the police officers who tried to stop them. Photographs of flaming helmets became a defining image of the protests. When contempt of court charges were eventually filed against the president and the secretary of the Madurai Bar Association for the role they played in organizing the motorcycle rally, busloads of advocates traveled from Madurai to the head branch of the court in Chennai to spread the rebellion, leading to violent confrontations with court police. Chief Justice Kaul, who later wrote the Perumal Murugan judgment, finally decided to call for new measures to disbar High Court advocates who broke the law when a group of them burst into his courtroom during a proceeding and told him to "go back to Kashmir!," where he was originally from. All of these events led one journalist to go so far as to describe the Madras High Court as a "judicial badlands" at the time.[14]

The confrontation between lawyers and judges that was hidden from public view before the ruling had taken on bewildering dimensions for a broader audience. All because of a court order about motorcycle helmets. Many news readers I talked to about this at the time referred to the advocates dismissively as *rowdies*, a term usually used to denote violent street criminals. There was a general acceptance that the courts have the authority to lay down the law, as it were, in a context where the legislative assembly and the police were widely untrusted and associated with corruption. When I asked A. Subramani, who had been covering the court for over fifteen years, first for

the *Hindu* and then for the *Times of India*, he was a little more understanding while also disapproving of the lawyers' methods: "You see, advocates,
they are the type of people who always question everything. It's their nature,
even if it's in the public interest. They were angry at being told to prove they
were not criminals and questioned why they should show anything to prove
it." Paul Kanagaraj had, in fact, argued as such, claiming that the judiciary
was besmirching their name and that it was all being carried in the newspapers in a hearing about the incidents in Madurai presided over by Justice
Kirubakaran. The judge insisted that there are a number of criminals and
charlatans among the advocates. In any event, the contempt of court case
against the two lawyers from Madurai was leading to another showdown at
the main Chennai branch of the Madras High Court a few months after the
helmet order that had been delivered there. This time, everyone was watching, expecting more violence on the court grounds.

It was an eerie scene. Police deployed heavy reinforcements in an effort to
secure the court. A large LED television screen was placed outside in front
of the buildings, surrounded by the types of heavy steel barricades used
to block the streets in case of construction or civil unrest. Advocates not
directly involved in the contempt case were barred from even entering the
courthouse, as was the general press. The corridors were also blocked with
steel barricades and police. For the first time in the history of the court, they
would have to watch the proceedings on-screen. In an interesting twist on
this restriction, television news stations were able to show the inside of the
court room during arguments for the first time as well, if not with very high
resolution. They did so by simply placing their cameras in front of the television screen outside the court. Audiences watched judges grilling lawyers
through a history-making live telecast. Only a few advocates arrived from
Madurai this time, and the encounter between the offending bar association
leaders and the judges of the Madras High Court unfolded without any serious incidents of violence. They were made an example of and reprimanded
before the television-watching world, and they were then released.

The helmet battle in a longer war had ended. Fought on the court grounds
and in dialogues between judges and advocates reported in the news, this
confrontation had pushed at the limits of sovereignty in judicial address, as
both sides appealed to a wider public through different means. As a news
event, it followed a peculiar narrative path from road safety to court security,
ending in a history-making, if temporary, reconfiguration of the public gaze
on courtroom events. Jurisprudence had been *forced* "off its elitist pedestal," to twist Goodrich's phrasing, as it resorted to police security measures

against those who were severely testing the highly mythologized majesty of the judiciary. The bare force of the law had to make itself explicit rather than hide behind ritual trappings or what Baxi terms the "mask" of judicial discourse.[15] The technocracy of biopolitical reason propagated through the judgment had been politicized and made subject to public scrutiny, even if most agreed with Justice Kirubakaran's reasoning in the end. But the threat of disbarring advocates who were found to be in serious breach of the law remained a live issue after the helmet melee, leading to fierce opposition from Paul Kanagaraj and his association and continuing to command a great deal attention in the legal press. In the weeks following the contempt hearing, the Madras High Court grounds were further restricted when Chief Justice Kaul ordered the Central Industrial Security Forces (CISF) to take over law enforcement and security on the court grounds from the police who had been doing this work. When I returned in December of that year to continue fieldwork after teaching for a semester at my home institution, I was no longer allowed to enter the court.

PRODUCING THE BODY FOR PUBLIC CONSUMPTION

The second story looming large in talk among reporters at the High Court when I arrived that summer, if not yet dominating the news cycle like the great escalation over helmets, began when a young man named Shameel Ahmed died shortly after being admitted to the Rajiv Gandhi Government General Hospital, just down the road from us. I first heard about this from the journalists I was following in court. His death was recorded as a small item in the newspapers because Shameel had been taken into custody for questioning a few hundred kilometers away, at the Pallikonda police station near the Andhra Pradesh boarder, ten days earlier. After four days of interrogation in the police station, Shameel was released and returned home but was immediately admitted to the hospital in nearby Vellore for severe internal injuries before being transferred to Chennai, where he died. Most news reports left it at that, and television largely ignored the story.

What later became clear is that Shameel, a married Muslim youth and the father of a young child, was alleged to have run away with a twenty-three-year-old woman named P. Pavithra, who was also married and a mother. The two had worked together in a shoe-leather factory away from their respective homes, and they had known each other for about one year. When Pavithra left home after a quarrel with her husband, a man by the name of Palani, he proceeded to file a petition for a writ of habeas corpus, a recourse demanding the production of her body in court normally associated with the tradition of civil liberties to be used against unlawful detention. Here, as in many cases when women choose to leave home in pursuit of relationships deemed undesirable by their families, the writ was used to demand that the police find someone who was said to be "missing." This use of habeas corpus effectively turns a civil right protecting people from the police into a search warrant empowering the police to apprehend the body.[16] In the words of Giorgio Agamben, "*Corpus is a two-faced being, the bearer both of subjection to sovereign power and of individual liberties.*" As he notes, *corpus* is the means by which a body is "detained and exhibited" before a public.[17] That Pavithra belonged to a Dalit community—thus doubly reduced to her body both as woman and as Dalit—was never mentioned in the mainstream news but was widely known and discussed among reporters and many others I talked to about the story.[18]

What appeared to everyone to be a case of death resulting from police torture would have remained a relatively minor news event to be handled by city reporters under normal circumstances. Custodial deaths are unfortunately fairly common, the journalists I was chatting with at court agreed, and media houses rarely have the appetite for public confrontation with a police force they rely on a great deal for their news gathering. But the story gained traction because Pavithra could still not be located by the police, and violence had begun to erupt in Shameel's hometown of Ambur, known for its large Muslim population. It turns out that Shameel was not the first young man to have been tortured to death by law enforcement in this manner, and people had lost patience with an unresponsive police force and government. Leaders of the Ambur community led by Shameel's father-in-law, who was the district head of the Indian Thouheed Jamaat, a Muslim social service organization, had already been protesting his disappearance after they failed in their attempts to contact the inspector of police responsible for his detention. After news of his death circulated, first through WhatsApp and Facebook and then through the mainstream Tamil media, protest turned into riot. Most of the crowd's anger was directed at the police and their vehicles, but a state-run liquor shop, public buses, and a few other stores were also severely damaged. A number of police men and women were injured, and around two hundred Muslims in the town were picked up for questioning. Many were allowed home after investigations, but ninety-five people remained in prison for over a week after the violence. Martin Premraj, the police inspector responsible for Shameel's torture, was suspended in absentia after the riot. Common local knowledge in Ambur had it that the same inspector was also in charge during the killing of another Muslim youth in police custody two years before. He had been missing since June 27, the day after Shameel died in Chennai. It was only because of his suspension that the English-language media started to cover the story more closely.

Meanwhile, Pavithra, who was last seen by her family in late May, was still in hiding. Although she had visited Shameel in the town of Erode after leaving her husband, according to a documentary later aired on Thanthi TV news, he asked her to return to Ambur, knowing the potential for violence that he would face should they be seen, a Muslim man and a Hindu woman together out of wedlock.[19] No one knew where she was. All the while, Ambur was still simmering with tension under the application of section 144 of the colonial-era Indian Penal Code, prohibiting public gatherings of any sort. Hindu nationalists, led by the BJP politician Vanathi Srinivasan, had worked hard to emphasize the communal aspects of the Ambur violence. The Hindu right had accused the Indian Thouheed Jamaat of systematically organizing violence against the state, using Shameel's death as a pretext, as part of a general strategy to mobilize Hindu support in this region against the sizable minority Muslim community. General media coverage of the violence involving thousands and the massive police repression that followed appeared distant from the perspective of readers in metropolitan Chennai, however. Stories were somewhat limited in the city's newspapers and television, with the exception of the daily newspaper *Dinamalar*, known to be more sympathetic to Hindu-nationalist politics. By that point I was following events very closely and clipping everything I could find in the newspapers. But several news editors I spoke with that week played down the importance of the story by explaining to me that it was the BJP that was trying to make it larger than it was for political gain. The editor at the *Tamil Muracu* evening daily went on to tell me more specifically that it was his job not to play into majoritarian hands by overplaying the story of the riots and their aftermath.

Then, on a Saturday night over one week after Shameel had passed away, I received a phone call from a legal reporter named Shekhar with whom I had become friendly. "Frank. Did you hear? They found Pavithra by tracing her friend's cell [phone]. She's been living in a women's hostel here in Chennai all along! Look at your Chennai High Court Reporters Group WhatsApp. Come to court on Monday." While Pavithra had gone to Erode to meet with Shameel after leaving home and shortly before he was tortured, police discovered that instead of returning to her village near Ambur as he had asked her to, she had moved to Chennai in an effort to escape from her family. A photograph of Pavithra being escorted to the police station was on the front cover of every paper the following morning. She had been remanded to the Vellore police, who had been charged with finding her, and they were told by the local judge to produce Pavithra before the Madras High Court. Already commanding the center of the usually slow Sunday news cycle, the stage was set for an even bigger media event. All attention would be focused on Pavithra's hearing at the Madras High Court that Monday, where she would be produced before the judges, the media, and her family, having broken no law whatsoever, but as a body summoned before the public by writ of habeas corpus.

The court grounds were full of onlookers when I arrived, as if some sort of festival were taking place. Amid the dust and crowds, most could barely see the police van carrying Pavithra when it rolled up to the building. A throng of camerapersons and photojournalists descended on the scene, chasing the police as they escorted her up the stairs for the hearing. I made my way to the press room, where older print journalists were sitting checking their emails and updating their editors on their cell phones. "Did you see the crowds [*gumbal*]?," Subramani asked in a flat tone without even bothering to look up from his phone. Senior legal reporters like him had seen occasions like this before and were unimpressed compared with the younger television journalists. Most journalists made their way upstairs to the packed courtroom, nevertheless, to witness the encounter with the judges themselves, although some stayed behind waiting for reports from junior colleagues who didn't mind getting caught in the scrum.

In court Pavithra was told to stand next to an appointed government lawyer before the justices S. Tamilvanan and C. T. Selvam while her husband Palani looked on. They were surrounded by her parents and a sea of spectators. The proceedings began when the judges asked, speaking in Tamil throughout, whether Palani was in fact her lawful husband and about the facts of the case.[20] The pivotal question from a legal perspective was, "Did anyone take you away from home unlawfully against your will?" to which Pavithra responded, "No."

After answering a few initial questions, Pavithra told them simply that she would accept returning to her parent's house and expressed her desire to leave her husband. It was in the course of this rather routine line of questioning that Paul Kanagaraj, who was standing in the front row of onlookers despite having no official role in the proceedings, interjected, to the surprise of many, "The Ambur riot arose only as a result of the ongoing investigation into this woman's disappearance!"

The judges responded they had read the news and then proceeded to question Pavithra aggressively: "Shameel Ahmed was married. You were also married. You had a husband and a child. Then what? Now this youth has died and his family has been harmed as well. It's only because of these problems that religious and caste riots are breaking out. Even unmarried men and women, if they belong to different religions, can only be married under the special marriages act. But here, both are married and with children. When this is the case, how can they get married?"

Then Pavithra tried to assert her rights by simply stating, "I want a divorce from my husband."

This statement of intent prompted a reply by the judge that would come to define the courtroom encounter. The judge replied tersely, "Is divorce something that is available for sale at the corner shop? Something that can be bought with cash? A divorce is something you must file for in another court, you think you can get one just like that?"

The government lawyer, Thambidurai, then added, "50 Lakhs worth of property and vehicles were destroyed in the Ambur riot. The investigations about the riot are still ongoing," to which Paul Kanagaraj elaborated what he took to be a legal dilemma: "The high court should not consider this as an ordinary habeas corpus case. This is because there are no clear laws to deal with problems connected to a man and a woman who are already married living together. Therefore, in light of the unusual problems that have arisen in this rare case it is important to develop some guidelines about how police should proceed under such conditions."

The judges inquired about where Pavithra was currently living and asked again whether she would return to her parents' house, when Kanagaraj again emphasized the danger of the situation and recommended that she be given police protection as more untoward incidents might occur. After consultations among the judges, Pavithra was eventually told to return to the women's hostel in Ambattur, where she would be under police security, until the case was to be finally adjourned three weeks later, on July 23, at which point she would return home to her parents. The "homology between masculinist and state power," to borrow from Wendy Brown's apt phrasing, could not be clearer.[21] Pavithra was finally escorted to a room in the courthouse to fill out some paperwork before she was returned to the hostel by the police.

Later in the day, once the hearing was over, I walked outside the court corridors and saw Paul Kanagaraj, surrounded by other lawyers wearing their black robes, giving a press statement to a large group of television journalists and repeating what he had said and what had occurred in the courtroom. Because video cameras and other mechanical recording devices were not allowed inside the court, this impromptu press conference by the president of the Advocates Association, along with an interview with the government lawyer involved, were the primary materials presented on the evening news shows to provide an account of what happened. It was only that evening that I saw, along with the wider television viewership, how Pavithra had covered her head and face with a purple dopatta (scarf) while being brought in and escorted out of the courtroom by her handlers.

The image of the young woman bent over on a desk following the proceeding with her face covered, reduced to a body without visage, became the predominant visual impression of the events that unfolded that day. But greater indignity was yet to come in print. The following day, the *Times of India*'s headline read, "Woman, Whose Disappearance Caused Ambur Violence, Produced before Madras HC." *Dinathanthi* had the same, in Tamil, reveling in the details of the judicial encounter in its reporting. The *Deccan Chronicle* went with "Divorce Not Sold in Shops: Judge," a headline that was repeated in *Dinakaran* and many other Tamil dailies and weeklies and that proved to be attractive ticker material for the twenty-four-hour news stations. *Dinamalar* provided the most detailed line-by-line transcript of the courtroom interaction (upon which I have based the passages above), and added a twist by coupling the story of Pavithra's public shaming and the ersatz legal problems her behavior was accused of raising with an article about how police were also investigating whether she had converted to Islam, once again playing to fears among Hindu chauvinists. The *Hindu* alone avoided the sensationalism of other papers and television, focusing instead on tensions in Ambur itself and refraining from focusing on the judges' statements.

In addition to the lack of respect accorded to Pavithra, which we will return to in a moment, what is remarkable about the judges' comments as they were circulated through news coverage is the absolute lack of concern with the custodial murder of Shameel Ahmed at the hands of the police inspector Martin Premraj. The apparently much more serious problem of a woman's compromised marital chastity across religious lines took center stage, obscuring what everyone privately knew to be the social violence against Muslims of which Shameel's demise was symptomatic. When hierarchies within hierarchies are transgressed in this manner, however, violence appears as a quasi-natural occurrence to many, thereby obscuring its political character. Pavithra's unapologetic assent to breaking the "sexual contract" took center stage as a scandal without legal basis demanding supplementary action.[22] What Pratiksha Baxi terms "the glare of publicity" served as a form of punishment.[23] With some exceptions, notably the popular weekly *Ananda Vikatan*, which was more critical of the role of the police, the mainstream press found this to be a perfectly sensible exercise in publicly shaming Pavithra for the violence she had been accused of causing in the narrative that had been built. It was, in fact, the Hindu-right Twittersphere and online media that lauded *Dinamalar* for how they had been covering the whole story, perversely recognizing the problem of communal violence at the center of events that the other papers ignored. While sharing in the misogyny that formed a common ground between Hindu nationalism and mainstream news reporting, they derided these other media for being "soft" on minorities. On the whole, news coverage from the court appears to have appealed to what editors construed to be a popular sense of substantive justice. If the law itself could not provide remedy for what a news consumer would have taken to be Pavithra's transgression, the words of the judges and the images of her suffering before the cameras served as a social sanction provided by the news.[24]

Returning to events in the courtroom, Pavithra's habeas corpus hearing, like all of the judgments and proceedings described in this chapter, can be read as an assertion of juridical sovereignty, as Agamben's analysis of the logic of habeas corpus already indicates. From a formal legal perspective, the hearing should have closed with her negative answer to the question of whether she had been abducted against her will. But this was, in fact, only the beginning of an exemplary pedagogical performance delineating "margins within the state" beyond the strict contents of the law, where Pavithra was "taught the difference between membership and belonging."[25] Her purported misdeed had become a problem for the law, raising questions about her capacity to belong and inciting discourse in lieu of a nonexistent legal remedy. The assertion of sovereign power, backed by the might of the law, was maintained, although the claim made by the judges was that they had no jurisdiction over her demand for a divorce, and the advocate Paul Kanagaraj argued in court that there is no law to deal with the wider problems allegedly raised by Pavithra's disappearance. As Justin Richland notes in his analysis of language and jurisdiction, "even when legal actors decide that the legal institution they enact (through language) has no authority to act, the force, authority, and legitimacy of that legal institution is nonetheless being enacted."[26] If Justice Kirubakaran's helmet judgment was explicit in its "traveling beyond" the bounds of normal jurisdiction and Justice Kaul's Perumal Murugan judgment addressed a wider societal struggle over creative expression in terms of transcendent rights, in this otherwise mundane case, judicial address spoke to the world through the very words renouncing its jurisdiction over Pavithra's demand for a divorce. The two former cases performed expansions of the court's reach while the latter case enacted a sort of punitive constriction by Justices S. Tamilvanan and C. T. Selvam. This "speaking the law" (the Anglicization of the Latin *juris-diction*, as noted by Richland) enacts the sovereignty of the court and the state it represents while making available textual materials for social sanction well outside the purview of the law in the very same gesture.

All of the cases I have described asserted and grounded legal authority in large measure through the mediation of normative news-consuming publics beyond the courtroom. Unlike the judgments in the Perumal Murugan and helmet cases described above, however, where the written statements of the High Court justices were widely cited in the news coverage of events, here it was spoken interaction with Pavithra herself that provided the content of most reporting. Whereas written judgments are explicitly addressed, not only to the parties directly concerned with a case but to the wider world, in Pavithra's hearing the widely quoted words of the judges were directed at her. The press and her family were what Erving Goffman would identify in his decomposition of participant roles as unaddressed "overhearers" who were "ratified" insofar as they had a right to be there and observe the proceedings.[27] And so, while the judicial address was directed at the person standing before the judges in the strict linguistic sense, in the wider social sense the juridical text was there to be picked up by all who were in the courtroom and furthermore disseminated as news for public consumption through the media of print, digital circulation, and television. These absent and unratified addressees would then act as citational vectors in the distribution of legal power beyond the law in a narrative that framed Pavithra as a voiceless but deadly agent in provoking a communal riot. A number of news websites continued to discuss this widely publicized encounter between Pavithra and the force of law embodied in the harsh words spoken in court in the following days and weeks. Her final hearing made for a small item in some newspapers, as a sort of coda to the drama that had culminated in her habeas hearing. For some in the press, however, the story was not quite finished.

"Mischief Committed by the Newspaper"?

Selvakumar looked worried when I entered the pressroom at court that afternoon. It was a few weeks after Pavithra's habeas corpus hearing. This legal reporter for the Tamil daily newspaper that had recently been started by the *Hindu* was consulting with his colleagues when he glanced up at me with an unmistakable expression of fear in his eyes. He and his fellow journalists were gathered around a piece of paper. It was a legal notice, issued from the High Court judges who had heard Pavithra's case, threatening Selvakumar's newspaper with charges of contempt of court. Unlike the civil proceedings discussed earlier in the helmet case, where the Madurai advocates where found guilty of "willful disobedience to any judgment, decree, direction, order, writ or other process of a court," as per section 2(b) of the Contempt of Courts Act of 1971, this notice concerned a different kind of offense. Section 2(c) of the same act defines criminal contempt "as the publication (whether by words, spoken or written, or by signs, or by visible representation, or otherwise) of any matter or the doing of any other act whatsoever which scandalises or tends to scandalise, or lowers or tends to lower the authority of, any court." The alleged infraction was not a matter of simply obeying the word of the court as the subject of a judgment. Instead, this was an order concerning the court's public image and how judges' words had been depicted in the press. In effect, this accusation of contempt is a special kind of criminal defamation charge.

When I joined the huddle of journalists to ask what was the matter, they explained that it was not Selvakumar's reporting on the case that had landed the paper in trouble; it was rather a special supplement in the Tamil *Hindu* containing opinions about observations made in court and the language used by judges in Pavithra's hearing.[28] Noting the debate that had emerged on social media in the days following the courtroom drama, the Tamil *Hindu* opinion pages had asked five women, writers and intellectuals, to comment on the proceedings. Apart from the often-quoted judicial response to Pavithra's demand for a divorce about commodities and corner shops, the paper also took up a related issue that was being discussed in the left-liberal end of the social media world. In the transcripts of the proceedings published in newspapers, the judges were reported to have been using the informal, singular (*orumai*) second person pronoun in Tamil (*nī*) when addressing Pavithra in court as opposed to the respectful plural "you" (*nīngal*) that would have been expected in an official public interaction. Commonly used to assert gender and caste hierarchies in everyday speech—both of which were at play in the context of the court hearing—this pronoun usage was argued to be offensive by a number of the respondents writing in the Tamil *Hindu*. For example, Rajini, a lawyer commenting in the paper asked, "is addressing someone in using the disrespectful '*nī*' ('you' singular) or '*un*' ('your' singular) appropriate? First of all, at age twenty-three, Pavithra is a major. During a habeas corpus hearing, no one has the right to tell her 'you (singular) go there, you (singular) come here.' It's against Pavithra's basic human rights." Similar opinions were shared by the celebrated writer Salma, who argued that Pavithra knew very well that she would not be granted a divorce on the spot. Other women lawyers and activists complemented these criticisms in the same article.

The contempt of court notice given to Selvakumar was taken up *suo moto* by the bench, that is, by the judges themselves upon reading the newspaper. It was addressed to N. Ram, the publisher, and his brother N. Ravi, editor in chief of the newspaper, requiring a response within four weeks. It read,

> Having gone through the report and the interview published in "The Hindu-Tamil edition" dated 13/07/2015, we are of the view that there are prima facie material [*sic*] to treat the same as contempt committed by the newspaper. We are of the view that it is the mischief committed by the newspaper misguiding the people. We are respecting all the persons, especially woman [*sic*] attending the Court. It is seen that the interview given by certain persons would show, as if the Courts are not respecting woman, which is totally false and irresponsible statement against Courts.

I accompanied Selvakumar to the photocopying stand across the street from the court complex, where he made copies for his colleagues and one for me after I had assured him that I would not be publishing about the notice until years later. The legal journalists at court that day were also asked to refrain from publishing news about this notice in an effort to avoid further confrontation with the judges by amplifying their accusations and drawing more attention to the criticisms published by the Tamil *Hindu*.

In this particular case, it appeared to be in no one's interest to allow this attempt to silence the press to be made into a news event by the newspaper so as to introduce the type of feedback loops of publicity discussed in the last chapter. The Tamil edition of the *Hindu* was a relatively new paper, and most reporters and their editors cherished good relations with High Court judges too much to jeopardize them over what many nevertheless considered to be an abusive accusation meant to keep them in line. After discussing the issue with his colleagues and photocopying the notice of contempt, Selvakumar then went to the *Hindu* offices on Mount Road to inform its bosses. In the end, based on advice from their legal team, the paper printed a small apology that very few readers would have noticed. But this gesture appears to have satisfied the bench enough for them to drop the charge of contempt against the paper. Like many of the criminal defamation cases discussed in the last chapter, this threat by the court to pursue charges of contempt against a newspaper drew little if any public attention. It was best dealt with silently, as a nonevent.

To Maintain a "Top Most Image of the Judiciary"

Charges of contempt of court can also become big media events, such as those making up the distressing case of Justice C. S. Karnan, a judge who threatened fellow Madras High Court judges with contempt and who was eventually jailed himself on the same charges brought against him by the Supreme Court of India in Delhi. Already in 2011, shortly after being called to join the Madras High Court, Justice Karnan, who is a Dalit, made news by writing to the National Commission for Scheduled Castes (NCSC) accusing his fellow judges of treating him poorly because of his caste background. Specifically, he said that he had been touched inappropriately by the shoes of another judge as a sign of disrespect while other judges smiled. The already noteworthy allegation became big news as a result of a press conference the judge held. Justice Karnan had broken with the tradition of strict public separation between sitting justices and news media (although judges sometimes give quotes to the press in more private settings). The accusations of casteism were made in public and *for* the mass public. Journalists I talked to following the press conference were enthusiastic about its event-making capacity, which would put their legal reporting on the front page, but they also expressed a hint of worry that things appeared to be going too far. "I don't think he should have spoken like that about respected judges" was an opinion that several in the legal reporters' group shared with me in conversation. The press also appears to have an investment in maintaining a majestic image of the court.

Accusing judges of the Madras High Court of systematic discrimination against Dalit judges, Justice Karnan called these incidents "a black mark on Indian judiciary" before a gathering of journalists he had invited to his chambers for the purpose.[29] The press conference itself had become a historic event in the annals of legal reporting. But it was only the beginning of a larger campaign to direct mass attention to the problems of inequality and inside dealing plaguing the higher judiciary in India, according to Justice Karnan. Public condemnations of caste prejudice where then followed by complaints about the cases that were brought before his bench, eventually leading to unspecified charges of corruption against the highest level of the judiciary. At one point, the judge burst uninvited into an ongoing hearing being overseen by other judges concerning a piece of public interest litigation about how judges were appointed to cases. In the one of the great halls of the Madras High Court, Justice Karnan claimed before the court and before the press that he was being belittled by being assigned cases that were not commensurate with his status and skills despite that fact that the High Court is supposed to assign cases to its judges on a rotating roster system.

Justice Karnan then continued to appeal directly to the public through news media, initiating *suo moto* stay orders to halt the chief justice's attempt to interview new judges for possible assignment to the court. He would eventually go on to threaten the chief justice of the Madras High Court with contempt of court hearings when Justice Karnan's stay was reversed by the chief justice. Seeking a way out of a difficult and very public legal battle with a judge from an oppressed community whose accusations were plausible but not substantiated, the Supreme Court of India eventually transferred Justice Karnan to another bench on the Calcutta High Court. This transfer order, too, was stayed by Justice Karnan, who wished to remain in Chennai to pursue his allegations in the Madras High Court. But his attempt to use his powers as a judge to stop his own transfer was dismissed under the principle of *nemo judex in causa sua* (no one shall judge in their own case) as his story was taking up more and more space as a national news event across media outlets. "You have insulted me in the general public consisting of a population of 120 crores in India due to lack of legal knowledge" declared the rebel judge in his response to the Supreme Court.[30] This is a serious accusation that invokes precisely the image of the judiciary before the eyes of the nation, reiterating his earlier argument that it was the court that was *in contempt of itself*. Karnan was situated both within the judiciary, as a sitting judge claiming contempt of court, and without, as one whose powers are curtailed by the same law of contempt as interpreted by peers he had deemed "corrupt," thus motivating his appeal to public opinion. In insulting him, the justice argued that the court was lowering its own image on the national stage, and it was on this very stage that he was determined to take the battle forward.

What was termed Justice Karnan's *populist sensationalism* had engendered a wide debate in the legal world and beyond, as experts and audiences worked to understand the entanglements of caste and the paradoxes of legal bureaucratic structure.[31] A widely recognized problem in a field long dominated by upper castes, especially Brahmins, had taken on new dimensions as the judge leading the charge against discrimination appeared to have little respect for the basic standards of legal bureaucracy and procedure even if he was zealous in his use of the law. For example, Justice Karnan wrote a letter directly to the prime minister of India in which he detailed his charges of corruption and even sexual assault on the premises of the Madras High Court. He urged the leader to take action in an effort to "save the Top Most image of the judiciary," and he went on to call on "all political parties of India to extend their fullest cooperation in maintaining an impeccable image at all times."[32] Writing to the prime minister and addressing the public as he also pursued legal avenues that were sought as much for their display value as they were in the hope of seeking official remedy, the rebel judge had clearly instrumentalized the law as a medium for news making. He had done so against the judiciary itself, and not as a pure outsider, giving the news-reading public the impression of the Indian higher judiciary exploding from within before their very eyes. Many newspaper readers I discussed this case with as it was unfolding took the justice be unsound of mind and interpreted his direct appeals to the public and unusual legal acrobatics to have made a mockery of an otherwise respected if imperfect judiciary.

This public attack on the courts, in turn, attracted the charge of contempt of court against Justice Karnan himself, this time leveled by a bench of seven senior justices of the Supreme Court of India. When he initially failed to attend the Supreme Court summons, the judge was issued a bailable arrest warrant. Justice Karnan responded by filing a legal notice demanding legal compensation from the Supreme Court for not letting him work and for distress, at which point the judge was apprehended by the police. In the contempt hearings that followed, he stood accused of "scandalizing" the judiciary and was found to be guilty. The Supreme Court judgment frequently makes reference to the breach of having spoken directly to the public by means of the news media in his attempts to bypass what he alleged was a corrupt higher court system. In the words of the authors of the judgment on contempt of court against Justice Karnan, "His public utterances, turned the judicial system into a laughing stock. The local media, unmindful of the damage it was causing to the judicial institution, merrily rode the Karnan wave. Even the foreign media, had its dig at the Indian judiciary." The accusation of producing a scandal here extends beyond Justice Karnan's actions to include those reporting on his statements and legal tactics, even if no media outlet was specifically charged with a similar crime in this case. That the justice's accusations had become an international news story, however, was particularly troubling: "The BBC also reported on the issue." The wave that they collectively "rode" is what had caused real damage to the authority of the court, but it was Justice Karnan who would face the most direct repercussions. He was sentenced to six months of imprisonment for leveling "obnoxious allegations" that were also "malicious and defamatory" against thirty-three of his colleagues while he "shielded himself from actions, by trumpeting his position, as belonging to an under-privileged caste." In the judgment, Justice Karnan was furthermore restrained from speaking in public until he had served his time in prison. Within an hour of being sentenced, however, he publicly issued a judicial order negating the Supreme Court's ruling, handwritten on a notepad from his guesthouse, before the Supreme Court issued a gag order restraining news media from reporting Justice Karnan's statements. The news trail concerning the rebel judge grew cold while he was incarcerated. When he was released he claimed that he planned to start a new political party and contest elections. Karnan had finally turned from the realm of law as sovereign justice, from which he had been banished, to that of politics proper.

Justice Karnan's case appeared as a catastrophe that had spun out of control, as several commentators argued in the press. For example, Kaleeswaram Raj, writing in *The Week*, notes, "Karnan in Mahabharata, after all, is a tragic character. The modern episode of Justice Karnan also is a judicial tragedy."[33] Part of terming this escalation of events a *tragedy* is to acknowledge the degree to which the agency of the actors involved in this drama was deeply mediated by publics and institutions well outside of the law's official purview even if overdetermined by the law's public presence. Many saw the judge as a sharp mind who was destroyed in the public eye by his own thirst for public recognition and as someone who was treated differently then he would have been otherwise because of his caste. Some noted that when retired Justice Markanday Kautju was charged with contempt of court for a social media post around the same time, he was treated with a great deal more respect among judges and in news reporting. And as Suraj Yengde argues in his important book *Caste Matters*, an analysis of casteism both within the judiciary and in the public sphere is necessary to understand the contrast between the treatment of Justice Karnan meted out by the press and the high public regard for four justices from the Supreme Court who held the first-ever such press conference in front of the court denouncing irregularities in their own court just months later.[34]

On a fundamental level, we are faced with a social drama unfolding around discrimination and a higher judiciary that is either unwilling or unable to address it. A long-standing silence had been broken. But because of the manner in which the rebel judge's accusations of caste-based malice were publicized and the cloud of suspicion hanging over the judge's motivations and his sanity, allegations of casteism were never seriously investigated. The Supreme Court issued orders for a psychiatric evaluation of Justice Karnan instead of looking into the charges he made against his fellow High Court judges when he claimed to be distressed. The evaluation was taken by Justice Karnan as "an illegal insult to a Dalit judge" when he issued a legal travel ban on the Supreme Court judges from a makeshift court he had established in his home office before his arrest. At another level, then, there is the tragedy of deep personal attachment to something claiming universality that is perhaps ultimately harmful to the socially vulnerable.[35] While pursuing justice in the face of perceived caste discrimination, Justice Karnan was seemingly obsessed with the law, with using the law against its official guardians even if he had to do so outside of the court, and with legal remedy more broadly as a response to injustice. But he was ultimately rejected by the law and the state it represents. In Begoña Aretxaga's insightful formulation, insofar as "law . . . has come to represent the sovereign power of the state . . . the intense affect of this power . . . has the capacity to drive people mad, madness that comes from being 'oversaturated with law' (Berlant 1991)."[36] Justice Karnan's passionate, reckless recourse to the court of public opinion through his own legal actions must be understood in the context of this awesome power that appears everywhere, structuring the very field of public opinion itself while claiming to stand aloof. Appeal to the public had failed the judge too. In these events, we can see more clearly how the judges' desire to read about themselves in the morning paper before coffee is part of a media dynamic of feedback loops that can take unexpected, devastating, even maddening turns.

Conclusion: Hazards of Juridical Publicity

We have traveled a long way from the majestic image of transcendent law invoked in the opening of this chapter in the Perumal Murugan judgment. In the very same courtroom halls where right-wing publicity stunts like banning books set the stage for liberal triumph, a judge might publicly shame a young woman who had broken no law, incite a small riot among lawyers over protective headgear, or bear the social embarrassment of having a fellow judge barge into proceedings, every move happening before the public eye. All newsworthy and spectacular in their own ways, the cases discussed in this chapter have been grouped together through the contingent fact of their having taken place while I was conducting fieldwork among journalists at the Madras High Court. It was, perhaps, a relatively unruly and eventful time in the long history of this august institution. And yet these stories all point to some underlying forces structuring the dynamics of juridical publicity while at the same time opening themselves to a broader set of questions having to do problems of sovereignty and vicissitudes of public representation.

First, the normative fantasy of the hermit judge whose lonely interpretation of the law locates itself outside of politics or broader social pressures so as to ensure impartiality appears more difficult to sustain than ever. As the language of law continues to dominate the news cycle, the pressures of mass mediation on legal reasoning are becoming more apparent. We need only read the numerous discussions of news media in legal judgments and observations as evidence of how judges are reflexive about the fact of mass circulation of juridical discourse. While there is a long tradition of the higher judiciary using its uniquely authoritative position to comment on and intervene in the world at large from the courtroom pulpit in India, the proliferation of news media technologies and formats is also changing the quality of judicial address. If judges had addressed the world largely through their written judgments, which are often adorned with a rich literary textuality as in the Perumal Murugan judgment, contemporary media logics demand more contained, easily circulatable texts and sensationalist affect. The moralist denouncement of Pavithra through comparing her request for a divorce to shopping provided just such a textual form. Even Justice Kaul's thoughtful prose in defense of the liberalism inherent in Indian traditions was easily reduced to a sound bite demanding that the author be resurrected. It was written in bold as if to call out to less diligent reporters that this was the "take-home" point. To be a successful judge in such an environment is to be media savvy, it appears, and to pay attention to one's public image.

The second, more abstract point to draw from these cases of legal spectacle has to do with what Webb Keane once called "the hazards of representation" and the question of law as the public face of state sovereignty.[37] That the law and juridical discourse are frequently cited across contexts far from official origins would appear, on the surface, to present a problem for state power as understood through the lens of unified sovereignty. Lack of control over representations of the law might seem to be a weakness. However, we owe to Das the insight that in the life of the state, this very "iterability becomes a sign not of vulnerability, but a mode of circulation through which power is produced," such that the legal discourse can penetrate into people's lives "and yet remain distant and elusive."[38] We might recall in this context how Justice Kaul's words served not only to liberate Perumal Murugan but also to project an image of legal authority over "Indian tradition" from afar. It is the same pervasiveness of judicial discourse and its citation across contexts that allowed the casual observations made to Pavithra concretize and legitimate a narrative that pins communal harmony back to the problem of a woman's chastity. Shameel's death at the hands of police was rendered irrelevant in the public circulation of this case, as if the state bore no responsibility for the riot. So it is not because of the iterability of law that the state is made weak or vulnerable.

The vulnerability of the power of the judiciary that results from its dependence on mass publicity has to do with an aspect of circulation not examined in Das's work. Taking a perspective that brings questions of interaction and popular sovereignty to the fore, we can better appreciate how the quasi-sacred majesty of the law requires recognition from the very people in whose name the law acts. When such recognition is not properly put on display, public representations of the law, and of judges in particular, are subject to accusations of contempt, as when the Tamil *Hindu* published observations that a judge had been disrespectful, or when advocates flaunted the court order on helmets, or when Justice Karnan accused his fellow judges in public, precisely in order to "save the Top Most image of the judiciary," as he put it. Charges of contempt and "scandalizing" the judiciary can themselves lower the estimation of the court in the eyes of the public when carried out with excessive force or when proving that the much-vaunted majesty of the court is in fact fragile. Legal sovereignty is thus vulnerable not simply because it is on display in public but because it demands from the very media of publicity a form of acknowledgment and a forum for displaying its power that can easily be withheld. To the degree that legal journalism owes allegiance both to logics of print or televisual capitalism and to the people it is addressing as a public, the requirement that the majesty of the judiciary be formally recognized might not always be met to the satisfaction of the judges who also form a small segment of this otherwise amorphous mass.

CHAPTER FOUR

Celebrity Outlaws

"They got him." I was greeted with the news one evening upon returning home to the village where I was living while doing fieldwork in 2004. India's most famous outlaw, Veerappan, had been killed. One of the older farmers accompanied me into the house and pointed toward the blaring television set. The large family I was living with had been binging on televised films since they had hitched up an illegal cable connection just a month before. This time they were gathered with their neighbors around the news footage of a white van riddled with bullet holes. As I walked in to join the crowd that had already spilled out onto the front veranda, the newscasters on Sun TV were describing details of the "encounter," a euphemism for extrajudicial killing by the state. The fearsome sandalwood and ivory smuggler had slaughtered well over a hundred police officers, kidnapped a major film star and a former minister, and terrorized officials and villagers living in the mountainous forests spanning the border between Tamil Nadu and Karnataka. My hosts were not completely surprised by his death at the hands of a special police force; it was bound to happen one day or another given the intensity of the hunt. But they were a little ambivalent about his final passing.

Koose Munisamy Veerappan had been a news mainstay for well over a decade. Sporting a massive *Kattabomman* mustache cascading past his jaw, he was usually pictured carrying a semiautomatic rifle slung over his lean shoulder. Like the colonial-era rebel chieftain after whom this style of facial hair is named, Veerappan had become the stuff of legend. Some projected him as a protective Robin Hood, generously redistributing his ill-gotten wealth to local villagers in this impoverished region. He was also likened to Osama

115

bin Laden, in part because of his ruthlessness but also because of his elusive whereabouts amid a haunting media ubiquity. The two shared the habit of communicating with the wider world through audio and video cassettes. Even those news outlets more closely aligned with the Tamil Nadu government, which had vowed to bring him to justice, displayed some mixed emotions in their coverage of the final event. It was rumored that Veerappan had tired of life in the forest and that he wanted to turn himself in. As we were watching reports of the encounter, some in the village where I was living contradicted the news, claiming that he had in fact surrendered peacefully only to be betrayed by the police who were seeking vengeance for their fallen colleagues. Many distrusted the official police narratives. Maybe ordinary Tamils shared the ambivalence on display in television reports because they would miss his phantomlike presence as a reminder of alternative imaginaries in an age where politics had become increasingly routinized, even cynical. Like other "social bandits" before him, Veerappan laid claim to regimes of justice and shadow sovereignty rooted in the forest, while his spectacular reign of violence outdid even that of a notoriously predatory state.[1] Replete with moral ambiguity, all in all, the celebrity outlaw made for great storytelling.

Veerappan's iconography was produced for mass consumption by journalists through print, photography, television, and analog video cassette technology belonging to the era of mass mediation before the widespread use of networked digital media in India. Like the "cine-political" film stars who became great leaders—such as MGR or Jayalalithaa—his image saturated public culture. Veerappan's mustache was a frequent reference point in popular media and conversation. He embodied a rough masculinity that harkened back to traditions of Tamil militarism associated with the subaltern castes who once ruled the Tamil-speaking regions in defiance of British colonialists.[2] But unlike the celebrities who could transpose their public commodity images into the idioms of state power, Veerappan had developed a language of rule and an appeal to the plebian imagination that was "incommensurable . . . with that of the modern state," according to the historian M. S. S. Pandian.[3] Although mass-mediated through journalism, his image circulated as much in the murky realm of rumor as it did through official news organs even after his death. Oral lore and news intertwined with one another over the course of his criminal career, as mythology surrounding the outlaw attracted coverage of his attacks and persona, the details of which were often known through networks of hearsay and not though forms of reporting premised on direct experience. At the same time, he craved media attention. And those journalists who *did* establish direct relations with Veerappan were, in turn, tainted with the moral ambiguity surrounding the subject of their reporting.

This chapter examines how the figure of the celebrity outlaw enters the news cycle. In following this story, it aims to understand the entanglement of broadcast and network regimes of circulation animating the more general phenomenon of news event making that we have been following in this book. The analysis centers on the dangerous dynamic of spectacle whereby the allure of penetrating into the "mainstream" of news exercises an important pull toward fame for the outlaw, while the outlaw's shadowy networks provide the journalist who can capture and transpose this netherworld into mass publicity with a great deal of value in the fields of print or televisual news production. Journalist and outlaw thereby develop cycles of reciprocal publicity. The greater threat a notorious "public enemy" poses to society at large, the more journalistic capture and publication are worth. Events of news publication become public events in their own right, heightening the perceived threat to public security the outlaw poses. Publication fuels more news about the event of news making as well as critical commentary on the ethical implications of publicizing violent outlaws, thereby animating the circuits of print and communicative capitalism. Once again, then, we will be following the intensification of a positive feedback loop. But here and in the next chapter we will be paying closer attention than previous chapters to the role of changing media technologies and their affordances for circulation in reconfiguring the relationship between the event being represented in the news and the event of representation.[4]

The first decades of the twenty-first century brought upheaval to a media system centered on broadcast that had significant consequences for how would-be celebrities could claim the attention of news-consuming publics. The ecology that produced a star like Veerappan over the course of the 1990s was defined by a cinematic cultural imaginary, the emergence of videotape distribution, and political party control over recently liberalized satellite television. These were coupled with a print market that was more independent than party-owned news but often reticent about provoking the wrath of state officials. Cinema, television, and print, all forms of relatively capital-intensive, centralized media sat alongside another world: a domain characterized by the reticulated logics of circulation associated with rumor and other speech genres that did not rely as centrally on technologies of mass mediation.[5] Broadcast media and networked oral circulation of information always interanimated one another, to be sure—as we have learned from subaltern studies scholarship on logics of communication and as we have briefly noted in the case of Veerappan.[6] But the ongoing technological mediatization of society appears to be reconfiguring this relationship. What Ravi Sundaram has conceptualized as the "pirate kingdom" of videocassette and then VCD circulation through unregulated informal urban networks provided an interface of sorts between capital-intensive broadcast and subaltern distribution in the 1990s and early 2000s.[7] The rapid proliferation of cheap handheld means of digital communication since that time, however, has provided for what Marshall McLuhan would have called "break-boundary" in the media ecology, enabling new regimes of circulation. Between 2010 and 2020, over seven hundred million Indians entered the world of cell phone use, radically expanding the very field of mass mediation and networked media in particular. Indeed, the process of digitalization has been interpreted by scholars like Sundaram as one where "stable audiences have vanished, and multiple information streams compete" to produce value through the "multiplication of event chains" in ways that have altered the architecture of public formation in India and elsewhere.[8]

The means of digital circulation have certainly massified quickly and on a scale that is difficult to fathom, perhaps also eroding a monopoly professional scribes might have enjoyed on legitimate claims to representing truth. But the conceptual and generic separation of the world of official news from that of unauthorized rumor networks produces powerful and enduring knowledge hierarchies. News journalism garners much of its authority from the place it can claim in the domains of centralized broadcast media, professional expertise, and the forms of public recognition that follow from these institutions. In his classic work on insurgent transmission, Ranajit Guha, for example, insists on a strict distinction between news and rumor along two lines concerning epistemology and participant roles.[9] Whereas news has an identifiable source who can be held responsible for content, rumor has no identifiable author, and "the purveyor cannot guarantee its accuracy or answer for its effects."[10] Just as importantly, unlike news that requires a distinction between communicator and audience, in rumor information travels through what Guha terms "absolute transitivity," where the encoding and decoding of rumor are collapsed at each point of relay within the network. Veena Das elaborates another, related feature of rumor concerned with the performative force of language "with the potential to make us experience events, not simply pointing to them as to something external, but by producing them in the very act of telling."[11] Whereas our intuitive understanding of news holds that it should be communicating something about the world to a mass audience, rumor appears to collapse a number of constitutive distinctions among author, communicator, and audience by explicitly acting in the world it also describes. And while our faith in the news and its guarantee of accuracy has certainly been shaken in recent times, many, especially journalists, have good reason to hold tightly to the epistemological contrast between news and rumor along with the corollary ontological difference between events in the world being represented in the news and the event of their representation. The field of news production must claim for itself the autonomy to represent a world of crime, law, business, and politics that is figured as outside of itself, "as something external," even though the value of news as a commodity is measured by its capacity to create events in the world through acts of representation. The value produced through the "multiplication of event chains" typical of the "circulation engine" fueling digital media exerts a great deal of pressure on news, and these conflicting regimes of value can leave journalists and editors in a double bind.

The figure of the famous outlaw provides for an interesting entry point into these changing dynamics of event making, circulation, and representation in Tamil India, where the news landscape diversified with the rise of nonpolitical party television stations coupled with the proliferation of cell phone–enabled digital media. If the voice of judicial address is clearly shaped and mediated by news-consuming publics, as we saw in the last chapter, Tamil outlaws, too, have always been deeply invested in their own public representation. We can imagine that even colonial-era rebels and outlaws—like Kattabomman, whose virile mustache style has come to iconize the type— would have been concerned with their wider reputation as carried in popular song and lore.[12] But the subject of bardic mythology, whose life story had begun to look more like a film by the time Veerappan dominated headlines in the 1990s, can now claim a greater role in the production and circulation of their own image for mass consumption. Older conceptions of fame had been reframed as celebrity through commodification of the image. Now celebrity itself appears to be undergoing a metamorphosis as access to the media of mass dissemination is being democratized and competition within the "attention economy" intensifies.[13]

The following pages focus on encounters between forms of mass publicity providing a basis of celebrity for the outlaw and emerging networked publics engaged in multilateral communication that has now been electrified through digital media, providing new means of publicity for the celebrity outlaw and posing new ethical dilemmas for journalism. Our pursuit of these generative moments of encounter and reflection must attend in particular to how the layering of media technologies conditions the temporality of cultural form, as old tropes of banditry or vigilantism take on new political significance. The method followed here is thus designed to be attuned to what Kajri Jain calls "the inertia and subtle mutations of older forms and processes, and hence the circuits and turbulences between newer and older forms, or remobilizations and resignifications beyond remediation per se."[14] The ancient figure of the outlaw who holds up a sort of inverted mirror to society has been both renewed and remade in relation to the media enabling the circulation of their fame, and the outlaw's relationship to society has changed as a result. In order to better understand these heterogeneous, nonlinear interactions between media and cultural forms, then, let us begin with an examination of Veerappan's rise to celebrity status through centralized mass media before returning to modes of networked publicity associated with digitalization that have allowed for the emergence of a somewhat different type of celebrity.

The Smuggler and the Scribe

Veerappan's reputation for lacing his criminal violence with a touch of nobility was built in large part through his relationship with Nakkeeran Gopal, the trickster journalist and editor of a political biweekly magazine whom we met earlier in chapters 1 and 2 of this book. One might go further and argue that these two men, who shared mustache styles along with a penchant for speaking about themselves in the third person, helped to make each other. If Gopal's magazine gave the bandit's image more complex dimensions, *Nakkeeran*'s unique access to and coverage of Veerappan played as large a role as its relentless campaign against Jayalalithaa in making it the most widely read among the political magazines. In fact, this journal's obsessive coverage of the deep "nexus" connecting political parties, bureaucrats, and organized crime might be said to have defined a whole genre.

IMAGING THE OUTLAW

The smuggler's deeds were reported in the press throughout the mid-1980s, at first through smaller news stories about his illegal sandalwood trade, his habit of killing hundreds of elephants for ivory, and an escape from police custody at a guesthouse in the Karnataka forest. While he had already committed murders, especially targeting informers and lower-rank forest rangers, Veerappan's name shot into the limelight in 1987 when he kidnapped a district officer from Satyamangalam and eventually chopped him to pieces with an axe when demands were not met. Veerappan's grisly reputation was then sealed when his gang killed a more senior Indian forest officer named Srinivas, whom he blamed for his own sister's suicide. In one of the most frequently told narratives about the macabre joy with which Veerappan pursued vengeance, his whole gang was rumored to have played a game of soccer with the man's severed head after leaving his body on the road.[15] This was followed by a series of attacks and the murders of several police subinspectors. The poacher and smuggler had graduated from being a local menace in the Western Ghats to attracting the attention of the central Government of India, eventually becoming the target of boarder security forces and being labeled a terrorist. The governments of Karnataka and then Tamil Nadu organized a special task force made of several battalions of police following this escalation.

Before any regular television broadcast other than the unpopular state-run *Doordarshan*, these deeds attracted attention from the daily press, especially *Dinathanthi*, a paper that already had a reputation for its willingness to depict gruesome crimes in detail. At the same time, this was the period when weekly magazines where increasingly going beyond the headlines to invest greater energy in sketching detailed investigative portraits of depravity for a voyeuristic reading public. Led by *Tharasu*, where Gopal began his journalist career as a layout artist, *Nakkeeran* had also been reporting on the colorful criminal's exploits since Gopal founded the journal, relying on secondhand accounts and the rumor mill into which his wide net of reporters was well integrated. The magazine eventually made a name for itself through the publication of the serial killer "Auto" Shankar's death row testimonials about corruption deep in the Tamil Nadu police force and government.[16] But the onetime graphic artist turned editor in chief had become especially frustrated with having to use an old police file photograph from 1980 for every article. Readers were beginning to wonder whether Veerappan was really one person or if many were carrying out crimes in his name. The chief minister, Jayalalithaa, even claimed that he had left the forests altogether in a speech she gave before the assembly. As the news of more mass violence began to pile up, stronger visuals had become more and more important. Gopal started altering versions of the police picture he had available to him before calling a general meeting of his reporters and offering a cash prize to any one among them who could capture a new photograph of the renowned bandit. In Gopal's telling of the story, he offered the reward for a photo at the very same time that the government had put a price of four million rupees on Veerappan's head, as he was now wanted dead or alive by the newly formed special task force.

In 1993, a reporter from *Nakkeeran* named P. Sivasubramanian finally made contact with Veerappan to arrange a meeting. Without addressing a single substantive question to him upon their first encounter, the reporter simply asked for permission to take his photograph. The bandit acceded, and within a couple of days the reporter ended up with the picture and more: the first interview ever to be conducted with the outlaw. But it was the visual image that appears to have caused the greatest stir in the journalist community and beyond. According to Sivasubramanian, "Although the police accepted the photo as real, *potu makkal* [the public] thought it wasn't. 'Why does he have [a] mustache like everyone at the [*Nakkeeran*] office? It looks like it was staged!' So, it was to rid them of these doubts that we knew we would have to record Veerappan on video on location." Gopal claims that it was only when he personally exposed the negatives of these photos in his darkroom that he realized they were sporting the same mustache, as he had never before seen an image of the outlaw other than the old police file shot thirteen years earlier. Once contact had been made, both parties saw opportunities for developing a relationship that could fuel mutual publicity.

The photograph *Nakkeeran* published on the front page of its April 23, 1993, issue shows Veerappan in army fatigues holding a rifle on his lap against a rock wall backdrop, with the headline "Our Reporter with Veerappan! Exclusive Photographs!" The bandit's old police file photo hovers above in the upper-left-hand corner, providing a before and after contrast. This blockbuster issue was published just two weeks after Veerappan's gang had lured senior police officer "Rambo" K. Gopalakrishnan into a trap and killed twenty-one policemen using landmines to blow up a bus in what became known as the "Palar blast." Although Gopal states that the photo was shot well before the carnage had taken place, his reporter Sivasubramanian was charged with abetting the slaughter under the Terrorist and Disruptive Activities (Prevention) Act (commonly known as TADA), eventually being acquitted of all charges. This cover photo and interview mark the beginning of the special relationship of reciprocal image making that would extend over a decade between the political journal and the outlaw. They were sold at a hefty price to *India Today* for reproduction and translation into English for a large India-wide readership.[17] Over the next three years Sivasubramaniam interviewed Veerappan several times for *Nakkeeran*, providing material that was quoted by every newspaper and magazine as fascination grew across the

FIGURE 4.1. Photo from *Nakkeeran* magazine of Veerappan reading about himself in the pages of *Nakkeeran*. Photo courtesy of *Nakheeran Biweekly*.

country. Many more photos were also published, often showing the outlaw reading the newspaper or listening to the radio. A number of widely published photos pictured Veerappan reading about himself in *Nakkeeran*, for instance, in an open acknowledgment and performance of their increasing mutual dependence on each other. In the words of the Indian police officer K. Vijay Kumar who led the operation that eventually resulted in Veerappan's demise, "He was worried about his image."[18] Somehow, putting a face to the name and depicting a criminal who was clearly concerned with what the world thought about him had made a large difference in public perceptions.

As if in exchange for exclusive access, *Nakkeeran* often wrote about Veerappan's loyal supporters in the borderland forests. These were marginalized communities who were thankful for the protection he offered from state violence even as they feared his threats of vengeance to be taken against any who were accused of crossing him. In a series of articles and videotaped interviews circulated on VHS cassettes during this period, *Nakkeeran* reporters documented the testimony of villagers from Adi Vasi (Indigenous) and other marginalized communities who had been tortured by the police or forest officers charged with capturing the outlaw. Among the most nightmarish of these attacks took place in the Dalit village of Vachathi, where police, forest personnel, and revenue officials raped over a dozen women, beat up over a hundred men, and destroyed all the houses and other property while on a mission to find illegal sandalwood and to coerce the villagers into giving information about the smuggler. Veerappan, for his part, began to claim his murders of state officials as revenge against these injustices through his new-found public stage in the pages of *Nakkeeran*. The Robin Hood mythology of justified banditry against state repression began to take hold for the public at large, adding greater social and political valence to a story that had begun as a simple list of monstrous crimes.[19] The protective guardian emerges as the alter ego of the bandit in a narrative world where both might be assimilated into kingship and even divinity.[20] But if bards have traditionally played the role of mythologizing the bandit's challenge to state monopolies on legitimate violence, here logics closer to the heart of print capitalism and a society increasingly addicted to media spectacle were at play.

DIRECT ADDRESS

The outside world got its first extended look into Veerappan's forest home and the unusual moral universe of a mass murderer who claimed allegiance with the poor and downtrodden through a nine-hour series of video tapes shot by Sivasubramaniam and another cameraperson. The reporter says it took a few days of simply being around Veerappan and his gang, shooting their daily activities, before he opened up to conversation. The grainy footage begins with Veerappan sitting against the rock outcrops on top of a hill where his gang had set up camp. He is flanked on the left side of the screen by his fearsome, dreadlocked young lieutenant, a man who the magazine's readers already know goes by the name "Baby." Wagging his finger in the air, the outlaw, again dressed in black fatigues, addresses the reporter sitting in front of him with an opening monologue echoing the ambivalent premises of social banditry:

> They tell thousands of lies in their attempts to destroy me. It's true, I have got many tricks to get them, and I've done it. But, for a common person I would give my life to protect them. These two sides of me exist. A politician will promise anything, get into power, and go up on stage saying "I'll protect you," while they line their pockets and that of their families, without doing anything for people. Veerappan is not that kind of person. I stay by my words!

The video then cuts abruptly to Veerappan looking straight into the camera with hands folded in humble welcome, as Sivasubramaniam gets up out of the way and the camera closes in on the protagonist of the story. Drawing on the more formal genre of the public speech, he begins, addressing his viewers directly:

> That is to say, to my nation's people, I mean, to my mothers my sisters and brothers, elders and youth, I am speaking to you as you see me and as this is being filmed. See what thoughts I offer. Am I wrong? Or is the state wrong? I am going to tell you what happened in my life story. How I became a person from a young age, and my experiences. I'll tell you.

He then raises his hands and salutes the viewer once again, saying "Oh God, Murugan!" as the larger narrative ensues. The video consists of both a life story as told by Veerappan and a demonstration of his techniques for hunting both animals as well as the police who chase him, with a defense of his motives. Veerappan tells of the hardships he faced from his humble beginnings in the small forest village of Gopinatham to becoming the leader of his own smuggling outfit. He demonstrates how he and his men worship their firearms every morning. Not shying away from the details of the massacres he orchestrated and executed, the outlaw consistently returns to his role as protector of the forest, its people, and the animals he hunts only because he is "hungry," in contrast to state officials who terrorize people and hunt animals for fun. In a passage from the video often quoted in the press, for example, Veerappan describes the humane methods they use to kill elephants by shooting between the eyes, providing a "good death" for the giant and "charity" for the small birds that feed on the carcass. Depicted as a local doctor who administers country medicine to the sick and as a political savant who has figured out all the ways in which political leaders had led their people astray, Veerappan is throughout concerned to project himself as a poor man who knows a great deal about the world but has been misunderstood.

When it was aired in the early days of cable television on the DMK-owned Sun TV station in 1996, the *Nakkeeran* video was a hit with viewers. Veerappan had become a household name and media star on par with, and in contrast to, the cinematic stars of Tamil politics whom he treats with such derision in his address to the world outside the forest. He was building a public shadow sovereignty to rival theirs. So captivating was the video portrait drawn of the man many previously saw as a monster that when the book of transcribed dialogues was published by *Nakkeeran*, M. S. S. Pandian felt compelled to write in the pages of the *Economic and Political Weekly* that "one can envision a new politics and a new mode of governance" in Veerappan's moral universe.[21] The video was welcomed by some among the police for altogether different reasons. A former inspector general, for example, claimed that the video amounted to a confession, and that other forms of evidence would not be needed. The new forms of publicity and direct address that Veerappan indulged in with the help of *Nakkeeran* had brought the police ever closer to the bandit, while Gopal himself was coming closer to inhabiting the role of an outlaw journalist. As proximity to the outlaw grew, so, too, did discomfort with Gopal's ethics in the journalist community. But it was an unease that was coupled with envy, as *Nakkeeran*'s print and video publications were providing more and more valuable material for others to cover as news events in their own right.

FROM JOURNALIST TO MEDIATOR TO CONVICT

When the subject of Veerappan arose in my extended interview with Nakkeeran Gopal, we were sitting together in his fortified office. As he told me the tale of their deep relationship from the time he first published the bandit's picture, he looked up occasionally through the glass walls and doors across from his desk into the hall outside. The long corridor was adorned with a life-size panoramic photograph of himself walking through the forest with Veerappan and his gang. It was from the time of the video his magazine had aired on Sun TV that Gopal began meeting with the bandit himself in the woods. Clearly a story he had told many times before, the journalist relished sharing details of their interactions with me, as their transactions also enabled Gopal to claim for himself the very media celebrity he had previously been generating for other larger-than-life figures like Veerappan or Jayalalithaa. When the *Atlantic* published an investigative profile about Veerappan in 2001, for example, Gopal himself featured as an important character in the story.[22]

Any pretense of simply reporting what the outlaw was doing and telling the world had gone out the window by the late 1990s. Gopal took it on himself not only to represent Veerappan for the wider public but also to begin acting as the bandit's confidant and negotiator. Gopal even thought of his work with Veerappan in political terms. The journalist claimed that it was his video tapes and reporting on the outlaw that had caused the downfall of the Jayalalithaa government in the 1996 elections, proving them incompetent in their search for him and in charge of a police force that preyed on the common person rather than protecting them. Gopal also argued that he was the first person who started to work toward Veerappan giving up arms, because the government was unable to. He explained to me, as I sat across his desk,

> I had only met him once when he started to discuss the possibility of surrendering with me. I went up into the forest with my *thambi* [little brother] Sivasubramaniam. They would pick you up in a town, say Karur. And then blindfolded we would be taken to three or four different locations before getting closer to where Veerappan was. After that, it was a walk of over twenty kilometers in woods so thick you would have to brush off vines and thorny bushes as you walked through. . . . Then I met him and he was very courteous, always addressing me with respect as the *āciriyar* [writer]. When he started talking about surrendering, I made a demand. (Gopal quoting himself) "Look I'll speak to both states (Karnataka and Tamil Nadu) about surrendering. But you need to give me a guarantee. That's to say, you've killed 150 people till now you say. With that, you need to stop. From now on, you can't kill anymore. If you stop killing, then I'll go talk about this (surrender)."

Although Veerappan told Gopal it would be difficult, he eventually agreed to the terms, and according to the journalist, abided by them for two peaceful years.

While Gopal claims to have been working toward an arrangement between the outlaw and those who were after him, the special task force was getting closer, having lost some of their earlier fears, until one day Veerappan broke his promise and abducted nine forest officers. "I heard it on the radio!" Gopal exploded when narrating these events to me. "I was angry with him!" The nine hostages were held deep in the forest. This time, rather than risk their lives with direct police intervention, then chief minister M. Karunanidhi, who was already fairly close to Nakkeeran Gopal, asked the journalist to negotiate with Veerappan. Upon returning to the forest to negotiate the release of the nine hostages, Gopal told me he was given a cold welcome by Veerappan. The bandit had been listening to the news on the radio when it was announced that there was no way the government of Karnataka would accept any form of amnesty for the outlaw. According to Gopal, "Veerappan was enraged, pacing around like an animal." The outlaw shouted at his prey, "Your government will only understand when I chop you all up and display your heads on the road!"[23] If Gopal was miffed to have initially heard about Veerappan's actions on the radio news, Veerappan's understanding of his own actions appeared to be increasingly shaped by how he was being portrayed in the news beyond the *Nakkeeran* magazine.

Fearing for the forest officers' lives, Gopal told me that after hours of argument with the raging bandit, he was able convince Veerappan that killing these men would result in a terrible public image. The journalist claims that this was an argument that worked to change his mind. In our interview he quoted himself persuading the outlaw, "Look, I have written about the just things you have done but must also write about your injustices." Upon initial acceptance to negotiate a price of fifty million, Gopal was allowed to leave with one of the hostages, but without a guarantee that they would all be alive when he returned. Gopal went down the mountain to communicate the demand to the government of Tamil Nadu. After forty-nine days of going back and forth, Gopal eventually arranged for their release, and he was feted by the government of Tamil Nadu for his public service. Many others wondered just how much money the journalist was making through these transactions, going so far as to imagine that Nakkeeran Gopal had colluded with Veerappan in a mutually beneficial transaction. As the outlaw became more human, his journalist publicist was becoming more suspect.[24]

Veerappan's most fantastic kidnapping was that of the seventy-three-year-old Kannada film superstar Rajkumar in 2000. The actor, whose stature in Karnataka equals that of Tamil Nadu's cine-political leaders like MGR, had in fact played the role of a forest ranger who subdues forest-dwelling ivory and sandalwood smugglers in the 1973 film *Gandhada Gudi* and was furthermore reported to have shared a wish to meet Veerappan just before his kidnapping.[25] Veerappan also appeared to be a fan of the actor, reportedly addressing him always as *periyor*, used for respected elders. Upon first nabbing the actor, Veerappan had left a cassette tape with Rajkumar's wife listing a secret set of demands to the government of Karnataka reportedly having to do with rights to the waters of the sacred Kaveri River, which flows down from Karnataka to the Thanjavur delta in Tamil Nadu. While there are competing narratives about how Nakkeeran Gopal was eventually chosen to be sent to the forest to negotiate with the bandit, he was eventually called by the governments of Karnataka and Tamil Nadu to intervene, as Tamils in Bangalore were being attacked by Kanadigas who were outraged as Veerappan's choice of hostage. In a scenario that appeared as if it might have been lifted from a film script, the celebrity bandit had managed to incite mass violence in the state of Karnataka by kidnapping the state's most beloved personality, and the journalist was to play the role of hero mediator. Popular imagination elaborated the cinematic potentials of the situation. A major rumor circulating in the early days of the kidnapping had it that Veerappan made the production of a feature film about his life one of his demands. He was said to have kept Shekhar

Kapur's phone number in his diary in the hopes of being immortalized by the director who had made the 1994 film *Bandit Queen* about Phoolan Devi.

Nakkeeran Gopal, for his part, accepted the role of go-between again because he, too, was portraying himself as a savior of Tamils living under the threat of violence in the neighboring state. As he put it when recounting his decision, "If I hadn't agreed, there would have been thousands of dead. That's why I went." Both the outlaw and the journalist claimed to be representing their people's national interest while portraying the government as unable to do so. When Veerappan's demands where finally published, Rajkumar was still in the forest. They made a number of claims for Tamils beyond those on the Kaveri River waters, including making Tamil a language of administration in the state of Karnataka, building a statue of the great Tamil sage Thiruvalluvar in the city of Bangalore, and freedom from prison for members of a Tamil-nationalist paramilitary group to which he had grown close. But Veerappan was also portraying himself as a champion of the poor by demanding higher wages for tea estate workers and a better price for Nilgiri mountain tea. Perhaps most interesting was his request to make public a government report documenting many acts of brutal violence that the special task force charged with arresting him had perpetrated in the mountain villages on the border between the two states, echoing *Nakkeeran*'s reporting on the same subject. Claims about the demand for a film production were never verified.

Meanwhile, the government of Tamil Nadu used Gopal to communicate with Veerappan regarding his demands because the DMK, not Jayalalithaa's AIADMK, was in power. Another giant wall-size photograph of Gopal surrounded by television cameras returning from the forest to deliver Veerappan's response to the government to Chief Minister Karunanidhi adorns the entrance to his office building, marking the apotheosis of his fame in the Indian public sphere. Gopal's brushes with danger had become almost as riveting as the news of Veerappan he alone could deliver with any authority. The journalist would later write about these experiences in his widely read book *Nānum Vīrappanum!* (Veerappan and I!) (2004), first published around the time of Veerappan's deadly "encounter" with the special task force and now running into its sixth edition. *Nakkeeran* also made the most of their editor's role by being the only news outlet to publish photographs and other news about the well-being of the aging actor during his time as a hostage.

While Rajkumar was reported by *Nakkeeran* to be in good spirits and well cared for by his kidnapper, a growing grumble in the Tamil press was questioning Gopal's credibility. Some had come to view him as merely opportunistic; others were harsher in suspecting him of being in on a plot with

Veerappan or with corrupt forces within the Tamil Nadu government and enriching himself at the expense of beleaguered Tamils of Bangalore he claimed to be protecting. As a senior journalist once told me, "He's a crook, and that's why he got along well with Veerappan." An audio cassette of Rajkumar's voice telling listeners how he was being treated "like a brother" was smuggled out of the forest and released to the press, appearing to corroborate what *Nakkeeran* had been reporting. After a prolonged period during which many shops and even schools were closed in Karnataka, the government had shown willingness to give into Veerappan's demands, but they were stopped from doing so by the courts. Rajkumar was eventually released by the outlaw after months in the forests for reasons that were never clarified in the pages of *Nakkeeran* or any other news publication. Gopal and his journal had played a large role in portraying Veerappan as a revolutionary bandit for the poor. But by the time of Rajkumar's release, most journalists in other newspapers had begun to suspect that other motives having to do with a granite quarrying racket were behind the kidnapping, as more stories of Rajkumar's son's dealing in the notoriously corrupt industry had begun to surface. In the months following the actor's return to Bangalore, Tamil publics who were following the story became increasingly suspicious of official reporting. Rumors about Veerappan's deep depression and his desire to negotiate a surrender with the help of his connections in the Tamil militant movement circulated with much greater intensity, and these alternative narratives themselves became the stuff of news in the mainstream press.[26] Gopal continued to echo the rumor mill and to portray himself as the man at the center of any possible surrender in the pages of his magazine.

The *Nakkeeran* editor had tied his fate to the Veerappan story. Although he had been in jail many times before because of his confrontations with Jayalalithaa (detailed in chap. 2), Gopal would pay a higher price for his role in the Veerappan affair. True to an election campaign promise she had made before winning a majority in the Tamil Nadu assembly to return for her second full term as chief minister, Jayalalithaa's government arrested the journalist with the outlaw image in 2003. This time, however, she had done so under the especially draconian Prevention of Terrorism Act (POTA), passed in the wake of the 2001 attack on the national parliament in New Delhi. Gopal stood accused of carrying illegal weapons and of conspiring to kill a police informer in collusion with Veerappan himself. The POTA act made it easy to incarcerate a suspect while evidence was being collected. He spent eight long months in jail before being set free on bail in response to a habeas corpus petition filed by his brother. Files were eventually dropped, and Gopal's reputation for provocation in the face of power was as strong as it had ever been even if his credibility as a reporter was declining among a significant portion of journalists and even among the wider Tamil public.

When the joint special task force finally killed Veerappan in Operation Cocoon just a year later, Gopal pursued his attempts to capitalize on his connection by writing a series of articles broadcasting the rumors that denied official police accounts of the "encounter." Instead of being shot on site in the fake ambulance police had used to lure the outlaw out of the forest, according to Gopal, the police tortured Veerappan for days in retaliation of the many deaths and humiliations they had suffered. They then embalmed the outlaw's body to make it look as if it had been recently shot for the news cameras that swarmed the site once his death had been made known. Gopal continues to release YouTube videos on the story of police deception in the Veerappan case and he still does the rounds of news talk shows with his version of the story.

SYMBIOSIS, PARASITISM, AMBIVALENCE

Nakkeeran Gopal has always been a divisive figure in ways that might exceed even the moral ambiguity of the outlaw who made him infamous. Of course, they made each other infamous. And to that degree their relationship was mutually beneficial, or symbiotic. It was in large measure because of Gopal's reporting that Veerappan represented a kind of rustic heroism for many— even those who were horrified by the scope of violence he unleashed. The folklore around Veerappan was granted the more respectable status of news for readers of *Nakkeeran*. The photographs published in *Nakkeeran* and the video they had made with the outlaw for Sun TV carry a strong aura of truth for readers and television watchers. Gopal, in turn, became the most notorious journalist in South India by playing his role in turning a demon who inhabited the domain of rumor into a legend with more human qualities. Gopal's near monopoly on representing Veerappan's image to the world in the realist idiom through broadcast circulation has certainly lessened over the years as it has ceased to live as "news." As Veerappan had hoped, many feature length films and a number of television serials have been made since his death. But even in representations that are now viewed from a "historical" perspective, it is difficult to ignore Gopal's role in the larger story of the forest bandit.

At the same time, Gopal's escapades in the bush were tarnished by what some critics took to be his direct collusion in Veerappan's reign of terror and what many others read as unpalatable self-aggrandizement at the cost of the victims of the outlaw's violence. Gopal enjoyed nearly exclusive access to events otherwise known only by the police or through unsubstantiated rumor, becoming rich by uncovering the secrets of an alternative world for the public to consume, eventually inserting himself as an actor in that world. But if Veerappan could claim to represent a world other than that of the banal violence of the state that everyone had grown used to, there was also something parasitic about Nakkeeran Gopal's role as media star and political mediator. The journalist derived his value from standing between worlds—while being invested in their separation—even if the larger story he produced was marked by a constant blurring of the distinction between law and outlaw, as good crime fiction often does. The wild forest and established state politics had to be conceived of as apart for the narrator to show us how closely they mirror each other.

The dozens of journalists I have interviewed over the years are remarkably split on the question of Nakkeeran Gopal's status in the field more broadly. Known as the editor with the deepest and most robust network of reporters in Tamil Nadu, he is just as often held up as an example of how debased journalism has become in recent decades. As an editor at a major daily asked me once, "Who needs to watch films when you can read *Nakkeeran*? That's not journalism. It's as if Gopal were acting in a film." In some respects, Gopal is exceptional. No other journalist has faced the wrath of the law with such severity and regularity, and no one else enjoys so much fame for being a scribe. Like the confrontations with the god Shiva that defined the image of the classical Tamil poet Natkīrar from whom Nakkeeran Gopal took his publication's name, the journalist's exceptionally combative persona make him unusual in a field marked by general docility before political power. One could almost as easily imagine making a film about Gopal as one could about Veerappan. But in other ways, Gopal is the quintessential contemporary journalist for whom the lines between fact and fantasy or right and wrong have been subsumed under the broader imperatives of defacing public secrets, telling a gripping tale, or simply producing a spectacle. Perhaps he disturbs so much because of how he makes salient the parasitic qualities of all crime journalism and other forms of reporting where value is measured as much in the profitability of event-making spectacle as it is in the dissemination of fact. What the leading scholar of South Indian literature, David Shulman, wrote about the figure of the outlaw in classic Tamil texts might equally apply to Nakkeeran Gopal as a polarizing journalistic icon: "This ambivalence within the individual persona corresponds to the basic ambivalence of the social order itself, which has incorporated its own antithesis."[27] Gopal, the celebrity journalist, represents the often-disavowed common knowledge that, similar to the oftentimes thin line between police and criminal, the border separating bandit and journalist can be extremely tenuous.

Networks Electrified and the Pluralization of Broadcast

Veerappan remains the most important reference point in the annals of South Indian banditry, having defined the very genre of the modern celebrity outlaw in collusion with Gopal. The forest brigand and his publicist thrived in a duopolistic political and media world where the two large political parties were in control of major satellite television networks and the public imaginary of a shadow sovereign power was ruled by film. Whereas the DMK-owned Sun Media network had quickly become a lucrative media empire by the time Sun TV was airing the videos of Veerappan in the mid-1990s, the AIADMK's Jaya TV served party propaganda vowing to destroy the outlaw to a devoted audience. Over time, every political party in the state had to start a television news channel to be considered legitimate, most of them running at huge losses. Newspapers had, for the most part, enjoyed greater independence from parties during this time even if they tended tacitly to support whoever was in power. This is especially the case with the most widely read daily, *Dinathanthi*, a paper that has also specialized in sensational crime reporting. Weeklies and biweeklies like *Nakkeeran* or *Junior Vikatan* were where readers had come to expect more critical and investigative reporting often mixed with wild speculation in the form of political gossip and rumor columns, a genre that became increasingly important in the 1990s and 2000s and embraced by the daily *Dinamalar*. Unfounded but plausible narratives that could not be attributed to any source had found their way into the medium of print through textual devices that would mark them off from harder news reporting.

This print and cable television market continued to thrive into the 2000s and the 2010s, but it also had to contend with and enter into digital modes of circulation enabled by widespread cell phone use. As noted in the introduction to this chapter, journalists and news consumers experienced a rapidly changing world where online content was largely distributed and consumed on handheld devices for the first time and where a great deal of media was produced on phones and with networked circulation in mind. A much-hyped turn to information technology and online access through publicly accessible personal computers in early 2000s India turned out to be important more for the charismatic promise of newness than for any real reorganization of media consumption habits. The first generation of widely available cell phones had nevertheless begun to affect practices of politics and commerce.[28] Between 2004 and 2007 the number of cell phones had tripled, and by 2020 the number of working cell phone numbers in India had overtaken the total population. Many of the approximately 750 million active cell phone users in India at the time of writing use multiple phones and SIM cards.[29] As a result, even a great deal of television news is watched on these devices in the form of short clips that have been forwarded through social media networks.

The massive expansion of data-enabled mobile phone networks have afforded the onset of convergence among multiple media interfaces precisely when the first nonparty television news stations, led by the upstart Puthiya Thalaimurai (New generation), blossomed.[30] The corporate-backed station was the first high-definition satellite channel employing the latest digital production technology to hit Tamil television. Within only a few months of launching in 2011, Puthiya Thalaimurai had overtaken the party-owned competition to become the most watched Tamil television news channel. Within a year it was watched by nearly twice as many viewers as Sun TV.[31] Advertising revenue started streaming in as news television, a medium previously conceived of primarily as useful for politics, had proved its capacity to generate wealth through the production of shows that would become news events in their own right. The relative autonomy of the news channel from party politics had made it a valuable commodity, and the nonpartisan corporate model was then replicated by the newspaper-owned Thanthi TV in 2012 and later by Reliance Industries–owned News 18 Tamil in 2016. It was thus over the course of the 2010s that the simultaneous proliferation of cell phone–enabled social media and independent news channels had begun to layer themselves firmly over the existing infrastructure of party-owned channels and print media in Tamil Nadu, thereby shifting the circuits through which news was produced and disseminated.[32] Printed news moved online slowly, led by the weeklies, while the world of television news was being remade by digital circulation of news video clips coupled with news production's interaction with and increasing dependence on information circulating through other media.

WhatsApp, a phone-based, multiplatform, voice-over-internet protocol application introduced in 2009, was by far the most important force in transforming the media environment for all forms of news production and circulation. WhatsApp motivated many to acquire smartphones with screens, forming a digital infrastructure that penetrated more deeply into existing popular networks than either Twitter or Facebook. This is especially the case in the regional languages to the extent that up to well over half of Indian Tamils had gone online through this application by 2016, more than in any other state. It was free, it was designed to work well on the limited 2G and 3G networks available to most people, and it allowed users to forward endlessly to groups of up to 265 users, enabling information to circulate through distributed networks at speeds and scales previously unimaginable. This application enables groups to share not only text but also videos, documents, and photographic images in addition to longer audio files. These files are housed in the phone itself, not online, and can be transmitted to other phones when cellular data is enabled or through access to wireless internet. WhatsApp messages are in an encrypted format that eludes surveillance even though the company started sharing user information with Facebook in 2016, two years after being acquired by the infotech behemoth. Messages on WhatsApp are furthermore not subject to the algorithmic logics or monitoring that can "filter dissent" on other applications like Facebook.[33] But the architecture afforded by bit technology, especially the unpredictable scalability and replicability of the digital image that danah boyd has identified as characteristic features defining "networked publics," is central to how information circulates.[34] The forms of volatility that WhatsApp introduced into the distribution of often inflammatory and deadly rumors in India eventually led the company to impose severe limits on forwarding capacity and group size as a result of government pressure and bad publicity for Facebook. In contrast to centralized broadcast media, where governments can censor production through targeted threats to distribution—for example, shutting down a press or a television station— both Facebook and WhatsApp afford radically decentralized circulation. When virality online spills out onto the street, the state's reaction has been to shut down internet connectivity altogether. Overall, WhatsApp has radically intensified the "democratization of modern events" that Pierre Nora noted long ago as one of the effects of the mediatization of society, a process, he also notes, that produces "monstrous events."[35]

The Love Police, Murder, and
the Limits of Journalism

The aspects of outlaw celebrity explored in the remainder of this chapter echo the rise to fame that Veerappan enjoyed in the 1990s and early 2000s while also marking some of the differences made by the new media ecology for how outlaws can enter the news cycle to address and enlist a wider public. These new conditions were also symptomatic of a political change: the rise of specific caste-based politics in a region where public expressions of collective political identity were largely subsumed under the broader non-Brahmin politics of Tamil nationalism and its cinematic populism. More specifically, a form of public hate, focused especially on relationships between Dalit men and caste-Hindu women, has emerged in the form of violence against Dalits in Tamil Nadu.[36] While Dalits have always been subject to violence, new dominant caste-based vigilante groups have formed to police sexuality across the state, mirroring in many respects the North Indian and Kerala-based Hindu-nationalist groups that have formed to counter what they term "love jihad," the alleged conspiracy among Muslim men to marry and forcibly convert Hindu women. Many among the dominant castes in Tamil Nadu subscribe to the theory that there is a concerted effort led by Dalit political parties to trick women from their communities into pursuing romantic relationships with young Dalit men in an effort to upend social norms.

The old genre of rumor thus appears as an important mode of address, circulation, and performativity native to the logic of networks but now subject to forms and scales of circulation that only digital technology can afford. At the same time gossip, the function of which is often to police sexual morality, has taken on monstrous and deadlier dimensions as the surveillance and targeting of those accused of pursuing inappropriate relationships break similar scalar boundaries. Leadership of caste-based vigilante groups that organize themselves both offline and through social media often involves a form of political entrepreneurship outside of established parties that relies on the reticulated, mimetic logic of older genres of communication now concretized in technological form as a "design feature" of social media. These new forms of communal hatred have all relied heavily on the infrastructural affordances of WhatsApp, in particular, allowing deep pasts of caste oppression to erupt violently and very publicly into the present through contemporary media.[37] As the "absolute transitivity," which Guha identified as a feature of rumor, becomes incorporated within the circulatory regimes of digital media, the capacities of the caste-vigilante outlaw to claim celebrity have expanded. By the same token, the morally ambiguous role of publicity through journalism has become even more pronounced than it was in the era in which Veerappan and Gopal coproduced each other. Journalists can easily become instruments of circulation as much as they are expert reporters on a world outside the field of news production. An asymptotic relationship between the event represented and the event of representation threatens to collapse altogether into one event-generating feedback loop, and greater rhetorical work is required to maintain a separation between the crimes of the outlaw and the function of journalism.

FROM HUCKSTER TO POLITICAL ASPIRANT
TO CRIMINAL SUSPECT

Whereas Veerappan was assimilated to a mythology of caste valor as a Vanniyar only after his long celebrity career and demise, the young S. Yuvaraj was a murderer who became a caste hero through WhatsApp-mediated vigilantism that also gave him value in the larger worlds of broadcast news and politics. Before entering politics it appears that Yuvaraj—whose day job was operating borewell drill rigs—was involved in a number of scams ranging from crooked real estate deals to a pyramid scheme where farmers were told that they could get rich quick by raising emus for export.[38] Hailing from the Kongu Nadu region of western Tamil Nadu and belonging to the dominant Gounder, or "Kongu Nadu Vellalar" community, his first political affiliation was with caste-based Tamil Nadu Kongu Ilaignar Peravai (Tamil Nadu Kongu Youth Federation). This political group is led by U. Thaniyarasu, an influential member of the legislative assembly allied with the AIADMK party, which was then in power at the state level.

After fighting with the powerful leader, Yuvaraj started a rival caste-based party in 2014 called Dheeran Chinnamalai Gounder Peravai. Like many caste organizations, this one was named after a chieftain, Dheeran Chinnamalai, who is said to have been a brave rebel warrior against the British East India Company along the same narrative lines as the famed Kattabomman, who lived farther south. In promotional materials for the party, Yuvaraj is depicted twirling his mustache against a backdrop of the party's green and red colors with an image of the mounted and armed colonial-era outlaw floating above his head. Although drawing on the common semiotic repertoire of Tamil militancy that also fueled the Veerappan image machine and many other dreams of masculine virility, Yuvaraj's party took a slightly different turn when it allied itself with the Hindu-nationalist BJP (Bharatiya Janata Party), for which he campaigned in the 2014 national elections. After the elections, Yuvaraj joined the ranks of those discussed in the beginning of chapter three, those who tried to halt to publication of the well-known Tamil novelist Perumal Murugan's *Māthorubāgan* (*One Part Woman*) because of its depictions of historical temple rituals involving intercaste sexual relations. This moment signaled a new convergence of Hindu-nationalist and local caste-based politics. Yuvaraj's leadership in the campaign to ban the book made him a more important player in this region of western Tamil Nadu, where the convergence is most marked. He had already become locally known for holding large rallies where he would demand an oath from his fellow Gounder caste-mate followers that they would never marry outside of the community.

Yuvaraj shot to statewide prominence when he was named as the prime suspect in a murder case. The case received little attention at first. The death of a young man named V. Gokulraj was initially reported in July of 2015 as a small news item about an engineering student who had committed suicide. In light of recent caste violence, just by reading the headlines many in the region might well have suspected that cross-caste love was behind the suicide, as social pressure to maintain separation between communities would have mounted on the young man even if the papers do not disclose the caste background of their subjects in such stories. In this case, however, social media networks were already circulating a handwritten suicide note and a video recorded on a cell phone featuring Gokulraj saying he committed suicide after "love failure." As these images were then shown on television and in newspaper coverage of the event, greater attention was paid to the fact that Gokulraj was a Dalit student who was rumored to be close friends with a young woman who studied at college with him named Swathi, from the Gounder community. It was only after police had completed their post-mortem analysis that the "suspicious death" came to be known as a case of murder. The young man had been strangled and stabbed by others with a sharp object. His body was then taken to the railway tracks to be framed as a suicide, as many caste-motivated murders are. The recent murder of another Dalit youth named E. Ilavarasan who had married a Vanniyar woman was on everyone's mind. He, too, was found on the railway tracks in what most believe to be a faked suicide.

After further investigation, it emerged that Swathi had last seen Gokulraj the day before his body was found. They had visited the well-known Arthenareeswarar temple in Tiruchengode together, the very setting of Perumal Murugan's novel that had already been the object of Yuvaraj's earlier protests. News channels had obtained security camera footage from the temple showing the two college friends being dragged out of the temple gates by a group of men, one of whom was identified as Yuvaraj and the others as his associates. Swathi's family later shared a recorded phone conversation in which she said that she and Gokulraj were only friends, and that Gokulraj was forced to enter a car bearing Yuvaraj's Dheeran Chinnamalai Gounder

Peravai party emblem that was waiting outside the temple. The men took her cell phone and told to go to her parents' house. The vigilante group had been notified of the friendship and their location at the temple through an extensive WhatsApp-enabled surveillance network that is common among caste-based organizations, and it remains unclear whether Swathi's family was involved in the abduction.[39] Based on video footage coupled with testimony from Swathi and her brother, both police and the wider public following this story were left to surmise that Gokulraj was forced to write the fake suicide note and was filmed by his kidnappers before being murdered. Several members of the gang were arrested, but Yuvaraj absconded when this evidence was made public.

SHADOW CIRCULATION AND CELEBRITY

These horrifying scenes were only the first act in a cruel drama that would continue to capture public attention. So far in this narrative, WhatsApp had been used as an instrument to organize the vigilante group, as a medium of surveillance, and as a means to try to frame the murder as a suicide through the circulation of misinformation. But Yuvaraj had, in fact, not left the public eye altogether, and social media, now amplified by television news, was at the center of what became a counterpublicity campaign. While in hiding in various locations across South India, Yuvaraj sent a series of audio recordings to his WhatsApp group, welcoming his extended relations (*uravukal*) and community/caste friends (*samūha nanbarkal*) and directly invoking "our people" (*namma makkal*, using the inclusive second person pronoun also to index his addressees as belonging to his caste).

These were immediately forwarded across groups at a furious speed. In one of the audio messages that was subsequently posted by one of Yuvaraj's fans on YouTube, the absconded outlaw explains his choice of medium: "If you ask why I'm giving this audio instead of speaking through a press meet or newspaper, it would be one hour's news or one week's news, if it came on TV or in a magazine. This audio will be in each of your phones. I know it will spread to your friends, your relatives, and your connections, and it will continue to be conveyed." This reflexive framing of the "audios" paints them as a truer, subterranean knowledge designed to spread through the channels and temporalities of networks as opposed to the punctuated logic of broadcast media. After the opening frame, Yuvaraj then shifts modes of address, exclaiming that his caste community is more important to him than anything else, saying that he will not be moved by the emotions of family or by the lust for power that characterizes formal politics. He then invokes yet another hero of Tamil masculinity, this time invoking the war for Tamil independence in Sri Lanka: "While fighting for the Tamils, LTTE Prabhakaran lost his entire family. This is nothing compared to that."[40] The audio goes on with a theory of police conspiracy to defame his community and Dalit parties' desire to destroy society. In another recording, Yuvaraj claims, "If I were to surrender they would kill my people, they were trying to kill me! And this whole affair is being used by caste [i.e., Dalit] organizations as an assault on social institutions [*samūha kattamaippu*], trying to keep people from living peaceably together, and live a simple married life, which is what everyone wants." The language of instrumental politics contradicts the earlier narrative that Gokulraj killed himself because of "love failure," and Yuvaraj eventually appears to accept the premise that someone murdered the young student. But he denies responsibility for the act while diminishing it as the unfortunate result of a disturbance in the natural order of things.

Supporters quickly posted the recorded "audios" on a range of social media platforms, including YouTube and Facebook, where they became the stuff of an underground network among Gounders and others who were simply titillated by the outlaw's audacity. In his attempt to redirect media reporting, Yuvaraj released at least six such recordings, on the one hand claiming his innocence in the case of murder and his reluctance to face the law but on the other hand proclaiming Gounder caste pride and surprise that anyone should be upset about what he saw to be a righteous end to an illicit relationship. Yuvaraj would repeatedly complain that the police never investigate the murder of Gounder men or women, and he consistently invoked the conspiracy that there is an organized effort on the part of Dalits to destroy the foundations of society. It was not just a different regime of circulation that Yuvaraj was cultivating, spreading his messages through technologically enabled "sharing" among friends, relatives, and connections; he was also invoking the very epistemological "region of rumor" Das has shown to be central to obliterating the solidarities of everyday life by activating stereotypes steeped in the language of kinship, communal difference, and betrayal.[41] These are narratives of "digital hate" that the official news producers are accused of hiding because of their allegiance to liberal norms that frame caste pride as antisocial.[42]

The Tamil news media, in turn, had begun to follow Yuvaraj closely, printing his words, publishing the tapes online, and playing clips during news broadcasts. Investigative reports also drew connections between Gokulraj's murder and earlier murders of Dalit men accused of cross-caste romances, usually delivered in a deep dramatic voice-over accompanied by photographs of the murdered youths and a disturbing piano and orchestra score evoking the feeling of tragedy for news watchers. While marking their distance from Yuvaraj's words being broadcast on screen and in print, as an external set of events, journalists had nevertheless become important communicative vehicles for his image and for his accusations to reach a wide public across the state of Tamil Nadu and beyond.

Two months after Gokulraj's murder, Yuraj released a recording of himself talking on the phone to the policewoman charged with finding him, Deputy Superintendent of Tiruchengode R. Vishnupriya, in a strange conversation in which he was sympathizing with her about the tremendous pressure she was under to capture him and disclosing his location in the neighboring state of Kerala. Shortly after the recorded conversation, the superintendent, who was also Dalit, ended her own life for reasons that were unclear to most, and the police continued to claim that they were unable to trace Yuvaraj's whereabouts. The release of the twenty-minute audio file after her suicide, played in full and accompanied by photographs of the outlaw and the recently departed police official on a number of news channels, added new layers of intimacy, melodrama, and violence to a gruesome story of which the news media could not get enough. We might say that the outlaw was "trolling" the news-consuming public, having incorporated them as nodes in a network by means of broadcast media while making a mockery of the police force.

OUTLAW ON THE AIR

For three months, law enforcement officers claimed to be unable to find the absconding killer because he was using a series of mobile phones to access the internet and circulate WhatsApp messages without SIM cards. The credibility of the Tamil Nadu police force was under severe strain as many had begun to suspect that they were simply unwilling to arrest Yuvaraj because of the political might of his Gounder caste. The search was eventually transferred to the national-level Crime Branch of the Criminal Investigation Department (CB-CID) in the hopes of bringing professional expertise from outside this sphere of power to catch the outlaw. Yuvaraj's celebrity was growing, too, through both official new reports and unofficial circulation of his audios and photographic image. The formerly marginal political aspirant had become a household name. He also appeared to be invested in keeping public attention focused on his story rather than disappearing into the woodwork altogether, as others who are accused of murder might have done. As it turns out, Yuvaraj was actively soliciting news coverage by calling the major television stations and newspapers to offer interviews and to promote his audio recordings.

It was over one hundred days into the search for Tamil Nadu's most wanted criminal suspect that he was eventually interviewed on the most widely watched news channel, Puthiya Thalaimurai. Yuvaraj's first television feature aired on the channel's hit debate show, *Nerpada Pecu* (Talk straight), a program whose motto is *Maunam kalaiayattum* (Let silence be disturbed). Two celebrated journalists from the new era of independent news, Gunasekaran and Karthigaichelvan, anchored this show, which had developed its reputation by probing a number of topics that had previously never been discussed or had perhaps been approached tangentially.[43] Issues like everyday caste discrimination and gender inequality in Tamil society spoke especially to younger viewers who had grown tired of what they took to be the rehearsed pieties and orthodoxies of political-party-owned news media.

In what was billed as an "exclusive interview," Yuvaraj spoke to the television-watching public from an undisclosed location. Unlike the normal *Nerpada Pecu* debate format with many participants, however, no questions were asked on the air, and Yuvaraj was pictured alone apart from a Puthiya Thalaimurai microphone shown in the frame. The escaped suspect calmly discussed police incompetence in the case while denying responsibility for murder, all while wearing a neatly starched white-collar shirt and speaking in the relatively formal register of Tamil used for broadcast news. He tried to project an air of civility that seemed at odds with the conspiratorial tone of his speech, which was aimed toward blaming Gokulraj himself for his misfortune: "That boy went out with five or six girls, but the police are not interested! All to publicize for the Dalit organizations that they are after me." This broadcast was not "live." Rather it was aired in delayed time, having been recorded earlier in the day and edited for prime-time television. Sections of Yuvaraj's speech in which he named officials he accused of wrongdoing were censored with beep sounds smothering his voice. Sections of his monologue were also clearly edited out with short interludes in which the anchors summarized what the interviewee had to say in an attempt to assert distance and control for the news channel that had gotten so close to a wanted suspect and caste extremist. The aura of "liveness" that attends the televised image persisted, however, affording a shared sphere of mediation among murderer, television journalists, and audience that was distinctly uncomfortable for many and downright offensive for some. Puthiya Thalaimurai received a number of complaints in the days following their exclusive broadcast.

Two more television interviews nevertheless followed, on Puthiya Thalaimurai and the rival channel Thanthi TV, respectively. These encounters were produced after Yuvaraj had circulated a WhatsApp message stating that he would be surrendering himself to law enforcement now that the CB-CID was in charge of the case. In both interviews Yuvaraj argued that it was the state police that he did not trust, whereas most news followers had the impression that it was the same police force that was protecting him while claiming to be unable to catch him. This time, in the second Puthiya Thalaimurai interview, the normal debate show format returned, with Yuvaraj live on screen speaking to the well-known television anchor, Karthigaichelvan, through the Skype video calling application while other guests listened. Yuvaraj quickly dismissed the premise of talking only about Vishnupriya as the journalist then asked him pointed questions about what happened at the temple the day Gokulraj disappeared. Having to respond to the video evidence, the suspect admitted that he had seen the two students with each other but then claimed that the young man was being abusive to his friend. Yuvaraj told his interviewer and television viewers a narrative about how he and his men had to protect the young woman and so escorted her friend out of the temple before sending her home. His account was barely plausible to most viewers, and it confirmed a number of stereotypes for those invested in the rumored conspiracy that Dalit men are on the prowl, looking for victims among women of higher caste status. The outlaw sat twirling his mustache while responding confidently to Karthigaichelvan's probing questions about what really happened and why he was trying to drive a wedge between castes, apparently satisfied that he had managed to have his rendition of the story broadcast on prime-time television. Other guests on this edition of the Nerpada Pecu who were also being recorded while listening included retired police officers and social activists. They looked on in disbelief, listening to Yuvaraj's manufactured version of events, also perhaps shocked by the fact that this was happening live on television and that they, too, were taking part in what was beginning to feel more like a publicity stunt than a news show.

The other televised appearance, on Thanthi TV, was also broadcast live. There, the well-known interviewer Rangaraj Pandey was shown in a television studio office while Yuvaraj appeared through a video conferencing application. In this final appearance before he would turn himself in, Yuvaraj fielded an even more aggressive line of questions about how he could know so much about the Gokulraj case if he was, in fact, not involved in the young student's murder. In response, Yuvaraj grinned, explaining that he has his own "spy department" (*ullu thurai*) among his men that is better informed than the crime bureau or the Tamil Nadu police force. Pandey then asked the caste leader why he thought it was his job to decide who should love whom, to which Yuvaraj said he was only trying to raise awareness of nefarious forces that where trying to destroy society and cultural traditions. Explicitly recognizing the performative dimensions of the televised interview and the potential for incitement, with dead seriousness the anchor, Pandey, simply replied, "Sounds to me like you're giving a warning, not raising awareness. We both know many of your supporters will be watching this." Both the Puthiya Thalaimurai and Thanthi TV interviews ended with the news anchors thanking Yuvaraj for participating and supporting his decision to face the law. The shows were hits for the broadcast networks that hosted them. Television watchers across the state were both riveted and disturbed to watch the suspected murderer speak serenely to them as he had to his followers through WhatsApp, now on television with all the power of liveness and presence that medium affords. In the lead-up to his grand surrender, I was told by senior journalists at the *Hindu* that Yuvaraj even called to ask whether this distinguished national paper wanted access to him, an offer they turned down. "That's not the type of thing we do," one of them explained disapprovingly.

AUTOCRITIQUE AND DENOUEMENT

A number of journalists and prominent voices in Tamil Nadu took issue with the decision by Puthiya Thalaimurai and Thanthi TV to give Yuvaraj, the prime suspect in a caste-motivated murder of an innocent student, a stage before the wider public. As both the journalists who interviewed him noted explicitly, his WhatsApp audio messages were full of casteist language attacking the most marginalized segments of society. Among the more powerful of these indictments of media coverage came from Ravikumar, a Dalit political leader and intellectual, now a member of parliament from the Viduthalai Ciruthaigal Katchi (VCK), who was also a well-known figure on television talk shows at the time. He argued that the basic rules of journalistic ethics were being flouted, all in order to partake in the gruesome spectacle that Yuvaraj had been staging. Whereas in the era of duopolistic party-owned television news, decisions about whether or not to air would probably have been based on political calculations, many began to view the channels of the "new generation" with the increasing suspicion that they were guided only by commercial concerns. However, Karthigaichelvan and Rangaraj Pandey, for their part, had labored intensely in their respective interviews to portray the function of the news program to be critical interrogation, not simply to give exposure to their interviewee. Difficult questions about the role of the police force also emerged as the press and television channels displayed amazement that they had access to a criminal suspect that law enforcement could not locate and apprehend. Both Puthiya Thalaimurai and Thanthi TV could claim to be beyond party politics, and it was for that reason that they could ask more difficult questions about both caste violence and state incompetence.

In response to public outcry over the first interview broadcasted on Puthiya Thalaimurai, the channel's head news editor, M. Gunasekaran, decided to host an episode of Nerpada Pecu in which the channel's decision to air a show with Yuvaraj was debated. The dynamic young journalist had already made a name for himself in print media before becoming Tamil Nadu's most celebrated news anchor and the public face of Puthiya Thalaimurai, known for his empathy toward the weak and his tough questions for the powerful. Now he would be using his critical journalistic skills to analyze his own channel's ethics in broadcasting a show featuring a wanted suspect who was still on the run. Guests on the program included their most vocal critic, Ravikumar, in addition to a senior journalist, G. C. Shekhar, a political leader from the Communist Party of India, and two retired law enforcement officers. After debate about whether the police were simply unwilling to apprehend Yuvaraj, the show focused on criticism of the channel's interview: was it right or wrong to air such a program?

Gunasekaran summarized Ravikumar's criticisms, welcoming his intervention to spur reflexivity among journalists, and then asked his guest, "Instead of seeing the interview as a stage for Yuvaraj's campaigning, could you not see it as our means of exposing the police's inability or unwillingness to catch a known criminal?" The political leader responded by first praising Gunasekaran and the television channel for having the debate and being willing to criticize itself, then turned to the question of whether or not that have any ethical guidelines when showing a wanted suspect on the air, the way the BBC does, or other self-regulating mechanisms, such as the reader's editor at the *Hindu* newspaper. At one point, Ravikumar compared Yuvaraj's publicity campaign to the mediatized beheadings carried out by the Islamic state, noting that there are clear limits about what news programs can show. Although one of the retired police offers kept interrupting—annoyed that everyone was comparing the television channel's capacity to make contact with a wanted suspect to the police who did not arrest him—a consensus nevertheless emerged among guests on the program that television news had no guidelines at all for what they should and should not represent on the air.

The anchor then turned to address his fellow reporter, Shekhar: "I welcome criticism, of the media, of the police, of political leaders . . . everyone, but how do you view Mr. Ravikumar's remarks?" Shekhar, a print journalist with the *Telegraph*, began by arguing that television is fueled by sensationalism and that journalists are all driven by what he termed a "fugitive syndrome," meaning that they thrive on getting exclusive access to wanted outlaws. "But that is their job!" He reminded everyone that an early BBC interview with Yassir Arafat was considered scandalous at the time. Shekhar continued,

> then there was Phoolan Devi, and of course Veerappan. In fact, it was the police who sent Nakkeeran Gopal to negotiate with Veerappan when Rajkumar was kidnapped. So, we have to see that it is the media's job. We're different than the police. It was Yuvaraj who decided the time, place, and what he would say, and it is the journalist's duty not to make him the hero of the story. But in this case, I think they did the right thing.

Other guests agreed, with the exceptions of the communist leader and Ravikumar. What was at stake in the ethical question at hand for Gunasekaran was whether Yuvaraj was framed in a manner that led people to believe and admire him, or, alternatively, whether this was an act of publicizing and thus exposing his attempts at deception. Did he project heroism or criminality? Was the television channel simply giving a stage for Yuvaraj to spread his poison, or where they showing him in a critical light? These were questions that could surely not be easily resolved on a televised debate show. A great deal would have depended on the kind of viewership the program had, not only while on the air via satellite television but also as a video clip that could be circulated through WhatsApp and other media of the digital networks that had already worked to spread Yuvaraj's celebrity. It was shortly after the debate show aired that Yuvaraj made his announcement that he would yield to the CB-CID, who had taken up his case.

Yuvaraj eventually turned himself in at the Namakkal police station in Tamil Nadu accompanied and celebrated by hundreds of his supporters after three months of media stardom spent evading a police force that appeared unable to bring him to justice. Because his appearance had been announced on WhatsApp and then on television ahead of time, the large crowd that had accompanied him as a caste leader could be seen in all news media. A local police officer was quoted in the *Indian Express* as saying, "He surrendered in style. Our officers had to receive him like a hero. We would forget this shame only if we can get him convicted."[44] Like the "internet Hindus" who have become so important to local right-wing nationalism in North India, Yuvaraj's capacity to wield mobile phone–enabled networks to penetrate a mainstream media that is always hungry for audiences was unprecedented.[45] And like his counterparts elsewhere, he could manifest once-virtual crowds in the actual world at crucial moments.[46] But his celebrity did not end there. Yuvaraj managed to send a WhatsApp audio message, while in the Vellore Central Prison where phones are banned, in which he accused the superintendent of police of trying to kill him. After allegedly admitting to the murder while in the custody of CB-CID, he was released on bail in June of 2016, again received by five hundred of his ardent supporters. He told reporters that he had evidence to prove that Gokulraj had committed suicide and deputy superintendent of police Vishnupriya who was investigating the case was in fact murdered. After three months of registering every day while on conditional bail, Yuvaraj was remanded to jail in August of that year because he was threatening witnesses in the Gokulraj murder case. The case was shifted out of Namakkal sessions court, and Yuvaraj was eventually convicted and sentenced to life imprisonment by a special court in Madurai for scheduled caste and scheduled tribe cases in 2022. Eleven of his associates were also found guilty of aiding and abetting the murder of Gokulraj.

When I finally had the opportunity to meet with Gunasekaran, which was after Yuvaraj was remanded to jail without bail, he had recently moved from Puthiya Thalaimurai to run the news department of Tamil News 18. This was another new nonparty channel, owned by one of India's largest corporations, Reliance Industries Limited. The celebrity anchor brought up the Yuvaraj interview while rattling off a list of his achievements before I could even ask the question. He defended his decision to run the initial interview, arguing that "such an important debate on caste violence, the police, and new media never would have occurred on prime-time television otherwise. And then we did the show where we debated the interview. Did you see it?" Echoing G. C. Shekhar's argument from the debate he said, "It was our job to show the world, we didn't make a hero out of him!" Shortly after my meeting with Gunasekaran, when I had coffee with Shekhar himself to ask him more about his thoughts on the Yuvaraj interview, he also sensed my ambivalence, responding, "Anyone would have interviewed Osama bin Ladin, but he never gave interviews. The question is, are you being used?" Television, he argued, tended to bend toward the spectacle of covering the suspected criminal as a celebrity, but it was still the journalist's job to let the public decide for themselves. "News is not like a court of law, there are different rules," he said.

Not everyone is convinced. One senior television journalist I asked about the decision to air the show with Yuvaraj on broadcast news called it "obnoxious," and another "bullshit." For many Dalit activists and other avid followers of the news I have interviewed beyond the community of journalists, to allow the person who was suspected of such heinous violence to speak freely on camera was to take part in that very violence.

Conclusion: Ethics of Representation and Communicability

The events surrounding the respective careers of Veerappan and Yuvaraj bring into focus the moral dangers of proximity between journalists and outlaws. They also illustrate the attractions suspects have for the journalist and vice versa. If spectacular lawbreakers provide invaluable narrative material for the news, the desire for celebrity that appears to accompany their wanton violence is sated most effectively through the organs of mass media. To be a legend in the realm of rumor, whether circulated orally or through digital transmission, is not quite the same thing as being a sensation on evening news broadcasts or inhabiting the front pages of the most widely read publications. Veerappan and Yuvaraj nevertheless penetrated the mainstream in different technological and political milieus. This difference in ecologies, in turn, raises questions about how proximity between criminals and those who would report on them is, in fact, established as well as what kind of proximity it is.

When Veerappan ruled the borderland forests, access to the channels of mass publicity was a relatively scarce resource. The heinous extravagance of his crimes would have assured the outlaw news coverage, but it was his connection to Gopal that allowed him to play a role in shaping his own public image, thereby "coproducing" the news. Journalists from *Nakkeeran* like Sivasubramanian and Gopal, for their part, undertook long, arduous journeys into the outlaw's forest lair. Physical and social distance thus played its role in creating an effect of separation between hubs of news broadcasting and the underworld of the jungle on which they were reporting. And even when capturing "live" footage of their subject, video tapes would have to be taken by foot and then by road or railway back to the center of production for reformatting as "broadcast news." When Veerappan wanted to communicate with the world outside, he did so with prerecorded audio cassettes, like the one he used to list his demands for the release of Rajkumar. Or he would schedule a meeting with his coproducers at *Nakkeeran* who would lend to these missives the legitimating function of mass publicity by refracting Veerappan's deeds through the language of journalism. The fact that Veerappan was an avid consumer of his own public image in mass-mediated form was then folded back into that image itself by the journalists at *Nakkeeran*. The outlaw was thus frequently depicted as listening to the radio and reading the pages of the journal that had made him the celebrity he was. Gopal's role in coproducing this metapublicity machine was morally dubious because he so clearly benefited from prolonging the drama while trading on the Robin Hood reputation of the outlaw that he himself had played a major role in defining.

Yuvaraj, on the other hand, had no news-media sponsor like Nakkeeran Gopal to usher an appropriate entry into the world of mass publicity. He had already become well known both through his violence and through his own reporting on it in the widely circulated "audios" he used both to bypass and to attract professional mediation. Yuvaraj also claimed a smaller scale of celebrity than Veerappan in an environment where he could speak live on television without the police knowing his location through the affordances of Skype and WhatsApp but where his story would eventually fade into a broader tale of caste violence. Contemporary television journalists like Gunasekaran, Karthigaichelvan, and Rangaraj Pandey, for their part, were potentially tainted by their "direct" contact with Yuvaraj by virtue of sharing a plane of mediation that simply did not exist in the time of Veerappan's collaborations with Gopal. The concerns over representation in the case of Yuvaraj on the news were not about the moral stance the respective news anchors had taken toward their interlocutor. No one would have thought that these journalists were sympathetic with the suspected murderer, nor would they have been accused of colluding with him, as some suspected Gopal of doing with Veerappan. Disapproval was clear and conducted in the idiom of rational debate. But this moral and epistemic stance was quite beside the point for some critics. The potential for incitement to future violence appeared to be built into the simple fact of Yuvaraj appearing as a participant on broadcast news. Harm was done simply though the fact of giving a "stage" for the suspect and allowing his image and words to circulate further, allowing him to address a general public beyond those who consumed his audio texts. Because he had established a network of counterpublicity that had become the subject of news to the degree that his "audios" threatened to overtake the vicious murder he was accused of committing as the central features of the story, putting him on the air could be construed as extending his celebrity status. The very fact that he was aired on the news had furthermore become news itself.

Contemporary media networks allow for technologically afforded "absolute transitivity" in Guha's sense of a collapse of the roles of an encoding sender and a decoding receiver animated through logics of selection and spreadability, as the same audio file moved seamlessly from Yuvaraj's phone to other phones, news websites, YouTube, and other broadcasts that then reenter WhatsApp through sharing. Renouncing authorship of any particular deed or narrative himself, through this regime of circulation Yuvaraj's message (*ceyti* or *takaval*) extended well beyond the Gounder community or western Tamil Nadu. As a result—not only of Yuvaraj but of a whole series of panics and violent attacks that were circulated through networked media, some explicit mimicries of Gokulraj's murder—the contours of the public secrecy that had long defined speech about caste shifted dramatically across the state. That this was a form of speech motivated by casteist hatred is central to understanding its potential to incite violence. And in this respect, Yuvaraj's speech was also transitive in the sense Judith Butler attributes to the performative utterance in that it publicly enacts injury by discussing the events of Gokulraj's death in the field of mass mediation.[47] This shared ground of performativity through circulation also enlisted the addressee or "audience" as another active node in a network that was incredibly abstract and seemingly limitless in its feedback effects.

The digital media ecology in which Yuvaraj and his journalist interlocutors were maneuvering affords a proliferation of this shared domain of communicability: the capacity for texts and images to be reproduced, repeated, and forwarded at speeds and scales previously unimaginable. If the rhetorical split between the subjects and events of the narrative (viz. Yuvaraj's violence and his audio missives) and the narrating subject of formal news reportage (the news anchor) is required to maintain the epistemic stance that also separates news from rumor, the domain of communicability as the space of circulation *shared* between these subjects threatens to overwhelm the distinction, haunting it at every moment. When initially interviewed on television, remember, a time delay was imposed artificially to mark the distinction between the event of interviewing and its broadcast circulation as news. But has the "Yuvaraj effect" not been produced in its very telling and sharing, not unlike rumor? Broadcast journalists must be well aware of this danger. And yet the compulsion to circulate was too great and also laden with the ethical charge to share and make known the truth of the outlaw's bigoted violence. Further deliberation on the ethics of representing the suspect then acted as yet another vector of communicability. Yuvaraj's story is thus symptomatic of a media sphere enabling the extreme communicability of semiotic form, linguistic or otherwise, to undermine claims to communication while deriving energy from those very claims. This is not to espouse the unquestioned virtue of communication, a process and ideal setting in which information is separable from the medium that sits at the core of modern modes of domination, as many theorists of the public sphere have argued. But it is to note its inseparability from communicability as a distinct modality of power in the contemporary age.

CHAPTER FIVE
Short Circuits

The image of a man in a yellow sports shirt standing on a police truck aiming his rifle has claimed its place in the annals of state violence. I first saw it as a still photograph that a friend had forwarded to my cell phone on WhatsApp, later realizing that it had been excerpted from a longer video featured as "breaking news" on television. He is a sniper firing into a crowd that had gathered to protest the extreme environmental degradation inflicted by the Sterlite copper-smelting plant on the town of Thoothukudi. Captured on a cell phone by an unknown person behind police lines, these images stand as evidence of a crime. Low resolution but high impact.

Tens of thousands had started out in procession from the Basilica of Our Lady of Snows, marking the hundredth day of protest on that searing hot day, May 22, 2018. Making their way to the district magistrate's office to demand closing of the plant, the protesters had no knowledge of the last-minute imposition of section 144 of the Code of Criminal Procedure restricting public assembly. Most were also unaware that the district collector, the Indian administrative officer whom they had come to address, had left town. When police charged into the crowd, beating them with lathi sticks (batons), a few responded by throwing stones. Then the shots went off. Thirteen people died of bullet wounds in total in the Thoothukudi uprising, killed by law enforcement on behalf of private interests. In an attempt to silence dissent, hundreds of first information reports filed by police in the name of "unidentified suspects" were then used in the months after the firings to harass anyone who raised their voice against Sterlite or the government violence. While the evidence of police malfeasance would appear incontrovertible, the families

FIGURE 5.1. Police sniper in Thoothukudi. Sent to author via WhatsApp.

and communities of the dead continue to await justice. Local administrators, police, and the courts seemed more interested in suppressing opposition than in representing residents, leading to widespread anger across the state and in the Tamil diaspora. The Tamil Nadu Environment and Forests Department did, however, close the copper plant, which is owned by the multinational Vedanta Limited, as a result of the protests. That the uprising and the massacre took place in the very same town that gave rise to the first political labor insurrection against the British, violently suppressed over a hundred years before, resonated in ways that few other than history buffs could appreciate. But the fact that the people had been betrayed by the state yet again was clear to all who had seen the photograph or video.

The Thoothukudi mass protests and the shootings recorded on cell phone cameras marked the culmination of Tamil Nadu's season of discontent. Soon after the passing of J. Jayalalithaa—"Amma" (mother) to many, a dictator to others, and a powerful force to all—a series of spectacular protests erupted across the state from the beginning of 2017. The compact between state and society forged through democratic politics had been growing increasingly fragile for some time in Tamil Nadu, as it had elsewhere. Everyday politics of the great Dravidianist parties had become untethered from cults of adulation surrounding their cinematic leaders, leading to growing disenchantment among ordinary citizens. If the disappointment of unmet aspirations had been captured by the majoritarian right in other parts of India and other countries, in Tamil Nadu it was much less clear what kind of politics were possible after half a century of Dravidianist party hegemony. But it was obvious to all that something was exploding, a vital force that the state-level government, long sustained by a combination of charismatic populism and adroit repression, could not contain or divert. For over a year Tamil people in revolt dominated news cycles across India and beyond. Bypassing established circuits of representation, energy was spilling out into the streets, onto the beaches, and across the television screens, newspapers, and social media–fueled smartphones that make up the infrastructure of mass publicity. Large, digitally enabled crowds came to embody both the potential for as well as the limits of mass democracy. The blunt police violence that ensued appeared to some as an almost inevitable, if lamentable, response to this loss of control. State criminality in quelling unrest had been recorded, in turn, and circulated for all to see in numerous instances, tightening a feedback loop that would spur new waves of discontent. The political public sphere was undergoing a profound metamorphosis, raising difficult questions about how popular sovereignty might be enacted in the digital age.

One of the less remarked on features of Michael Warner's classic essay on "Publics and Counterpublics" is the argument he makes about the relationship between temporality and the political force of publicity:

> A public can only act within the temporality of the circulation that gives it existence. The more punctual and abbreviated the circulation, and the more discourse indexes the punctuality of its own circulation, the closer a public stands to politics. At longer rhythms or more continuous flows, action becomes harder to imagine. . . . In modernity, politics takes much of its character from the temporality of the headline, not the archive.[1]

Warner was writing before the fuller implications of digitalization had become knowable, and he was making a specific argument about why the genre of scholarly writing carries little political weight compared to journalism or activism. But his broader point about publics acting according to the temporality of the circulation that animates them remains an important one. We might add to this line of reasoning that politics in postmodernity has taken much of its character from the continuous flow of 24-7 television. And we are now living in a world characterized by the volatile temporalizations and scalability of publicity afforded by the networked circulation of images and discourses across media platforms.

For thinkers engaged in the debate about mass publics and politics under conditions of digitalization, these new temporalities and scalability through which publics act have resulted in what is often thought of as the "short-circuiting" of established forms of mobilization and representation. The varieties of networked digital circulation analyzed in the previous chapter as means to claim celebrity have also enabled novel forms of collective action, bypassing some of the mediating power of political parties or traditional sources of news. Crowds articulating public grievances often appear to be self-organizing because of their decentralized or distributed media of assembly in contrast to older movements led by a political vanguard. If the temporality of the headline was an enabling condition for the mass politics of the twentieth century, new logics of circulation therefore demand new ways of conceiving the political and its relationship to the formal institutions of politics in the twenty-first century.

Some see liberating potential in the turn away from older structures mediating the representations and actions of a collective agency represented by "the people." In their book *Assembly* Michael Hardt and Antonio Negri envisage a democratic space opened by technologically enabled "multitudes" for the "production of subjectivity necessary to create lasting social relations" no longer dependent on institutions and representative leaders.[2] Writing about anticorporate globalization protests, Jeffery Juris notes, "the horizontal networking logic facilitated by new digital technologies not only provides an effective method of social movement organizing, it also represents a broader model for creating alternative forms of social, political, and economic organization."[3] What participants experience as the "live," emergent character of networked circulation gives publics a means to become even closer to a democratic politics beyond traditional conceptions of sovereignty in these analyses. But for many others, this desire to escape the traditional demands of representation so celebrated by techno-anarchists and autonomists is profoundly ideological and ultimately debilitating.

It is precisely the "more continuous flows" of publicly circulating texts and images that appear to inhibit action for some contemporary critics or, when leading to political mobilization, not the kind that leads to substantive change. According to Stiegler in his book *Telecracy against Democracy*, for example, "debating . . . in the time-delayed mode of political and social organizations . . . is what has been destroyed by the 'real time' of live

communications," leaving in its wake "herd-like collectivities" that are profoundly desocialized and as a result politically moribund.[4] In a parallel set
of articles focused more on populist politics in Asia and the occupations of
2011, Rosalind Morris interrogates "publicness beyond the public sphere, in
the nonspaces of a networked world."[5] In the "ephemeral coalescence" of
crowds to make claims on the political under such media conditions, Morris
finds "violent short-circuitings of a process that would have been necessary
for the development of a fuller political subjectivity."[6] In Morris's account,
this new publicness is furthermore defined by a distinctive mode of address
in which "being seen to speak" overtakes "being heard," and image replaces
voice as the dominant trope of popular representation.[7] These critical formulations of what is sometimes also referred to as the "postpublic sphere" have
moved rapidly from the problem of the "prepolitical peasant" that the left
tradition had inherited from Marx to that of the *post*political "digital native."
Neither figure appears to inhabit the punctuated temporality of modernity
required for the development of an adequate political subjectivity. The media
chronotope of real-time/nonspace is debilitating because of its thin social
underpinnings from the perspective of these theorists, whereas for Hardt and
Negri this sense of immediacy forms conditions for the assembly of heterogeneous social labor against the capitalist logic enabling the chronotope in
the first instance.

This chapter works to examine these concerns about the work of representation in the space-time of deep digitalization from a different perspective, to think specifically about the explosive energies and forms of public
contestation enabled through "short-circuiting." It does so without deciding
on what counts as sufficiently developed political subjectivity, which appears
to be the question at stake in this debate. It also takes a perspective on media
that seeks to understand the "newness" of new media through the questions
digital affordances raise for how people conceive of their capacity to act in the
political field.[8] Drawing on the ethnographic archive of protests that erupted
over the course of Tamil Nadu's season of discontent, we will interrogate how
short-circuiting occurs through the introduction of techno-political "switchpoints" with the potential to divert the flow of social energies, reconfiguring
the possibilities of how popular sovereignty is imagined in the process. This
is a politics firmly ensconced *within* the logics of communicative capitalism,
however, and for that reason there are serious limits to its transformative
power. Silicon Valley giants, WhatsApp, and its parent company Facebook
have acted as media necessary for these new forms of political assembly, most
often distributed by India's largest cellular telecom service, Reliance Indus-

try's Jio. The corporate role in facilitating communication was never problematized. Protests have thus been enabled by a highly centralized political economy that extracts value through the profoundly *de*centralized movement of discourses and images.

What the protests analyzed in this chapter have in common is an emergent logic of event making in which the professional news media's role in recording and thereby making historical events public had been short-circuited alongside more traditional forms of political representation. Evidence of the police shooting in Thoothukudi, for example, had become "news" not only because video images caught on a cell phone were broadcast on television but just as importantly because of the speed and scale at which they circulated through other cell phones, with or without the mediation of professional journalism. The news story shown on television channels Puthiya Thalaimurai and News 18 Tamil—the first stations to broadcast the video footage of police snipers—was a classic "news event" in which news media were reporting as much about the fact that the images were already "viral" on social media as they were about the fact of police shooting into a crowd of protesters. These two facts, separable at the level of abstract logic, slip easily into one another in the phenomenology of digital network politics. But this collapsing of the event of widespread circulation and the event being represented as news at the level of experience is only one aspect of the story. Equally important are the claims to documentation and evidentiary status made by image-texts that are produced and disseminated outside of the field of professional expertise.

A new age of mass forensics has come into its own. The very same cell phone–enabled media of assembly also act as media of surveillance, or what some scholars term *sousveillance*: the observation and recording of state power from below its sway.[9] Inexpensive digital capture and circulation of image-texts have enabled a massification of "reversing the forensic gaze," to borrow from Eyal Weisman in a different context.[10] As a result of this popularization of forensics, however, disclosure and communicability can become difficult to disentangle from one another in the experience of the event of documentation, challenging epistemological regimes for establishing the truth of the event documented. The facticity and importance of an event are increasingly measured by its circulation as an image-text—its *communicability*—and the primary "forums" before which evidence from the field is presented are none other than those of popular justice and mass affect. As popular documentation of acts of violence against the citizenry accumulates, whether or not people can hold the state legally accountable remains to be seen, in southern India as elsewhere. The juridical standards for introducing such images as evidence are certainly different from those pertaining to the court of public opinion, and the law has been notoriously slow to act in cases where reason of state is pitted against the claims of protesting crowds. But an obsessive public scrutiny of digital evidentiary traces of state negligence or criminality that travel with great velocity—sometimes without identifiable authorship—has almost certainly led to greater disaffection with established structures of representation and an intensification of techno-political processes of short-circuiting.

Seasons of Discontent and the Network Imaginary

The tense collisions between networked crowd protest and state repression that characterized the year and a half following Jayalalithaa's death were not wholly new. The crowd had long stood as an exemplary sign of popular will in Tamil Nadu as it has elsewhere in South Asia and beyond.[11] Also like other regions, this one has a history of state-sanctioned violence against dissidents even if there was something different and shocking about the image of a police sniper firing into the protest in Thoothukudi. Mythili Sivaraman had documented how the rise of the Dravidianist politics of the Dravida Munnetra Kazhagam (DMK) in the 1970s, for example, was coupled with the subjugation of labor actions and public claims to equality made by marginalized castes.[12] M. G. Ramachandran (MGR), known as a champion of the poor, was equally ruthless in quelling dissent. And Jayalalithaa herself was quick to deploy the punitive wing of the state to suppress any criticism of her policies in her first term as chief minister in the early 1990s, as we have seen in earlier chapters.

A series of protests against the construction of a nuclear power plant in the southern Tamil town of Kudankulam, however, marked a turning point by linking small fishing communities to a wide set of activists who were able to command larger scales of attention through alternative media networks. Local opposition had already taken root shortly after an agreement to build the plant with Soviet support was announced by the Government of India in the late eighties. When the Fukushima Daiichi disaster in 2011 raised wider public awareness of the dangers posed by nuclear energy, an uprising began in which the Catholic Church had also become involved. But it was a series of high-profile protests led by S. P. Udayakumar and the People's Movement against Nuclear Energy shortly thereafter that attracted India-wide and international attention in ways earlier expressions of discontent had not, making visible a new network imaginary while attracting more extreme forms of state repression.[13] The whole fishing village of Idinthakarai, over eight thousand people, were eventually charged with sedition because of their resistance to the plant, while many state officials accused foreign NGOs of fomenting unrest. The mass arrests, in turn, led to protests outside the Indian high commission in London and a public letter addressed to the governments of India and Tamil Nadu signed by prominent British MPs demanding that charges be dropped, adding another dimension to the dynamics of globalized networking at play in the Kudankulam protests.[14] Such extreme police measures could be read as a sign of fragility before a people whose recognition of the government as the legitimate representative of popular sovereignty was waning.

So, when hundreds of thousands took to the streets and the beach in Chennai to claim their cultural rights to a Tamil cattle-wrestling sport called "jallikattu" in early 2017, followed immediately by the tens of thousands who descended on the villages of rural Pudukkottai and Thanjavur to protest hydrocarbon extraction, many were surprised at the scale of these gatherings but not at the fact of mass unhappiness with the political status quo. The energies first witnessed in Kudankulam had reached a tipping point and were now allowed to spread in a political environment in which the major parties' capacities to channel discontent had weakened significantly. "Under *Amma* (mother) this never would have happened" was a refrain I heard from nearly everyone I talked to who took part in the protests in Chennai and Pudukkottai, referring to the chief minister who had passed away three months earlier. For her supporters, this was a claim about Jayalalithaa's superhuman strength and will to defend the Tamil people from the Government of India. For her detractors, the very same statement invoked her ironclad grip on politics and her broader control of what could be said and done in public. The implication of the latter position was that her disciplined party machinery would have quelled protests through negotiation or force before they gained public traction. Both positions were in agreement that a powerful political regime had collapsed. And the fact that Jayalalithaa's nemesis, Karunanidhi, had retreated from political life because of illness and old age right around the time of her passing appeared to augur the end of an era.

Participants also attributed the scale of protests and the speed with which they assembled to the new technologies enabling multilateral communication, thereby bypassing potential chokepoints in the distribution of information. The distributed logics of circulation that had always fueled crowded gatherings and insurrections, as Ranajit Guha noted long ago, appeared to have found a technological counterpart in cell phone communication.[15] WhatsApp, in particular, had brought to life a new world of peer-to-peer circulation, electrifying and thereby greatly expanding networked social imaginaries that had joined the ranks of print and broadcast news imaginaries in political importance. The techno-political challenge to state power was so great in the case of the Thoothukudi protests that the government shut down internet and phone data services altogether in the whole of southern Tamil Nadu for days on end. In fact the media of assembly appeared more threatening to authorities than the discursive content of protesters' demands, which were hardly revolutionary. What was equally striking to many observers, and was connected to fears of losing control, was the fact that the new protests were not being led by the kind of leaders or political parties long associated with mass politics in Tamil Nadu. Charismatic individuals did emerge as public faces and voices of discontent, but the protests were conspicuous in their explicit rejection of both leaders and political parties as media of organization and representation. The idea of direct connection among people facing a hostile state and an outdated media system long connected to party politics was charged with an affective energy that could not be contained by existing forms of representation. Over the course of the year, short-circuiting had become a problem for media houses, major political parties, and the government of Tamil Nadu, too, not just a conundrum for left-leaning political thinkers.

By the time the protests against the Sterlite Copper Plant in Toothukudi had gained wider attention, the Indian press was beginning to ask questions about the new politics of civil unrest emerging in the southern state. The Delhi-based *Hindustan Times*, for example, ran an article investigating "A State of Protest: Why Tamil Nadu Tops List of Most Protests in India since 2009." An article published in the *Hindu* around the same time cited official government data reporting 20,450 different agitations in the state in the year 2015.[16] As astute observers, like the journalist Kavitha Muralidharan, noted, the culture of protest flourishing in the state had its roots in Dravidian-nationalist mobilization of earlier generations even when directed against the very parties that had institutionalized these politics. Protesters all claimed to be representing the Tamil nation while distinguishing their visions of nationhood from those offered by the DMK, the AIADMK (All India Anna Dravida Munnetra Kazhagam), or any other major political party. What also became clearer to commentators as protests spread like wildfire from one arena of confrontation to another was the fact that nearly every one of these major agitations was focused on some sort of issue having to do with ecological breakdown. If the sinews securing state-society relations had snapped, something else was being forged: a renewed claim to connection with the nonhuman world that was, perhaps paradoxically, given life by digital technologies of circulation and the rise of a corresponding globalized network social imaginary. No longer investing fantasies of shadow sovereignty in the figure of the cine-political leader, the people could now create a representational and affective commons in the idioms of clean air, fertile land, and native animal life. The Tamil nation had come to imagine itself increasingly in terms of indigenous natural wonder.

Shadow Sovereignty as Bovine Virility

Tamil Nadu's political power surge began in the weeks following Jayalalithaa's passing, however improbably, with human relationships to a usually placid creature: *Bos indicus*, the Indian bull with a distinctive hump on its shoulders known elsewhere in the tropics as "zebu." It was a calm early morning in January of 2017 when ten people assembled in front of the iconic colonial "Ice House," now the peachy-pink colored Vivekananda Memorial at the beach front in Chennai, singing, "We want *jallikattu!*" That is, they were demanding the right to practice an ancient bull-wrestling sport, commonly held in rural areas of southern Tamil Nadu around the harvest festival of Pongal. In this contest, groups of young men attempt to subdue bulls that have been purposefully enraged for the occasion by grabbing their hump and holding on while the animal bucks up and down, thus gaining the admiration of their peers and the crowd assembled to watch. In jallikattu lore, the sport is imagined in quasi-Darwinian terms as a stage for the selection of the bravest among village bachelors and the most virile studs among the bulls. The Supreme Court of India, however, had banned the sport in response to animal rights activists' litigation alleging cruelty to the bulls. The ban had been in effect for some time, and a number of similar protests had occurred the year before, abating when a state-level ordinance allowed the sport to take place. This year would be very different. By midnight of the same day, about six thousand people had gathered on Marina Beach demanding their rights. By the following day about fifteen thousand had assembled. And by the end of the week the number of people participating reached the hundreds of thousands, amounting to the largest protests the city has seen since the anti-Hindi agitations that helped the Tamil-nationalist DMK party ride to power in the mid-1960s.[17]

FROM VICARIOUS ATTACHMENT TO SYNECDOCHE

This heaving mass had gathered to protest the ban on a sport almost no one, in fact, practices in the city of Chennai. Most would have seen the famous competition in Madurai's Alanganallur on television during Pongal celebrations, or at least watched movies where the sport is depicted as a backdrop against which the hero gains the affections of a village belle. Many among the protesters had probably never paid much attention to jallikattu, but lack of direct experience with the sport was beside the point. The Tamil people were under attack. In the jallikattu narrative emerging from the protests, deep interdependence and love between humans and bulls was being misrecognized as animal cruelty by the likes of People for the Ethical Treatment of Animals (PETA) and North Indians who cared nothing about the cultures of the South. The Government of India and the Supreme Court representing these forces had once again overstepped in their claims to dominate this region that had once threatened to secede from the union, and the image of the bull had captured the public imagination as a sign of Tamil sovereignty, pride, and virility.

Soaked in deeply gendered imaginaries of the nation, the jallikattu protest on Marina Beach had a distinctively urban middle-class feel to it while claiming cultural heritage in the rustic idiom of bull wrestling. Whereas young men typically lead political action on the street in Chennai and elsewhere, women and children of all ages participated equally in this celebration of an ethnicized and animalized masculinity. This is a vision of virility that the writer and scholar Stalin Rajangam notes is based also on caste-based domination over Dalits who have been excluded from the sport in rural Tamil Nadu, a prohibition that sits at odds with the inclusive image of nationality the crowd sought to project.[18] The same type of *communitas* that is reported to have characterized a number of recent political movements enabled by distributed forms of communication was a powerful force here as well.[19] For example, young women who participated reported amazement that they were never treated poorly or aggressively, as they normally would be in large public gatherings. Local restaurateurs and shop owners spontaneously organized food and water delivery to the massive crowds that had gathered.[20] In a rousing speech that the usually comical radio personality R. J. Balaji gave on the beach, he proclaimed, "Look here, we're cleaning the road, giving food . . . I've brought my little sister here . . . we're not just showing South India or Bombay, we're showing all of India!" This was a collectivized patriarchy that distinguished itself from others through imagery depicting Tamil women as both strong and protected by their brothers in ways unimaginable elsewhere. The crowd had surprised itself as well as onlookers in its capacity for civility and spontaneous restraint that seemed to correspond with its high-tech modalities of assembly. This was a responsible mass gathering inhabiting a virtuous virality, not a mob.[21]

Unlike the anti-Hindi agitations of earlier generations that were organized by student groups and commandeered by political parties, this one rejected leaders, and an organizational structure emerged only after the fact of mass mobilization. Despite efforts of the ruling AIADMK to absorb their energy and the opposition DMK to latch onto it, protesters repeatedly and self-consciously fended off attempts by political parties to lend official support and co-opt the movement. The jallikattu agitation was more of an occupation-style movement that echoed the events in Tahrir Square, Zuccotti Park, and elsewhere from five years earlier.[22] The famous film star Vijay attended the Marina Beach gathering incognito with a bandanna over his face to the wide approval of those experiencing the events online who had spotted him in photos protesters on the beach were posting. Crowds on the beach held signs circulated across media emphasizing their ecumenical break from established and divisive regimes of representation, exclaiming "no colour, no caste, no religion, no politics: only jallikattu! Dear fellow Indians, this is how you protest. #jallikattu." A more important division was driving action, that between ethnically external enemies of the sport and its Tamil protectors, which did not include the state government. As Balaji proclaimed at the top of his lungs in his speech, "They are going to pass an ordinance in the coming days and when they do it, it will not be because of the MPs we elected, it is because of only YOU!" Balaji was not claiming the role of a leader addressing the crowd; he was serving instead as a conduit for the crowd to address and enthuse itself as it rejected any other forms of representation. He was not sitting above the mass on a stage or on screen. Balaji was figuring himself as one of them, drawing from the relatively nonhierarchical intimacies of the radio jockey–listening public relationship. His broadcast persona had become networked, as Balaji's video circulated both on YouTube for the wider public to enjoy and within the crowd on the beach itself.

As in Vicente Rafael's account of cell phone–enabled crowds in Manila fifteen years earlier, the mass in Chennai "imagined themselves able to communicate beyond the crowd, but also with it, transcending the sheer physical density of the masses through technology, while at the same time ordering its movements and using its energy to transmit middle-class demands."[23] The very restraint and discipline that characterized the massive crowd action taking place on Marina Beach as "middle class" might almost be said to result from the fact that they wanted to be seen by the world at large in terms

FIGURE 5.2. Popular meme circulating during jallikattu agitations. Sent to author via WhatsApp.

different from those that normally attach themselves to crowds. Also comparable to the secular crowd in Turkey analyzed by Kabir Tambar, "The crowd, whose movements are not formally coordinated as they were in the older tradition of state ritual, appears spontaneous and enthusiastic. As a sign, the crowd can be deployed to achieve a political end: the crowd creates a tangible representation of 'the people.'"[24] In this case the obvious contrast was between the crowds of Marina Beach and those who regularly attend massive political rallies held by the Dravidian parties in the nearby Island Grounds. The former's digitally enabled savviness and self-discipline were frequently opposed by attendees and observers alike to the ritualized instrumentality, cynicism, and even "rowdyism" now commonly associated with the latter, who are usually thought to be enticed by party workers with liquor, biriyani, and cash.

It should not be a surprise that WhatsApp and Facebook were the main media though which people came to know of and be attracted to the protest. Similar to the time lag noted by Jonathan Rosa and Yarimar Bonilla regarding different social media platforms in the #Ferguson movement, however, WhatsApp significantly outpaced Facebook as the primary vector of circulation such that participation in WhatsApp felt closer to participating in the event itself rather than engaging with representations and updates removed from events on the beach.[25] Imaginative memes proliferated over the course of the week. Among the most popular images to emerge intertextually evoked the DMK's party insignia of a rising sun, only to wrest it from the political party and reclaim it for the Tamil people as a whole. These platforms also became important media for the dissemination of jallikattu culture among protesters and beyond. A seven-minute film about the grand funeral fans held for a famous bull called *Appu, King of Jallikattu* had been downloaded from YouTube to become one of the most widely circulated videos of the year among Tamil youngsters around the world, and it was watched on the beach itself among protesters. While acting as media of assembly, WhatsApp and Facebook also acted as media of information about the world outside of the protests. In fact many Tamils learned a great deal about native varieties of cattle, like the *kangayam* and *pulikulam* bulls used in jallikattu, that they had never considered before the uprising on Marina Beach. The sport was represented as an important link in the reproduction of autochthonous breeds, and public concern grew about Jersey and Holstein cows replacing *desi* (Indian) cows. As scientific expertise about the different milk produced by these European breeds mingled with more outlandish claims about corporate plots to sap the vitality of the Tamil people, alarm spread about the ravages of neoliberal capitalism on nature among more radicalized youth.

The image of a virile bull had become the "empty signifier" par excellence, one that had formed a chain of equivalence connecting a wide range of otherwise disjoined demands and grievances, as in Laclau's analysis of the general logic populism.[26] While national and global media focused on what they took to be the peculiar nature of the agitation and its bovine fixation, journalists from Chennai were more attentive to links being made to a broader regional dissatisfaction with the national government. In Balaji's words, "we're not just talking about jallikattu, we're talking about Pepsi, Coke, Sri Lanka! . . . we're talking about the farmers' problems! Have you seen any politicians confront this? We have the courage!" It was Thirumurugan Gandhi, leader of the May 17 Movement, named after the final day of massacres in Sri Lanka's civil war, who made efforts at the protests to connect this perceived assault on Tamil identity to the plight of Sri Lankan Tamil refugees. The South Chennai district secretary of the Communist Party of India (Marxist), on the other hand, told a local journalist that he "saw at least 15 of [Prime Minister] Modi's effigies being carried out on top of a bamboo made item (called *paadai* in Tamil in which a dead body is carried to the burial ground) and later they were smashed in the sands as the police did not allow them to burn the same."[27] No single person or party was in control of narratives that were seen to emanate from the crowd itself.

REACHING, RECORDING, AND CIRCULATING FLASHPOINT

Granting permission to conduct jallikattu in the state of Tamil Nadu was not, and could not be, enough to satisfy the crowds gathered at Marina Beach. The rather meek chief minister who replaced Jayalalithaa, O. Paneerselvam, had gone to New Delhi to ask for permission to hold these sporting events only to be rebuffed by protesters. When an ordinance was eventually given amending the Prevention of Cruelty to Animals Act to allow for jallikattu to take place under new regulations to protect the bulls, some went home, but masses of protesters continued their occupation. Their dissatisfaction with the current state of government was too widespread and dispersed to be calmed by such assurances while antipathy for the BJP's national government had grown considerably. Protests in support of those on Marina Beach had sprouted among the Tamil diaspora in cities like New York, Toronto, and London, from where videos were also sent to those on the frontlines in Chennai and other locations of protest in Tamil Nadu. The state was running out of options while the world was watching.

There were still thousands of protesters who were waking up after having spent the night on the beach when police arrived at five in the morning to evict them, one week into the occupation. Many fled once the police threatened to charge the camp later that morning, claiming that the protest had been infiltrated by "antisocial elements," while a number of youth stood fast on the beach. Those who remained were eventually attacked by the police with batons and tear gas. Some were chased into the ocean while others found refuge in the Nadukkuppam fishing community housing project nearby, where police went on a rampage in their attempts to arrest protesters. Several police cars parked in front of the Ice House, where the protests began, were lit on fire, and the protests on Marina finally ended in this violent dispersal. Protesters organized themselves through WhatsApp to escape the police and regroup in different parts of the city, and demonstrations continued for days among radicalized young men. But the heterogeneous crowds of ordinary people who had suddenly been energized to make their presence felt in the public sphere had gone home.

On the following day, I was reading about the police assault on protesters in the newspapers when I received a one-minute video on my cell phone, forwarded to one of the many journalist WhatsApp groups I belonged to.

Shot at a forty-five-degree angle from an apartment building rooftop just in from the beach, the shaky cell phone footage begins by zooming in on a road running under the elevated commuter railway track. Small figures in khaki police uniforms can be seen running around when a spark flashes next to some three-wheeled auto-rickshaws, then bursts into flames. The man filming exclaims, in English, above the din of crowds, "Police is keeping [sic] fire to autos, FUCK! What is happening? See, see, see, that lady, she's firing a second one! See. This is the real face of the police. What the fuck?" Those in plain clothing approaching the scene below were being handcuffed by police while other police officers set fire to all the autos under the railway track. Another set of hands holding a cell phone filming the same event enters the frame before the video clip ends abruptly. A few hours later, another video surfaced of police walking through the alleys of the Nadukkuppam fishing settlement vandalizing parked motorcycles belonging to the fishermen because law enforcement officers had earlier claimed that protesters had been violent. This clear documentation of police burning and vandalizing vehicles and then blaming protesters for being "antisocial" was corroborated by yet another street-level video of burning auto-rickshaws, also circulated through social media later that day.

Popular recent entrant to the Tamil television scene News 18 Tamil was the first channel to broadcast these videos, which had already circulated widely online and through WhatsApp. The Chennai police commissioner responded in a press conference shortly following the news reports that "The videos of police surfacing on social media are morphed. It is a matter of investigation." But public anger had already boiled over as the image first circulated through WhatsApp, and then broadcast on the news, immediately reentered circulation on social media. The senior film star Kamal Haasan, for example, had recorded the cell phone videos of police setting fire to autos as they were playing on his television set on News 18 Tamil with his own cell phone, and he posted the footage on his Twitter feed, which boasts over six million followers, demanding an explanation.

In a moment of what Bolter and Grusin might call "hypermediation," Haasan's tweet was then rebroadcast on News 18 Tamil as further evidence of public outrage over police malfeasance while garnishing positive publicity for the channel's "exclusive" reporting on the original videos taken from the streets and the rooftops by unknown youngsters.[28] Other prominent personalities followed suit in expressing their dismay online and in the press, including opposition party leaders from the DMK, illustrating attempts on the part of more traditional figures and institutions to reabsorb the explosive energies unleashed through the techno-political short circuit within these older circuits of representation. Over the longer term, two independent investigations led by prominent intellectuals and researchers pointed to the videos captured by cell phone and oral reports of state violence on the last day of protest, confirming widespread public belief that the police used violence as a pretext to forcibly shut the occupation of Marina Beach down. The police department, for their part, continued to question the veracity of these images.

The damage to state legitimacy had already been done, although not through systematic investigations by journalists or civil society activists. The exposure of duplicitous violence had been circulated by some youngsters who happened to be sitting on their rooftop examining the chaos below while armed with cell phones. Claims to primary indexicality, that existential connection in time and space to the event being recorded, were built into the formal qualities of the initial pixilated cell phone video. The voice of a young man cursing in disbelief is loaded with affective qualities transmitting shock as if directly to those who experience the video. The poor image quality speaks of its authenticity in the world of popular forensics, while the instantaneous and infinite reproducibility of the digital moving image subjects it to dynamics of circulation that elude filtering, censorship, or any sustained argument. Arguments were for television debate shows, and investigations for print media. Both proliferated during the protests and in the days following their violent end, as news organizations attempted to gain some mastery over the situation. But the gaze from the handheld cell phone point of view is what would increasingly set the sensorial and experiential foundation for these other types of knowledge practices to work with and through. If cell phone–enabled crowds like those analyzed by Rafael had long fetishized this technology's capacity to transcend societal divisions through communication, the new forensics from below have energized a popular fixation on transparency that the professional news organs meant to supervise the state could not deliver without amateur help.

ENTANGLEMENTS AND NETWORKED ADDRESS

The forms of short-circuiting energizing the events on Marina Beach are instructive in regard to recent changes in the entanglements between the journalistic text and the world it represents in the age of digitalization. At one level, the genre distinction between professional journalism and information traveling through other media, or "citizen journalism," had become more difficult to sustain. Whether or not one watched Balaji speak to the crowd on the beach as a direct upload on YouTube or through the excerpts that were broadcast on the Puthiya Thalaimurai news channel was not so important. The effect was similar, and stations like Puthiya Thalaimurai are now watched on their YouTube channel on hand held devices just as they are through other satellite television distribution networks on television sets.[29] It did not matter much whether one received the video of police burning the autos from a friend on WhatsApp or whether one saw it on Tamil News 18, on Twitter, or whether one watched Tamil News 18's coverage of Kamal Haasan's tweet showing the earlier News 18 broadcast of the video. People's conclusions that the police had acted in bad faith in the final days of the protest were forged through the same footage no matter where they encountered it first. Each act of representation and remediation appeared to build momentum on the others. Most people I have talked to about the police video encountered it in all four forms in addition to others, giving the videos a strange ubiquity, a kind of public knowledge that no amount of denial through accusations of "morphing" on the part of the police force could unmake.

Turning to the crowds on Marina Beach and their many supporters in other locations, we must appreciate how they addressed themselves to journalism as an authoritative medium for speaking to the world at large and "being seen to speak," as Morris would put it. At the same time, the events of the jallikattu protest could claim a wider and more dispersed world of circulation than that provided by professional news production, much of which was preoccupied with that very world of circulation. The events represented in professional journalism were just as likely to have taken place in the realm of digital images as they were in the world of bodies assembled on the beach or police violence on the street. Strict ontological distinctions between these domains would be misleading. But we may note the explicitly framed meta-representational quality of news broadcasts that often focused on what they construed as the "virality" of other media genres like memes and videos captured on cell phone—moments of representation and circulation figured as "outside" the representational regimes of news production itself.

News organizations had become an important node, aiming to claim the status of a hub, in a network that expanded well beyond the capacity of any actor or agency to shape, to comprehend, or to effectively represent. In fact most journalists I have interviewed who covered the jallikattu protest on Marina Beach where quite perplexed as to how it escalated so rapidly, feeling that they had been unprepared to understand the logic and scale of what was unfolding before them. "People were just forwarding messages to their friends and family and showing up like it was some temple festival [*thiruvizhā*]," remarked a reporter for the *Hindu* I was talking to at the time who was explaining the challenges he was facing as a political reporter in covering an event that was organizing itself in such a distributed fashion. The fact that this form of assembly clearly mimicked earlier occupations elsewhere did not necessarily help in understanding this strange event that attracted people who would normally not participate in street politics. Enthusiastic messages urging people to show up to protests on the beach or elsewhere in Tamil Nadu were just as likely to be sent from extended kin from abroad as they were from people situated in the state itself or others parts of India. The jallikattu protests thus stand as the event that firmly established virtual and street-level crowds as coconstitutive in the public imagination, one vector of public action feeding off the other while decentering existing regimes of representation.

This was a crowd both for itself and for the larger non-Tamil Indian public from which it distinguished itself: "Dear fellow Indians, this is how you protest," says the meme. As such, we can detect a tension between the "immediacy of copresence[,] . . . the auratic power of 'being there,'" and a simultaneous craving for recognition from the world figured as outside.[30] Some of the "double consciousness" that Bishara has identified as characterizing mass-mediated gatherings that are being watched on the world stage through news coverage was certainly at play here, too, but now it was subject to very unpredictable trajectories of circulation.[31] Journalist reports from local news channels, national channels like NDTV, and international channels like the BBC folded back into social media and across the cell phone screens of the flesh and blood assembly on the beach as protesters shared digital news clippings and videos from mainstream coverage of the event. However, the narrative of collective agency emerging from the protests was not about a simple exchange of mutual recognition between actors "on the street" and institutions that could claim to represent them before a wider public. Nor was jallikattu as dependent on professional broadcast mediation as earlier protests would have been for its status as a historical event. We might, then, go one step further than the argument about "coconstitution" to say that the proverbial "street" had gone virtual in the experience of protest, actualizing itself in various nodes, and that Marina Beach became a critical anchor point that was energized by news media representation and its recirculation in situ. But it was not wholly dependent on such representation. News had, in some sense, been engulfed, serving as fuel for the self-propelling engines of circulation that had come to define the jallikattu protests, an event that would have lasting consequences for how people might concretize the emergent network imaginary of politics.

In Defense of Lush Life

The second phase of networked insurrection I would like to examine in this chapter appeared to flow directly from the first outburst in Chennai around jallikattu but in a different context. Just three weeks after the police crackdown on Marina Beach, a series of protests took place in the kind of rural community in southern Tamil Nadu where jallikattu is an important event in the festival calendar. Neduvasal, an otherwise unremarkable village of about five thousand residents, suddenly claimed its place as the new epicenter of discontent when farmers in the tens of thousands gathered to protest a move by the government to allow a private firm to extract natural gas from the land underneath its fertile fields. Representations of mass mobilization around the state in defense of jallikattu served to propel energies in this village that no one outside of Pudukkottai district would have heard of, giving credence to the notion that protest in the age of networked publicity can indeed proceed along trajectories of circulation that can only be mapped after the fact.

These protests also happened to erupt in a village located only seven kilometers from where I had been visiting friends and conducting fieldwork intermittently for the last two decades. The type of news story I had become accustomed to following through journalists in Chennai had come to be shaped by members of a rural community I knew quite well, allowing me to develop a more textured ethnographic perspective on event making in a world increasingly defined by digital media. In telling the story of the Neduvasal uprising below, I take advantage of my greater social proximity to some of the important actors involved to follow two interlocking tracks: one focused more on the virtual networks enabling mass mobilization in this remote village, and the other more attuned to deeply embodied forms of protest that were nevertheless radically mediated by digital and broadcast media, as jallikattu had been too. The following narrative examines how "the temporality of the headline" that Warner argued had set the character of politics in the twentieth century continues to play a role in the twenty-first century, but now in a new media ecology defined by strong "continuous flows" across digital space-time. It also allows for a more sustained analysis of the dynamics of deterritorialization and emplacement that can be said to characterize protest in the age of networked media. Following the emergence of rural unrest in the wake of jallikattu from the "global" to the "local," our story begins not in the lush Tamil countryside but in a desert far away.

"WE ARE THE MEDIA"

On February 15, 2017, a twenty-eight-year-old software developer employed by a multinational firm in Abu Dhabi was finishing up the day's work, absent-mindedly watching Puthiya Thalaimurai streaming live on his cell phone, when he saw it: a ticker flashed across the bottom of the screen reporting that national finance minister Arun Jaitley of the ruling BJP had announced the opening of thirty-one new hydrocarbon projects across India. These had been awarded in the latest round of bidding under the Small Discovered Fields policy, including one in the village of Neduvasal in Pudukkottai district of Tamil Nadu. As he turned on the television set to follow the news more closely, Nimal Raghavan was shocked and angered. The software developer hails from the smaller village of Nadiyam, about twenty kilometers away, but he knows Neduvasal as if it were his own. The two villages, along with another dozen or so in the same region, are bound tightly to each other through generations of marriage exchange, much of which is cross cousin. Like very many youngsters from this area, Raghavan had spent his early working life abroad after completing his electrical engineering degree at Anna University in Chennai. This region of southern Tamil Nadu boasts a large labor diaspora living not only in the Gulf states but also in other parts of India, Southeast Asia, Europe, and North America. Agriculture had become an increasingly precarious occupation in these southern reaches of the Thanjavur delta because of fluctuating prices and years of drought. But for this IT professional, the thought of a once green and fertile farmland turning into an oil-rich desert like the one he was now living in as a labor migrant was intolerable.

Raghavan was already taking screen shots of the news flashes on his phone and tweeting them when he received a message from a friend back in Chennai picturing a temple, a fertile irrigation tank, and rice fields and also announcing the news that hydrocarbon extraction was approved from Pudukkottai. He posted these on his personal Facebook page, framed by the following text, in an effort to incite circulation:

#PleaseShare #Breaking
[in Tamil] *O' people prepare yourselves for the next struggle!*
This time it is for our farmers and our soil!

*The central government has granted permission to a company called
GEM to extract natural gas from Neduvasal in Pudukkottai!
This struggle is to stop them from doing that!*

Lets [*sic*] trend this hashtag

#SaveNeduvasal

#StopExtractingHydrocarbon

#SaveFarmers

#SaveAgriculture

The earlier struggle invoked in the first line of his text is none other than the agitation against the Supreme Court ban on jallikattu, which had brought hundreds of thousands of youngers onto the Marina Beach in Chennai a few weeks earlier. Raghavan had honed his skills orchestrating the online conditions for mass action during those protests. "I handled jallikattu in UEA," as he put it to me, where street protests would never be allowed on any scale worth notice but where this kind of online activity could proliferate unimpeded. The engineer spent the rest of that night with phone in hand doing everything he could to get his message to fly. He proceeded next to WhatsApp, personally messaging groups of Tamil friends and fellow villagers in Abu Dhabi, Dubai, Qatar, Chennai, Bangalore, Neduvasal, Nadiyam, and elsewhere. His Facebook page racked up hundreds, then thousands, of "likes," comments, and shares from the thousands of followers he had already accrued as a sort of communicative capital through the jallikattu protests. Others who had seen the television report that evening where also lighting the fires of agitation, connecting to each other through Facebook and WhatsApp, as an increasingly widespread panic started swelling among those connected through these channels. "The only medium is social media," Raghavan likes to say.

People from the regional diaspora in the city of Chennai had seen his Facebook post or received a WhatsApp screenshot of it and heeded its call to share widely. About a dozen among this group of several hundred families contacted each other to organize a face-to-face meeting over coffee at a restaurant in the city early the following morning. Living in different working and lower-middle-class neighborhoods across the urban sprawl, some had kept loosely in touch over the years in large part through the pleasures and efforts of attending temple festivals or weddings and other life cycle events, like ear piercings, required to maintain positive standing back home on the peripheries of the Kaveri delta. Many would not have seen each other outside of their region, the threat of the hydrocarbon project acting as a catalyst to activate the lower delta diaspora of Chennai as a group with shared interests back "home," as it were.

Among those in Chennai who would meet the following day was another villager from Nadiyam, a genial man in his fifties named Neelakanthan who had come to Chennai with an engineering degree in the 1980s to take up a job in a central government plastics research institute. Neelakanthan's *kula dēvankal*, or ancestral village gods, reside in Neduvasal's Nadiyamman temple. He already had experience with activism from his days as one of the founding members of *Pūvulagin Nanbarkal* (Friends of the Earth), the organization that first started translating environmentalist literature like Rachel Carson's *Silent Spring* into Tamil in the 1980s. Whereas Neelakanthan brought scientific and political expertise from his social movement background, he was constrained about what he could express in public owing to his working for the government. A younger, bearded man sporting a tight T-shirt and bright diamond earrings named Senthil Dass announced at the meeting that he would take up the work of public outreach. Senthil Dass, who had fled from Neduvasal to Chennai as young labor migrant, had since become a well-known playback singer in the Tamil film industry. When he is not in the studio he is usually on tour in places like Singapore, Malaysia, or Canada as one of the famous film composer Iliyarajah's singers. Even while the Chennai meeting was taking place, everyone was busy on their WhatsApp contacting others in the Neduvasal and regional diaspora around the world to alert them to the emerging struggle and to elicit support.

From the beginning of the digital campaign, tweets marked by the #SaveNeduvasal and #StopHydroCarbon hashtags usually featured the headline *nām thān ūdagam* (Only *we* are the media), using *nām*, the "we" that explicitly includes both addressor and the addressee as media.[32] This framing grammatically links the principle of "absolute transitivity"—which Guha argued underpins rumor as a form or circulation where encoding and decoding happen in the same moment—with the logic of modernist public address to strangers. A hybrid form of address emerged, equally at home in the idioms of rumor and public broadcasting, while reflexively marking itself as a realm independent of official news. The alarming message thus spread as discrete packets of information through fiber-optic network cables across the Arabian Sea and disbursed through the radio waves of 3G spectrum via cellular phone towers through the air. But the media that had come into being must also be conceived of in terms of dormant or potential social relations made active in the world as a network of networks with wide and even profound reach. Quickly spilling over beyond loose affinal webs of reciprocity into the broader Tamil world, this network of networks had core regions and hierarchical relations built into its infrastructure, with influential characters like Nimal Raghavan and Senthil Dass, for example, playing more prominent roles in "trending" hashtags. The velocity and geographical spread of its expansion, however, gave those who forwarded its messages a sense of being swept up as relay points in a communicability that had a different participatory feel to it than that of being addressees of the broadcast media news headlines they were circulating.

THE VIEW FROM NEDUVASAL

In the village of Neduvasal, back in 2008 people were initially curious when a farmer named Kulandai Velar—a member of the community of potters who lived outside of the main village settlement—leased his land out for hydrocarbon exploration. The Oil and Natural Gas Corporation (ONGC), a public-sector undertaking of the Government of India, had planted an eight-foot-tall wellhead into the fertile ground on his property north of the village, near the satellite settlement called Nallandarkollai. Since that time, Kulandai Velar had left his fields fallow while receiving his checks from the government. Once planted, curiosity faded over time, and the wellhead was largely forgotten: an iron ruin standing only as a distant reminder of one of the many get rich quick schemes that periodically sweep through such rural communities. Inspectors from ONGC would pass by maybe once a year, but everyone assumed that the project to explore the hydrocarbon reserves below had been dropped.

So, it came as a shock when Nimal Raghavan's friends back in Neduvasal heard the news about their village being chosen as one of the Small Discovered Fields to be tapped. And that too, through sublease by a private firm based in Bangaluru that no one had ever heard of called GEM Laboratories Private Limited. Some of the underemployed young men who were biding their time in the village contemplating futures abroad started asking questions of elders in the village about the wellhead in the fields, only to receive vague memories in response from most. Upon further inquiry, it turned out that another villager living in the main settlement in Neduvasal, named Subramanian, remembered when his farmland had also been surveyed by ONGC and the revenue department as a possible site for drilling at the same time as Kulandai Velar's. Unlike his neighbor, the muscular farmer with a sharp jawline had told the surveyors to get off his land because he was pursuing agriculture and wanted nothing to do with the hydrocarbon project. Farmers from this region like Subramanian are known to be quick with the *aruvāl*, the country machete many keep tucked between their belts and their veshties. The surveyors were scared off and never returned. When asked by the young men the following day, Subramanian assured those who had come to call on him that he had not changed his position, even if his neighbor was willing to lease his land. And from his large house, those assembled started plotting their next moves, including contacting local officials and planning a public meeting that very day in the main village square.

Owing to energies still coursing through the region following the jallikattu agitations, many young men from the Thevar community were especially primed to look for new venues to stage their fight for Tamil pride with the Indian state and with the Modi government in particular. By late morning on February 16, within twelve hours of Arun Jaitley's announcement and hundreds of WhatsApp messages later, village youth were ready to protest. They had decided to occupy the square next to the Nadiyamman Temple and the giant temple tank extending from it in the center of the village. Preparations began to assemble a *shamiyana* (shady covering) made of industrial tarp, to ensure sufficient water, and to begin printing giant digital "flex-board" signs declaring the village of Neduvasal to be a "hydrocarbon free zone." A local reporter from the Puthiya Thalaimurai television station who had been contacted by the Chennai-based group of Neduvasal diaspora was already on the spot by evening of the first day, broadcasting the emerging opposition from its inception and giving it reason to believe people would be watching from afar.

Many in Neduvasal, however, were still not sure that protest was necessary or wise. They argued with youngsters they thought too hotheaded that the community should learn more about potential employment opportunities that might come with a natural gas project. "I just thought they should educate themselves about the science behind it, and whether there might be some benefit to the village," explained Vivekanandan, Subramanian's neighbor whose agricultural land had also been surveyed for drilling. "But kids [*pasanga*] were really riled up after jallikattu." A number of older residents also feared that the militant tone in which some of the opposition to the hydrocarbon project was pitched and the fact that the young men leading the charge were from the dominant caste might prove to be divisive in the village itself. Positions began to change when rumors started flying through social media and by word of mouth that once natural gas had been extracted and the environment trashed, ONGC would then go on to search for petroleum deeper underground and finally open a lignite coal mine in the same area, as they had done elsewhere in the state. Vivekanandan remained nearly alone in questioning the veracity of these claims. Within a few days, the climate of fear appeared to have weakened potential divisions within the village by solidifying the line between defenders of the land and their enemies from outside the state.

THE MOMENT OF GENERALIZATION

Villagers from a wide range of caste backgrounds I interviewed in the months following mobilization all referred to videos they had watched as the main reason they came to take part in the mass protest that, until then, had consisted of young men from the dominant landholding community. The most widely cited was a documentary film called *Pālaivanamāhum Kāviri Deltā* (The desertification of the Kaveri delta) that had been produced by the May 17 Movement, a group founded to protest Sri Lankan government atrocities again ethnic Tamils on the island that had become a training ground for all sorts of activism including the defense of jallikattu. The film combines footage and testimony from agricultural communities in nearby Nagapattinam, which had been damaged by hydrocarbon projects, with computer animation of how hydraulic fracturing or "fracking" works. Similar animation videos depicting the effects of drilling on ground water—showing the lowering of the water table, withering crops, desertification, and the entry of seawater into the aquifer—were also sent to people by Suresh Ramanathan, another overseas worker who calls Neduvasal home and who had been working in the oil fields of Qatar as a technician for a petroleum company. Suresh furthermore circulated testimonial videos of fellow Tamils working in the Qatar petroleum fields about the harshness of life in a desert that was sustained only through oil extraction. And perhaps the final blow was delivered by the viral video of a women named Shelly Vargson from upstate New York lighting the water coming out her faucet on fire with a match to demonstrate the amount of methane released into her well as a result of nearby fracking. Nearly everyone I met had this short clip saved from WhatsApp on their cell phones. The documentary form itself had become communicable. It was all terrifying.

Village youth who had found a new calling in activism projected these films in makeshift screenings on village walls at night in Neduvasal and surrounding hamlets, generalizing the problem posed by the hydrocarbon industry. Other castes, older farmers, and women, especially, joined what had until then been group of Tamil-nationalist young men from the Thevar community who were looking to prove their virility in a fight. Stimulated through global networks of people and images, the fear of environmental devastation had prompted the people of Neduvasal to revalue their land, its vital energies now palpably threatened by the possibility of its imminent desertification. Everyone would be affected, from the landowning Thevars to those who worked the fields for desultory sums as *kūli*, or daily wage laborers, most whom where Dalits. Video evidence of crimes committed elsewhere had brought the village together in ways difficult to imagine before.

Over the next days, the village poured itself wholeheartedly into the project of resistance. From the beginning, the people of Neduvasal had decided that any political leader or celebrity would be welcome to show support, speak in the village, and take part in the protest, but they would have to do so under the strict condition that they not show their party insignia or flags. The protests were figured as a people's movement to protect Tamil land from the nationally owned oil company's complicity with private interests from outside the state, not the politics of cutting deals through parties for compensation as usual. The villages connected to Neduvasal through marriage were electrified, attracting daily visits from farmers hailing from across the Pudukkottai and delta regions. Each one of the interconnected villages took the organizational lead, in turn, on designated days. The central square in Neduvasal served as ground zero of what became a monthlong sit-in organized around rotating hunger strikes and a series of performances as tens of thousands from the region and beyond had come to support the struggle. As had happened during the jallikattu agitations, villagers organized massive food deliveries to feed their protesting guests as if it were a giant wedding party or temple festival.

The protests that ensued consisted of an intensely performative project of animation, breathing urgent politics of life and death into elements of an ecology that had until then existed primarily as silent background for human activity. Some of the most remarkable protests also took place out in the Nallandarkollai fields, where Kulandai Velar had leased his land. Making use of the striking image provided by the hydrocarbon wellhead that had been installed to provide an interface with the potential energy reserves below, villagers held a series of funeral rites for the land before news television cameras that would relay the scene for viewers around Tamil Nadu and other parts of India. Dozens among the older women of Neduvasal gathered around the eight-foot-tall monument of faded blue iron pipes, bolts, and pressure valves to sing *ōppāri pāṭṭu*, funeral dirges evoking a disturbing anguish through voice modulation that sounds like intense crying at times.[33] The singers embodied abandonment itself, beating their chests energetically for hours as they did to the dusty ground with open hands, stopping only to reach for the sky with palms upturned in supplication. Streams of tears poured down their wrinkled cheeks, framed by gray disheveled hair. Even members of the legislative assembly who visited during this phase of protests had to take off their crisp white shirts to take on the role of mourner when entering the village.

A few days after the funeral rites, men from nearby Vadakkadu marched in procession to Naduvasal, blocking the state highway dressed in only lungis and towels wrapped around their heads as they would for farm work and carrying plows on their shoulders. Women, in turn, carried stalks of kombu, a millet traditionally grown in the region, along with other agricultural products, forming a green parade on the hot pavement and stopping traffic on the main highway for the day. Later that week, a more grotesque demonstration was planned in which farmers covered in dark mud crawled on their knees in large groups, offering written petitions to a row of cows that had been lined up for the occasion next to two people wearing masks depicting prime minister Narendra Modi and BJP president Amit Shah on their faces. As neither the cows nor the BJP leaders responded, the petitioners begged them before the news cameras, bringing tears to the eyes of some in the crowd watching on. On another day, farmers from nearby Peravurani sat in the central square in Neduvasal eating mud and straw and posing with rats in their mouths while being surrounded by women singing another village musical genre called *kummi pāttu*, from the festival season for the smallpox goddess Mariamman, and dancing in a circle clapping hands, all while the hunger strikers were lined up behind them.

The idea was to put on a new show every single day. Highly performative and deeply felt, this was street theater evoking idioms of rural life that were designed to circulate on television and through social media networks. This meant devising ever more spectacular imagery to cement the struggle in the minds of news readers and watchers while also sustaining a certain level of energy among protesters who were thrilled to watch their protests being covered on all the Tamil channels and even by national outlets like NDTV news. Nimal Raghavan visited frequently from Abu Dhabi, as did Senthil Dass and Neelakandan from Chennai, taking photographs and using their considerable social media followings to widen the sphere of circulation to include IT workers in Huston, Texas, who held feasts in hotels there to help fund the protests back in Neduvasal. It was through Senthil that major film directors from Chennai joined the movement, many of them making symbolic trips to the village. Protesters themselves were energized, watching the world watching them. The spatiotemporal scaling of protest entailed a change of quality as

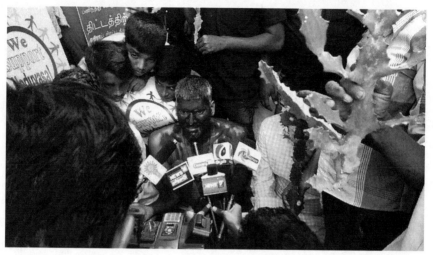

FIGURE 5.3. Neduvasal protestor covered in mud and speaking to television journalists. Sent to author via WhatsApp

viral networks enabled embodied crowds, who energized further circulation, and so on into the open-ended sphere of mass publicity.

"Nature" even appeared to take part in this mass-mediated revolt, or, according to some villagers I talked to, maybe it was the fearsome goddess Nadiyamman, whose temple opens onto the village square and whose duty it is to protect Neduvasal. The day before I visited the protest site, the effluent tank full of a tar-like substance next to the wellhead out in the fields had caught on fire, as if in willful resistance to imminent drilling. The pixilated video of flames shooting out of the ground at the break of dawn had been captured by Kulandai Velar's neighbor on his cell phone. It was circulating across WhatsApp groups in the region and beyond, renewing media attention to the protest and emphasizing the gravity of the danger posed by GEM Laboratory's plans to extract energy from erstwhile farmland. Tamil news audiences would be glued to their televisions around the state that evening, watching reports of the bursting tower of fire in the now-famous village of Neduvasal. The news reports, in turn, found their way right back into the hundreds of WhatsApp circles and Facebook sites that arose in the anti-hydrocarbon movement, proving once again how the mass forensics image-text can energize a highly combustible network imaginary.

The event of short-circuiting as global interconnection was transposed quickly into the realm of representative parliamentary negotiations proper to the state. Fearing the further spread of crowd protest to other locations—as it already had in nearby Kathiramangalam, just north of Neduvasal, and in an equally spectacular form in the generalized farmers' agitation in Jantar Manter in Delhi at the same time—the ruling AIADMK and BJP sent their leaders to negotiate extensively with protesters from Neduvasal. The district collector of Pudukkottai had already met with the protesters in Neduvasal many times. Eventually, the Tamil union minister Pon. Radhakrishnan of the BJP finally brokered a preliminary agreement representing the Government of India in New Delhi. Throughout, the Oil and Natural Gas Corporation and GEM Laboratories maintained a stony silence. When drilling proceeded despite protests in Kathiramangalam and led to a toxic leak, GEM eventually petitioned the ministry of petroleum and natural gas for a lease transfer to another location. It has not been granted.

MEDIATION AS ARTICULATION

The Neduvasal protests arose out of a moment of articulation in which radically heterogeneous elements where brought together through an interconnection superposed by new threats and media of circulation.[34] They had recruited a range of nonhuman actors as participants, for example. Cows had come to be addressed as sovereigns immune to the cries of their human supplicants. Humans had turned animal, eating rodents and cattle feed. The land responded, too, its fury captured on video. The imminent death of this fertile soil required a funeral: at once an enlistment of the carbonized life below to speak to politics of death and destruction above and an impassioned plea to death itself that their village be spared the disasters that had been wrought in neighboring villages as evidenced in the series of documentary films circulating in Neduvasal. The wellhead, which had been animated as an industrial monument pole of sorts, acted as an interface among worlds of gods, carbon, and human desire that are not easily made commensurate but were forced into collision with one another.

A contagious fear for the future of the land propelled the movement of images, texts, and people along a plane of communicability other than, and relatively autonomous from, the social world overdetermined by deeply embodied caste divisions within the village of Neduvasal itself. The "networkability of event transmission" had introduced a moment of social indeterminacy, or "indifference to difference," to borrow from Madhavi Menon.[35] But this moment of impersonal communicability and subjective indeterminacy arose precisely from an encounter with networked mediation that was as much discursive as it was affective.[36] To the degree that marginalized communities, including many Dalits in Naduvasal and beyond, were swept up by the movement against hydrocarbon exploration, then an emergent sociality could be said to have momentarily short-circuited the caste-based denial of society that otherwise forms the basis of village life.[37] It is not that caste domination had been erased or even bracketed but that the land of Neduvasal and its surrounding fields could be experienced as commons to be protected—perhaps for the first time. The water, which flows along strict hierarchical socialities as it circulates for consumption above ground, knows no caste below the earth. The fields, which are strictly divided up as property, owned by some and worked by others for marginal wages, all faced possible destruction according to the videos everyone had watched and rumors of a future coal mine. And so in addition to the shadows of nonhumans that do not normally have a voice in politics, shadow relations among humans were also animated, rapidly hitting the tipping point via the mediation of globally dispersed networks. That caste division within the village would reemerge shortly after the groundswell should not and did not surprise anyone. But that Neduvasal had been brought together by fear in the way that it was did amaze everyone.

Conclusion: Network Culture and Incendiary Documentation

Many have commented on the ramifications of networked technologies and the political imaginaries they enable in more ambivalent terms than those rehearsed in the introduction to this chapter, where I juxtaposed the utopian vision of distributed democracy with declarations about the foreclosure of politics entailed by short-circuiting. Taziana Terranova, for example, argues that the rise of what she terms *network culture* has led to a profound reconfiguration of the psychic and informational space within which political action unfolds without announcing an end to politics as such. Unlike earlier analyses of the society of the spectacle premised on the obfuscating power of propaganda, network culture refuses earlier models of representation, trading instead on the modulation of informational milieus.

> It is no longer a matter of illusion or deception, but of the tactical and strategic deployment of the power of affection of images as such. It is no longer a matter of truth and appearance, or even of the alienating power of the spectacle as "opium of the masses," but of images as bioweapons, let loose into the informational ecology with a mission to infect.[38]

Terranova is responding years later to the postmodern critiques of the sign-as-commodity with which we began this book: namely Debord, Baudrillard, Virilio, and company. "If this world could appear to some as a world where appearances or spectacles have triumphed over reality, this is only because of a metaphysical prejudice that needs images to uphold the value of a truth that must always be uncovered."[39] By contrast, in this latter model—which shares some conceptual terrain with Brian Massumi's theorization of a politics of affect in what he argues is the postideological age—the fact of circulation and the image's intensity matter more than the truth-value of a representation that claims to be disclosing something about the world outside of itself. Or, to return to the theoretical vocabulary I have been developing in this book in a formulation closer to that with which we ended the last chapter, communicability appears to have eclipsed the model of communication as the most important grounds on which political struggle is fought when traditional modes of representation have been short-circuited.

These insights into the crisis of representation emerging from the early theorists of networked affect remain compelling so long as we hold onto a robust concept of mediation. Terranova's argument that network culture "envelops the multiple durations of disparate cultural formations and milieus" rather than marking a unidirectional architectonic shift from reasoned communication to image warfare is helpful for thinking of the heterogeneity in temporal forms that characterizes politics.[40] In consonance with this general theory, Tamil Nadu's season of discontent, too, was certainly marked by the newly volatile scalability and retemporalizations that characterize digitally mediated publics and image politics while drawing on traditions of mobilization that owe their vitality to earlier articulations of Tamil nationalism. And these protests are thus different in important respects from the relatively staged displays of sovereignty as representational spectacle that had marked earlier party-based Dravidianist politics or from the everyday grunt work of political education that has long characterized mobilization of cadres in the communist parties. In fact, when they started, the protests on Marina Beach that had launched this string of agitations struck many onlookers in the city and elsewhere in India as quixotic at best and aimless or simply foolish at worst, yet another symptom of social media's corroding effects on a youth looking for a quick revolutionary buzz instead of doing the hard work required to organize through political institutions representing the sovereign people or to educate through debate. Indeed, many of the political challenges to existing structures appear as shorter-term events compared to the ethno-linguistic nationalism that Dravidianist politics had massified even as they

sever nationalism from cinematic or party politics, englobing nationalist discourse and sentiment within the network imaginary.

The role of *disclosure* in the affect-laden political upheavals marking
Tamil Nadu's season of discontent, however, foregrounds new questions
about truth, representation, and temporality in the age of digitally mediated
politics. Incendiary documentation fueling the fires of protest discussed in
this chapter made strong representational claims on the truth of events even
while the circulation of such documentation could be construed as an event
in its own right, whether we are considering the cell phone footage of police
burning auto-rickshaws in attempts to frame protesters on Marina Beach,
films depicting environmental devastation on the Thanjavur delta, or the
exposure of police snipers firing into the crowd in Thoothukudi. In the case of
the Thoothukudi protests and police violence, the widely circulating images
were furthermore accompanied by exhaustive written reports documenting
environmental degradation, the violence that was unleashed on protesters
by gunmen, as well as the ongoing harassment the residents of this city had
to endure in the days following the crackdown.[41] Widely read books have
been written about the dangers of hydrocarbon, and a whole world of science regarding native breeds of cattle in India now appeals to a wide swath
of youngsters who first participated in the jallikattu protests to protect what
they saw as cultural heritage. What now appear to be older forms of political
mobilization remain as essential as ever in the world of "new" media.

This feature of tighter, more explosive temporal loops intersecting with
longer-term formations such as nationalism or environmental activism is
afforded by digital technology. In each protest we have examined, images
exposing official malfeasance therefore played an important role in crystal-
izing protest within broader, enduring discursive frameworks that had been
developed by activists over the much longer term. By the same token, these
perduring frameworks for mobilization and representation have been significantly reworked as they are recruited in the image warfare that can be said
to characterize political action in the digital age of network culture. Drawing
on Karen Strassler's conceptualization of "image events," we can argue that
particular acts of representation had become "the material ground of generative struggles to bring a collectivity into view" around the very problems of
credibility and truth.[42] To assert a crisis in representation, as many have for
a long time and for very good reasons, should therefore not be to assume its
irrelevance in favor of the purported immediacy of affect. Crises of representation are perhaps better thought of as an interpretive coming to terms with
transformations in the media ecology, and as such, these crises constitute

an ongoing problematic as long-standing institutions strive to keep up with technological acceleration.

Returning to the dialectics of communication and communicability, we can see in the events recounted above that the claim to a hidden truth is precisely what adds fuel to the "circulation engine."[43] Communicability, so highly valued in both the politics and the economic models of our times, has *not* been severed from communication (in which the medium can be separated from the message). The capacity to represent is important to models of democracy as deliberation; it also appears to be a critical ingredient in the contemporary quest for communicability. Some representations, because of their compelling claims on a reality that many suspect is being hidden by nefarious forces, have wings that allow for wide-scale networked circulation. What appears to have changed dramatically in recent years, however, is the distribution of the technological means of representation allowing for a redistribution of the capacity for extreme communicability.

EPILOGUE

Environmental Engineering

This book has drawn on our experience of digital media to ask new questions about the recent past. It has focused in particular on the intensification and metamorphoses of positive feedback dynamics—whereby news becomes the eventful subject of further news—that have demonstrable roots in the pre-digital era. I have sought to avoid the overdetermination of a widely shared narrative implying a historical anteriority when disembodied reason oriented toward reaching understanding simply gave way to politics premised on unmediated corporeal affect and the raw force of images inaugurated by digital "virality." We have seen how print has long been entangled with deeply embodied populist politics, for example, or how the vitality of digitally mediated crowd politics has a great deal to do with practices of representation, disclosure, and even deliberation that we often attribute to older media and classical models of the public sphere. We have also opened up questions about how news events, in particular, become grounds for claims to legitimate power across different media of representation. Attempts to censor aggravating representations of political leadership or judicial power, for instance, can easily lead to the proliferation of more publicity for the news organ that has been censored while also standing as displays of sovereignty for the actor who seeks to control what can be represented in public. Through the analysis of such events, we have learned that claims to sovereignty are inherently vulnerable to the vicissitudes of public uptake and editorial calculation while the uneven distribution of such vulnerability is conditioned by the embodied, enduring logics of caste, community, and gender shaping the public sphere.[1]

To argue against common interpretations of the causes and character of techno-political change, however, is not to assume that there is nothing new under the sun. Transformations in politics afforded by the redistribution of the very means of technologically enabled representation and circulation, thereby breaking the monopoly professional news makers enjoyed on the means of mass circulation, have thus also emerged as an important part of our story of intensification. The imaginary of a vital popular sovereignty cathecting with the image of a leader who projects strength by policing the domain of the representable, for example, can also be detached from institutionalized absorption through news events in which the crowd is figured as an embodied collective agent and as a circulator of its own image. As a result, political parties and leaders are increasingly invested in extending their powers to create conditions in which news events that are thought to emerge directly from "the people" can be framed for political advantage. The question of communicability, which has long characterized the phenomenology of rumor, had already became a feature of news from its very beginnings as a mass-mediated commodity form. But communicability—as the potential for an image-text to be forwarded, repeated, and to thus circulate widely and thereby produce news events based on this circulation—now emerges as central to politics that have incorporated the logics of communicative capitalism into their strategy and practice in twenty-first-century India and elsewhere.

Digital media may well have opened new avenues for this potential for communicability to actualize itself and, just as importantly, for us to become more aware of it and its political significance. The human body, with all its fleshy identifying features, similarly emerges as both a central conduit and medium in the production of political publicity in the twenty-first century. It is perhaps paradoxical that digital media, the product of a long tradition that treats information as strictly separable from the material medium that is said to "carry" it, should become such an important social force in reflexively foregrounding the role of the body as a medium—a role that the body has always played while being obscured in thought about mass publicity focused on the norm of self-abstraction.[2] But this reemergence of our awareness of the body as medium appears to be a pervasive effect of digitalization in politics as well as in other domains of life. Extending our analysis of this phenomenon to realms of collective action, we might also note that the auratic pull of copresence animating the embodied crowd that worried social thinkers of the late nineteenth and early twentieth centuries experiencing the mechanized mass mediatization of society has resurfaced in the age of networked digital media. Crowd politics in the last decade or so appear to be mediated by digital technology, but it is this condition that also allows us to better appreciate how crowds had already been both mediated by print and a medium through which print might exert its political force. Something old reappears in a novel form, precipitated in important respects by the massification of a technological innovation that allows us to appreciate the past differently. The newness of form matters a great deal, however, as does the changing media ecology through which form reemerges, transfigures, circulates, and thereby comes to define the field within which agonistic politics are fought out.

Networking the News Event

In the wake of Trump's presidency and in the shadows of Modi's tenure as prime minister of India, the obvious intensity of what Ravi Sundaram terms the "crisis machine" fueling contemporary communicative capitalism demands renewed attention to how the staging of political spectacle might be moving in some new directions.[3] A broad concept of the news event can be useful in identifying how political power has sought to enlist the affordances of the current media environment—with all the uncertainties that come with massively distributed means of circulation—to particular ends. My more specific conceptualization of short-circuiting in the last chapter, for instance, already leads us beyond positive feedback loops to reconfigurations in the spatiality and temporality of politics allowing for crowds to appear as relatively independent political actors through digitally mediated redistributions of the capacity to represent. What concerns me here is how the progressively decentralized and distributed qualities of media circulation are nevertheless subject to very sophisticated attempts at political manipulation, or what we might call "environmental engineering." Recognizing the publicity-making potential of both legal and extralegal repressive measures, political strategy now seeks to rearrange the very networked environment within which events unfold while amplifying older police functions defining what can legitimately be said and shown in public.

When members of the ruling party in India discuss building a new "ecosystem" more conducive to the pursuit of their Hindu-nationalist goals, as they often do, they explicitly recognize what our academic theorists have been arguing: that "media is now atmospheric (Hansen 2012, McCormack 2017), in that it has become a more widespread, even an 'elemental' part of infrastructure (Peters 2015), existing in the background of personal devices and infrastructures."[4] Power thus articulates itself though reticulated forms of association organizing the whole field of circulation within which events can be made to happen across platforms. At the same time, media person-alities acting as influential nodes within this latticework of personal devices and other infrastructures animate events in such a manner as to divide "the people" from their purported enemies. This is where the volatile qualities of "network culture" that have concerned us in the later chapters of this book are given ideological form by older Manichean structural dynamics of populism explored in earlier chapters, a crucial difference being the manner in which Hindu nationalism is premised on the public degradation of bodies considered to be Other.

Tamil Nadu—the birthplace of media politics in India, where Dravidianism has long defined popular imaginations of a shadow sovereignty within and against the Indian nation-state—has not survived unscathed from Hindu-nationalist attempts to redefine who counts as "the people" through a reengineering of mediatization. We have already encountered the repressive and event-making capacity of Hindutva politics in this book when members of the Hindu Munnani stormed the stage during Puthiya Thalaimurai's debate show (chap. 1); when the same group organized a caste-based campaign against the author Perumal Murugan (chap. 3); when violence in retaliation for the custodial murder of a Muslim youth named Shakeel Ahmed served as a pretext for mobilization (chap. 3); or when a campaigner for the BJP turned into a caste-vigilante icon (chap. 4). This project of refiguring the subject of popular sovereignty as upper-caste Hindu remained fairly marginal to Tamil politics as a kind of background event-making machine, however, until more recent attempts to arrange the very media environment within which such events can unfold and be used to political advantage. Some events in the news-making business that become the subject of further news coverage can change the contours of the sphere of circulation itself through a reorganization of key nodes in the network. Agitators seeking attention through digital media platforms available to anyone with a cell phone have proven their ability to stage events that resonate with much larger scales of political power and thereby work to redefine the "mainstream" of broadcast media. This is precisely what happened to the celebrated television personality, M. Gunasekaran, who was responsible for airing the interview with Yuvaraj in chapter 4.

Gunasekaran became the target of what was framed as a grassroots defamation campaign that would end up having serious consequences for news making in the state. Gunasekaran was at the top of his game in 2020. Having grown up in a village in Dharmapuri, the poorest region of the state, he had started his media career in the rough-and-tumble world of Tamil newspapers before moving up in the perceived hierarchy to report for English papers, including *Deccan Chronicle, Times of India,* and India's most respected newspaper, the *Hindu.* Gunasekaran had thus already seen all aspects of print media, from the wild side of political reporting in Tamil to the most sober of the English-language dailies, before becoming the most widely recognized personality on Tamil television as the public face of Puthiya Thalaimurai when the new station was launched 2011 and quickly surpassed all the competition (see chap. 4). When I met him in 2016, he had just been recruited by the Reliance Industries–owned Network18 media empire to head their new Tamil-language channel, where the sharp and charismatic news anchor would go on to win the Ramnath Goenka Excellence in Journalism Award. In the interview Gunasekaran granted me as they were launching the new station, he gently admitted that there would be some limits on what they could report on because Jayalalithaa, who was chief minister of Tamil Nadu at the time, was known to menace those who were too critical. She had been using the nationalized Aracu Cable distribution company to threaten anyone who broadcasted news considered inconvenient to her AIADMK government. The prospect of being taken off the air altogether, as had happened before at Puthiya Thalaimurai, was a blunt weapon and a fairly effective one because of the centralized nature of distribution in this medium. But Gunasekaran never thought that he would be vulnerable to the machinations of Hindu nationalists, who had almost no visible presence in Tamil broadcast news media.

Members of the BJP and other Hindu nationalists had long been unhappy with Tamil journalists who, unlike their counterparts elsewhere, have never been docile toward them because of the party's association with North Indian Brahminism and their electoral irrelevance in a land ruled by Dravidian parties. After another failure of the national party to make regional inroads in the 2019 national elections despite a resounding landslide in their favor in most other states, Tamilisai Soundararajan, the BJP's state president, declared they would no longer participate in debate shows she claimed were biased against them. A report prepared by the state unit of the party had concluded that Tamil news media were "not BJP friendly" and were clearly "antagonistic."[5] But withdrawal from the news media landscape could not be a long-term solution for the party or for the broader project of Hindutva. Instead, a remaking of the media environment that had been built through Dravidian politics was in order and events had to be produced to enable this process of integration with regional infrastructures of representation and circulation.

An opportunity presented itself from the peripheries when a Hindu nationalist named Maridhas took to his YouTube channel, followed by about

350,000 subscribers, to denounce a relatively unknown group of YouTubers for posting a video making fun of the devotional song *Kanda Sashti Kavasam*, originally composed in the nineteenth century in praise of the god Lord Murugan. The offending video was part of a series that had been posted by the "Karuppar Kūttam: Odukkappadum Makkalakkāna Kural" (The black collective: A voice for oppressed people), so named because of the color associated with the militant atheist stream of Dravidian thought and a broader rejection of the lightness associated with upper-caste complexions. What first appeared to be a low-stakes targeting of the missteps of a fringe atheist group scaled up rapidly, however, when film stars started to show their outrage on social media and Maridhas began to connect the group to some of the most powerful figures in Tamil news, most importantly Gunasekaran. Pointing out the fact that the famous anchor was married to the daughter of a member of the Dravidar Kazhagam (DK), the social movement to combat caste and Brahminical religion dating from the 1940s, the vlogger claimed that the whole of Tamil News 18 and Tamil media more broadly were anti-Hindu.

Naming several journalists in Tamil News 18 and also targeting news channel Puthiya Thalaimurai's star anchor and news editor, S. Karthigaichelvan, Maridhas and his fellow Hindutva activists had managed to capture the attention of larger political forces (i.e., if they had not already been guided by the BJP in making these accusations in the first place). As if on cue, a former journalist named Madan Ravichandran went on his Channel Vision YouTube channel describing how radical Dravidianists were spreading their attack on Hinduism across news media in a post that was circulated widely in Hindutva media like #Swarajya.[6] Having successfully attracted a swarm of attention on Twitter and elsewhere along strictly divided lines between those who supported Gunasekaran and those calling for his resignation, Maridhas then posted a tweet in which he displayed an email from the associate executive editor of news18.com accepting all of the YouTuber's allegations as true. The news channel along with Gunasekaran quickly filed a case with the cybercrime branch under section 465 (punishment for forgery), section 469 (forgery for purpose of harming reputation) and section 471 (using as genuine a forged document or electronic record) of the Indian Penal Code and section 66 B and section 43 of the Information Technology Act 2000. It turns out that the email was fake, but the consequences of the storm that had been whipped up where very real.

The Network18 media conglomerate, which is owned by the industrial multibillionaire Mukesh Ambani, also known to be very close to the BJP under Narendra Modi's rule, first demoted Gunesekaran from his position as chief editor at Tamil News 18. He was expected to remain as the public face of the channel, having lost his leadership role. But the powerful anchor soon left the channel altogether to join Sun TV News, the older channel run by the DMK party family. And so, the era of a relatively independent Tamil television news that began with the launch of the first nonparty channels in the early 2010s appears to be coming to a close. Gunasekaran, the news media personality who promised to free news from the constraints of party politics, was forced to find protection in an organization with a rather explicit agenda to support the DMK. Deep ties between the BJP and India's largest media empire have thus served to challenge both the Dravidianist media environment, by particularizing its claims to hegemony, as well as the new one that had emerged in satellite television to claim political neutrality and even objectivity. As the state government in Tamil Nadu still controls distribution and frequently uses major corporations' nonmedia operations as potential targets of harassment to control what can be said on their news channels—like Puthiya Thalaimurai, which is owned by the SRM conglomerate—party-owned channels have proven their longevity.[7] To be completely subject to capitalist logics and the political pressures that can be exerted through control of the market is also to be working on a different temporal scale than that of political parties. "Nonparty" news clearly does not equate with autonomy.

Having entered into digital politics a decade before other parties, the BJP has proven itself the most adept in India at reengineering the whole milieu within which such events can be made to resonate effectively with large-scale political forces. Once again, public displays of offense took center stage, as they had before when the novel *Māthorubāgan* was alleged to have hurt the honorable sentiments of the Gounder community. This time, however, the capacity of mainstream media to portray Maridhas and his followers as irrelevant was limited by the obvious consequences of their agitation in the "offline" world of broadcast news offices. The self-styled grassroots vlogger had managed to collude with a political power that includes India's richest capitalist to decenter Tamil Nadu's most influential newscaster, and one can assume that future hires will be vetted accordingly. That News 18 denied accepting his allegations via email now appears to be beside the point. Whether or not collusion was preplanned by the party itself, old boundaries had been breached as the event of outrage had a "networkability" that was actualized in an ecology purposefully arranged to make a virtue out of the volatility introduced by new media.[8] As the major Tamil parties have striven to adapt to this new environment, they also started "information technology wings," the AIADMK having founded theirs in 2014 and the DMK starting one only as recently as fall of 2017. How they will reformat their political image long built through "cine-politics" in this age of millennial ferment and networked logics of assembly and publicity remains to be seen. What is clear is that the capability for rapid reconfiguration afforded by new technologies has changed the political landscape and that it is this mediatized landscape, the broader ecology itself, that is coming to stand as the very object of political manipulation.

Politics as Resonance Planning

A number of thinkers have sought to further our understanding of the production of political subjectivity when media can be said to form a prevalent role in the very environments within which our experiences emerge and unfold. Developing Weber beyond the question of causality that was of concern in his thesis on the Protestant ethic, for example, William Connolly has theorized a "media politics of resonance" amplifying and even animating complementary dispositions among evangelical and capitalist forces on the political right in the US that otherwise have differing explicit ideological orientations.[9] The concept of resonance—also developed along somewhat different lines in William Mazzarella's work on the vital energies of publicity in mass society—is helpful to think through recent tendencies in India and elsewhere.[10] If positive feedback has long worked as a circular dynamic escaping simple causes and effects to be tamed in pursuit of divisive politics where the momentum of one's foe could be used against them, there is now a growing awareness among actors that influencing the possible effects of particular nonlinear event spirals is perhaps no longer as important as working to create the very conditions for the emergence of types of events that can resonate across scales. The uncertainty inherent in circulation in the digital era is thereby harnessed to a political project.

If political scientists have conceptualized "political engineering" as the design of particular political institutions and laws to achieve certain effects, the emergence of this kind of resonance planning clearly demands a theoretical framework more squarely focused on networked media of circulation and their entanglements with recent transformations in a capitalism that is increasingly reliant on such media for the production of value.[11] To sweep the complexity of these assemblages under the umbrella of a theory of informational capitalism that knows ahead of time where politics is headed, however, would be to miss the constitutive and generative role of instability, or elements that cannot be subsumed *within* the system. Hence my focus throughout this book on what Kajri Jain has argued for as a methodological maxim of sorts in the study of capitalist modernity: to examine "the concurrence of universalizing forces and the exceptionalities that make their spread possible."[12] The role of capital remains as foundational as ever in this era when theories of media ecology and associated strategies of planned resonance have become axiomatic in political thought. Governing by means of events that reverberate through mobile networks and satellite distribution so as to modulate public spheres and pathways of circulation allows one to bypass a number of political institutions, but it remains an expensive business. The BJP's close connection to Reliance Industries was the necessary infrastructural condition under which Maridhas's defamatory stunt had the potential to resonate as it did, for instance, both in the public sphere and in decisions that were made about editorial power at the television channel. More generally, this connection is what has allowed Reliance-owned Jio to wield a near monopoly over cellular communications in many parts of India, including Tamil Nadu. The BJP and other parties imitating their IT wing strategies have furthermore invested in sophisticated systems of software "bots" to circulate certain events widely across algorithmically driven platforms like Twitter and Facebook, becoming the stuff of a field of broadcast news that has become remarkably docile in most of India. Editors of newspapers and satellite news channels live in fear of tax raids and other punitive measures the government might take should they not display utter enthusiasm for its policies. Entanglements between party politics and market rationalities have even ensured that because of their national dominance, the BJP's political manipulation of Facebook policy allows the party much greater freedom to program misinformation campaigns using this platform than rival parties.[13]

As importantly, however, parties employ a vast army of human workers whose job it is to develop and perpetuate environments suitable to the circulation of preferred events both on algorithmically driven media and, much more crucially, on networked social media like WhatsApp that rely wholly on human-initiated but technologically enabled acts of citation or viral "forwarding."[14] The "surplus populations" that have long been at the center of debates on the nature of postcolonial capitalism, or subjects of investigative journalism on wild aspiration in the face of relative deprivation, also form a labor pool readily enlisted in such projects to engineer ecosystems in the service of politics.[15] On the event-making side of this paradigm, the attraction of becoming a microcelebrity, and thus grabbing the attention of the politically powerful through acts of majoritarian violence that can circulate widely in the digital sphere, has become a powerful lure for a number of underemployed young men.

Whereas much of the best of North Atlantic media theory seeks to come to terms with a world in which the figure of the human appears almost fully colonized by what Katherine Hayles calls the "non-conscious cognition of computer systems"—or what has been conceptualized as "feedforward loops" that can "only be felt *indirectly* and *after the fact* by higher-order modes of human experience"—I would argue that human nodes in the assemblage of resonance politics in India and beyond also demand theorization of what Sandeep Mertia terms "sociotechnical relationalities."[16] This is to say that the socially mediated structures of desire attracting the would-be digital vigilante (chap. 4) or globalizing environmental activist (chap. 5) are precisely what cannot be sidestepped in any account of what Hayles sees as "the rapidly escalating complexities created by the interpenetration of cognitive technologies with human systems."[17] This is where anthropology remains essential to a media studies approach to politics. Nor can the political economy of "surplus populations" be ignored as a standing reserve of political labor in the service of networking, affective and otherwise. Human nodes in these media networks are indispensable. But the fact that the human is increasingly shaped by a media environment that exerts agentive force on this structure of desire, often below the threshold of consciousness, is what appears to be more and more important in our analyses. This is where anthropology must take more seriously the claims of media theory: "Twenty-first century media call into play elements of worldly sensibility that are *within the human* even if they do not (and cannot) belong to the human, they bring out hitherto unacknowledged elements of human experience, and in that sense make possible a veritable reinvigoration of the human."[18] Mine is therefore not at all an argument for a return to deliberation among integrally human agents as the guiding principle for our understanding of politics but instead to insist on the centrality of media that have already been mediated by other media to our experience of the world today. Deliberation does not disappear in this understanding, nor does affect come to be purely programmable. The point is simply that it is no longer possible to extricate the integral human from digital media environments that are already implicated in our politics of representation and our claims to truth.[19]

When the World Is Always Already Other Media

What does this mean for journalism and news media? It no longer comes as a big surprise that news media events form a great deal of the content of news media representation as it once did to thinkers like Stiegler, for whom such "event-ization" represented a collapse in the order of historical representation and a reorganization of temporality itself. If distributed, technologically enabled means of news production and circulation form the very environment within which human experience emerges, how could it be otherwise? News is still largely about human experience. But the question of journalistic judgment and the principles of selection for what counts as a news event based on real facts has become more complicated even as this question appears more remote than ever from the chimera of "objective" reporting devoid of "politics."[20]

Twenty-first-century journalism in India, and elsewhere, increasingly begins with the premise that high-velocity nonprofessional media representations produced through cheap and widely available digital technology are already involved in shaping the story that must be represented as news. Acts of journalism are always already "rerepresentations" and remediations of other media in this sense, image-texts that are often seamlessly reabsorbed by nonprofessional circulation engines. And such nonprofessional media representations are thus also facts, out there in the world, but now thoroughly imbricated with the nondigital facts that have long stood as the stuff of news. The problem that such representations are often purposefully designed to deceive has become a source of great anxiety, and for good reason. Scholarship on journalism in "posttruth" regimes in Italy and Russia, for example, shows the limits of the distinction Hannah Arendt famously drew between "factual truth" and "opinion" in the face of political power founded on the circulation of misinformation.[21] One need not wax romantic over a bygone era when acts of representation were clearly delineated from events represented to recognize that the legitimacy crisis facing news media today is very real and very much global.

The circulation of "truthiness" in the service of extrainstitutional power seems to be a pervasive tactic afforded by distributed media networks that are nonetheless subject to regimes of planned reverberation.[22] Offline violence against journalists proliferating in many parts of the world is impossible to disentangle from online events and swarms that are enabled by the resonance chamber. When combined with the amplification of repressive legal measures facing journalists in a place like India—where simply reporting on protests against government policy can draw charges of sedition—media environments that have been engineered to instrumentalize what are framed as transgressions against the nation would appear to leave very little room for responsible news production.[23] For what such metrics are worth (and there is reason to question them), the fact that India ranks 150 of 180 countries in the World Press Freedom Index published by Reporters Without Boarders indicates that attacks on press freedom are ubiquitous but that the news still really matters to people.[24] The very fragility of traditional media institutions in the face of these pressures has produced a context where much of the most interesting, and honest, journalism today therefore happens wholly online with relatively little overhead and therefore less to lose when targeted by those in power.[25]

Although all news media now pay special attention to "media" as a discrete topic on which to report—like "crime," "politics," or "business"—it is becoming clearer by the day that none of these latter spheres can be understood without reference to the background media environment in which events take place, whether we are considering tech industries, financial derivative trading, election campaigning, cybercrime, or the latest videos of police violence captured on a cell phone to be introduced as evidence in high-profile trials. What is of great concern is that these very sociotechnical entanglements are often difficult to get at through traditional methods of journalism insofar as the discipline has routed its claims to truth primarily through human protagonists or paper documents that have identifiable authority-grounding sources. This difficulty is partly because, like all media consumers, journalists, too, are subject to what Louise Amoore has identified as the algorithmic arrangement of "new regimes of verification, new forms of identifying a wrong or of truth telling in the world."[26] Beyond the ontology of algorithms working as cybernetic circuits closed off from the surrounding world, there is the also the question of authoritative representation in an age where the technological means of representation are subject to great suspicion because of the ease with which they can be manipulated. And the two, machine learning and human designs to misinform, often work in tandem to pernicious effect. Journalists would appear to have fewer and fewer means to grasp the conditions of their own knowledge production in such a world while we rely on them more than ever in our search to know how such disinformation is happening in the first place. But it is not for this reason that they stop trying to come to truth through the mediation of other media or that we have given up on the institution of journalism as somehow redundant. Nor is journalism peculiar in this respect.

For Achille Mbembe, the undermining of methodical and systematic processes for validating the empirical ushered in by the computational age signals nothing less than a "reconfiguration of what counts as knowledge" for *all* disciplines.[27] The proliferation of digital media in the past two decades has indeed been disorienting for anthropology as well as journalism insofar as both disciplines' reliance on "direct experience" that long stood as the basis for making empirical claims about the world has slowly melted away. And while this book has been framed explicitly as an anthropology of media, like our journalist colleagues we are now expressing varying degrees of reflexivity about the fact that we all do some kind of media anthropology these days. It is when media strike us as particularly "new," because of how sedimented regimes or habits of communication and circulation are troubled, that such reflection on technological mediation appears to increase, usually coupled with anxieties about how new media might be infringing on our autonomy as human subjects of anthropology.[28] For Mbembe, it is precisely this infringement on the myth of sovereign subject that gives him some hope that the computational age in Africa might be coupled with renewed attempts to decolonize theory informed by cosmopolitics despite his well-founded fears that all knowledge is also being reduced to "data" at another level and in the same moment.

It is in this spirit that I have proceeded in this book to open anthropological methods to the pharmacological imagination that has already defined the practice of journalism in the digital age, where the poison afflicting a thoroughly technologized social body might also be turned to as the means of collective life.[29] For all the philosophical critiques of the sovereign subject that have informed our critical theory for decades, the experience of journalism and politics in the age of deep mediation might well prove more important in making the point: beyond the sharply drawn *opposition* between autonomy and heteronomy that we have inherited from the Platonic tradition running through Kant lie technologies of *composition*.[30] And it is how we engage with and care for such technologies of mediation that compose our situation that matters in our attempts to navigate the decidedly stormy waters of news and politics in the twenty-first century. There is no return to immediacy nor should it hold any special value in attempts to revitalize news media. The quest for relative degrees of collective freedom that are only afforded *through* media, however, remains as compelling as ever.

Acknowledgments

More than a decade worth of accumulated debts has accrued in the making of this work. I would first and foremost like to express my gratitude to the reporters and editors whose work has shaped these pages. Among the countless journalists in Chennai who selflessly allowed me into their professional lives for some time, a number of whom also became friends, several demand special mention: P. Dhanasekaran, Dennis Jesudasan, B. Kolappan, R. Malaramuthan, Jaya Menon, Kavitha Muralidharan, R. Ramasubramanian, Sandhya Ravishankar, A. Subramani, Kathir Vel, Wilson, and Sruthisagar Yamunan. R. Mohan and Kosal Ram, both models of generosity, passed away all too early during the course of this research. It is from the insights and struggles these scribes shared with me that I generated the questions guiding this ethnography. N. Ram and R. R. Gopal were both extremely kind and free in recounting their stories of friction with state power. A. S. Panneerselvan joyfully pushed me to refine my research both empirically and analytically. And S. Balasubramanian Adityan graciously granted permission to access the *Dinathanthi* newspaper archives. In Delhi, interviews with Paranjoy Guha Thakurta, S. Srinivasan, and J. Venkatesan opened whole new lines of inquiry. The Alangudi reporters' circle, with indispensable help from S. A. Karuppiah, provided important spaces for reflection on how journalism is imbricated with local politics. SAK was also a crucial guide to understanding the events that unfolded in Neduvasal. Ravindran Gopalan gave boundless support for this research at the Department of Journalism and Communication at the University of Madras.

I have been blessed to work with brilliant friends, colleagues, and students at the University of Toronto. I have drawn a great deal of inspiration in particular from Naisargi Dave, Andrew Gilbert, Kajri Jain, Tania Li, and Andrea Muehlebach. Students in my Media and Mediation class have posed numerous questions I am still wrestling with, and I would like to acknowledge Aakash Solanki in particular. At U of T and beyond, Alejandro Paz has been a critical interlocutor and friend for over two decades now. I am furthermore incredibly grateful for questions and comments from colleagues and friends at numerous workshops, talks, and conferences elsewhere that have pushed this work in directions I could never have imagined. Among the very many forums where I have shared and discussed this research, I would like to note four of particular importance. At the wonderful Sarai/Center for the Study of Developing Societies workshop on "The Act of Media" in Delhi, Arudra Burra, Lawrence Liang, Jinee Lokneeta, Siddharth Narrain, Nivedita Menon, Ravi Sundaram, and Ravi Vasudevan all provided critical feedback and encouragement. As a visitor to New York University's Department of Media, Culture, and Communication, I had the pleasure of being hosted by Arvind Rajagopal and Anupama Rao as well as the honor of sharing ideas on the stage on several occasions with Venkatesh Chakravarty. Arvind's early support has been critical. At two different iterations of Yale University's South Asia Workshop, Paula Chakravartty, Karuna Mantena, M. Madhav Prasad, Srirupa Roy, and S. V. Srinivas graciously shared their queries and enthusiasm with me. Perhaps most significantly, friends at the Chicago Tamil Forum, hosted by the University of Chicago, have seen and helped refine early versions of nearly every chapter over the years. I am especially thankful for the care and erudition with which E. Annamalai, Sasha Ebeling, Swarnavel Eswaran, Stephen Hughes, D. Karthikeyan, Constanine Nakassis, and Amanda Weidman have each engaged with this work. Costas, a source of endless insight and warmth, has been a crucial companion on this journey. Others who have commented, formally and informally, on aspects of this research in ways that have made a lasting impression include Yasmeen Arif, Anuj Bhuwania, Lisa Björkman, Lawrence Cohen, Michael Collins, Veena Das, Ned Dostaler, Daniel Fisher, Susan Gal, Ilana Gershon, Andy Graan, Jessica Greenberg, Thomas Blom Hansen, Miyako Inoue, Aasim Khan, Paul Manning, Lisa Mitchell, Bhrigupati Singh, Sanjay Srivastava, Per Ståhlberg, Sahana Udupa, Shriram Venkatraman, and Rihan Yeh.

In addition to two extremely helpful and erudite reviewers for the press, Amahl Bishara, Nusrat Chowdhury, Bhavani Raman, and Eliot Tretter have gifted me with wonderfully insightful readings of chapters. William Mazzarella has been a key interlocutor for a long time now in addition to being an inspiration for the practice of a critical anthropology of publics. Ravi Sundaram will surely recognize our chats over the years in these pages. In many respects, his work and Sarai/CSDS more generally have been important grounding locations in the development of intellectual paths taken in this book. William and Ravi both gave gracious readings of parts of the manuscript that have raised more questions than I have been able to address here but for which I am incredibly grateful. Two mentors who commented on early versions of this work, Barney Bate and Michael Silverstein, both passed away during the writing of the book. The force of their ideas and their personalities continues to propel so many of us. Their laughter, wit, and passion for anthropology are dearly missed.

The research for this book project was made possible by a Social Science and Humanities Research Council Insight Grant in addition to start-up funding from the Vice Principal Research Office at the University of Toronto. Portions of this book have been previously published. Chapter one consists of a substantially revised and expanded version of "Populist Publics: Print Capitalism and Crowd Violence beyond Liberal Frameworks," *Comparative Studies of South Asia, Africa and the Middle East* 35, no. 1 (2015): 50–65, published by Duke University Press and reprinted in *Media and Utopia: History, Imagination, and Technology*, edited by Arvind Rajagopal and Anupama Rao (New Delhi: Routledge, 2016). Some parts of chapters four and five were published as "Metamorphoses of Popular Sovereignty: Cinema, Short Circuits, and Digitalization in Tamil India," *Anthropological Quarterly* 93, no. 2 (Spring 2020): 57–88.

The entire team at the University of Chicago Press has been wonderful to work with. My editor, Mary Al-Sayed, guided this manuscript through the publication process with expertise and clarity of purpose that are deeply appreciated. I am grateful to production editor Beth Ina and copyeditor Steve LaRue for their help. Thanks to Lee Gable for the index.

Finally, friends and family have given endless support without which none of this would have been possible. In Chennai, Senthil Babu, V. Geetha, Shashank Kela, A. R. Venkatachalapathy, and Karuna Dietrich Wielenga saw me through the research and writing with care and affection. SAK, R. Neela, and their extended families in Pudukkottai remain essential kin and comrades. Nagaraj Adve, Aparna Balachandran, Madhav Raman, Rupali Nair, and Padmini Auntie have enabled me to count Delhi as one of my homes, and in Bengaluru, Chandan Gowda has been a longtime fellow traveler. A very special note of gratitude goes to my in-laws, Mohan and Uma Raman, as well as Aruna Ratnam and the extended Ramachandran family. In Toronto, Max Ackerman's extraordinary care for my children made writing possible during numerous COVID-19 lockdowns. Edward Cody, my father and a journalist, set me on this path long ago in ways I am only now discovering. Ariane and Ronald Thompson, Melinda Cody, Lola and Chloe Ennis have all been immeasurably supportive, and I was happy to be able to share some of my life in India with them over the course of this research. The research and writing of this book was punctuated by two life-changing events: the births of my daughters, Minakshi and Naima Codyraman. They are my sunshine and sources of boundless joy. Most importantly, I dedicate this book to Bhavani Raman, a scholar whose example I hope to emulate, and my partner without whom life itself is unthinkable.

Notes

INTRODUCTION

1. Schudson argues against many of the myths attributing to the news the power to mold history, from the Spanish-American War, which is often thought to have been started through sensationalist (and false) journalism about the sinking of the USS *Maine* in Havana, onto the Watergate Scandal. See Michael Schudson, *The Power of News* (Cambridge, MA: Harvard University Press, 1995).

2. The phrase *media event* is also a term of analysis used by Dayan and Katz, but it refers to events that have been staged for the news that nevertheless take place somewhat independently of this staging. It is therefore different from the conceptualization of the "news event" guiding this book. See Daniel Dayan and Elihu Katz, *Media Events: The Live Broadcasting of History* (Cambridge, MA: Harvard University Press, 1992).

3. The order was issued under section 19 of the Cable Television Networks (Regulation) Act, 1995, which enables an officer to prohibit a cable operator "from transmitting or re-transmitting any particular programme if it is likely to promote, on grounds of religion, race, language, caste or community or any other ground whatsoever, disharmony, or feelings of enmity, hatred or ill-will between different religious, racial, linguistic or regional groups or castes or communities or which is likely to disturb the public tranquility." See also A. S. Panneerselvan, "My Days at Sun TV," in *21st Century Journalism in India*, ed. Nalini Rajan (New Delhi: Sage Publications, 2007), 193–205.

4. Ravi Sundaram, "Publicity, Transparency, and the Circulation Engine: The Media Sting in India," *Current Anthropology* 56, no. S12 (2015): S297–S305.

5. Guy Debord, *Comments on the Society of the Spectacle*, trans. Malcolm Imrie (London: Verso 1998), 6.

6. Jean Baudrillard, "Toward a Critique of the Political Economy of the Sign," trans. Carl R. Lovitt, and Denise Klopsch *SubStance* 5, no. 15 (1976): 114.

7. Paul Virilio, *The Lost Dimension*. trans. Daniel Moshenberg (Los Angeles: Semiotext(e), 1991), 93–94.

8. See Jürgen Habermas, *The Structural Transformation of the Public Sphere: An Inquiry into a Category of Bourgeois Society.* trans. Thomas Burger (Cambridge, MA: MIT Press, 1991).

9. Jodi Dean, *Democracy and Other Neoliberal Fantasies: Communicative Capitalism and Left Politics* (Durham, NC: Duke University Press, 2009); Yann Moulier-Boutang, *Cognitive Capitalism* (London: Polity, 2011); Shoshana Zuboff, *The Age of Surveillance Capitalism: The Fight for a Human Future at the New Frontier of Power* (New York: Public Affairs, 2018).

10. McKenzie Wark, *Telesthesia: Communication, Culture, and Class* (Cambridge: Polity, 2012), 9.

11. Paula Chakravartty and Srirupa Roy provide a powerful analysis of this explosion in news media, explaining how "up until the early 1990s there was only one news channel in the country, the state-owned Doordarshan. Over the next two decades, a staggering total of 268 news and current affairs channels were licensed by the Ministry of Information and Broadcasting." Paula Chakravartty, and Srirupa Roy, "Media Pluralism Redux: Towards New Frameworks of Comparative Media Studies 'Beyond the West.'" *Political Communication* 30, no. 3 (2013): 353. At the time of writing there were at least a dozen Tamil-language news channels in India and nearly as many major Tamil-language daily newspapers.

12. See Bernard Bate, *Tamil Oratory and the Dravidian Aesthetic: Democratic Practice in South India* (New York: Columbia University Press, 2009).

13. Besides *Murasoli* and C. N. Annadurai's own *Drāvida Nādu*, prominent Dravidianist papers include *Nam Nādu, Pōr Vāl*, and *Kathir*. See E. Sundaramoorthy, and M. R. Arasu, eds. *Tiravita Iyakka Italkal* (Chennai: International Institute of Tamil Studies, 2008).

14. Including *Kungumam, Muttaram, Vannatirai*, and *Sumangali.*

15. See M.S.S. Pandian, *The Image Trap: M. G. Ramachandran in Film and Politics* (New Delhi: Sage, 1992).

16. M. Madhava Prasad, *Cine-Politics: Film Stars and Political Existence in South India* (New Delhi: Orient Blackswan, 2014).

17. Lauren Berlant, *Cruel Optimism* (Durham, NC: Duke University Press, 2011), 228.

18. For an analysis of what this story means for the politics of television distribution in India, see Nalin Mehta, *Behind a Billion Screens: What Television Tells Us about Modern India* (New Delhi: HarperCollins India, 2015), 128–30.

19. See Arvind Rajagopal. *Politics after Television: Religious Nationalism and the Reshaping of the Indian Public* (Cambridge: Cambridge University Press, 2001); and Purnima Mankekar. *Screening Culture, Viewing Politics: An Ethnography of Television, Womanhood, and Nation in Postcolonial India* (Durham, NC: Duke University Press, 1999).

20. Ravi Sundaram, *Pirate Modernity: Delhi's Media Urbanism* (New York: Routledge, 2009). For a fascinating account of the role of videocassette news magazines, see Ishita Tiwary, "Unsettling News: Newstrack and the Video Event," *Culture Machine* 19 (2020), https://culturemachine.net/vol-19-media-populism/unsettling-news-newstrack-and-the-video-event-ishita-tiwary/.

21. See Paranjoy Guha Thakurta, "What Future for the Media in India? Reliance Takeover of Network18," *Economic and Political Weekly* 49, no. 25 (June 2014): 12–14; Paranjoy Guha Thakurta and Aditi Roy Ghatak, "The Immaculate Conception of Reliance Jio," *Wire*, March 4, 2016, https://thewire.in/tech/the-immaculate-conception-of-reliance-jio.

22. William Mazzarella provides a helpful definition of a medium as what "makes society imaginable and intelligible to itself in the form of external representations." William Mazzarella, "Culture, Globalization, Mediation," *Annual Review of Anthropology* 33, no. 1 (2004): 346.

23. Bernard Stiegler, *Technics and Time, 1: The Fault of Epimetheus*, trans. Richard Beardsworth and George Collins (Stanford, CA: Stanford University Press, 1998), 17.

24. Neil Postman, "The Humanism of Media Ecology," *Proceedings of the Media Ecology Association* 1, no. 1 (2000): 10.

25. See N. Katherine Hayles, *Unthought: The Power of the Cognitive Nonconscious* (Chicago: University of Chicago Press, 2017).

26. John Durham Peters, *The Marvelous Clouds: Toward a Philosophy of Elemental Media* (Chicago: University of Chicago Press, 2015), 3.

27. Benedict, Anderson, *Imagined Communities: Reflections on the Origin and Spread of Nationalism*, 2nd ed. (London: Verso, 1991).

28. Patrick Jagoda. *Network Aesthetics*. (Chicago: University of Chicago Press, 2016).

29. See Peters, *The Marvelous Clouds*, for an approach to media as infrastructure of being.

30. Esser and Strömbäck define mediatization as "a long-term process through which the importance of news media as an institution, and their spill-over effects on political processes and political institutions, has increased." See Frank Esser and Jesper Strömbäck, eds., *Mediatization of Politics: Understanding the Transformation of Western Democracies* (New York: Springer, 2014), 22.

31. See S. Theodore Baskaran, *The Message Bearers: The Nationalist Politics and the Entertainment Media in South India 1880–1845* (Madras: Cre-A, 1981). In anthropology, recent ethnographic scholarship on mediatization demonstrates how "the objects of media attention do not simply exist in the world, but are in important ways made by, for, and through their mediatized circulation, taking shape in relation to media technologies, institutions, and modes of circulation as 'communicable.'" Daniel Fisher, *The Voice and Its Doubles: Media and Music in Northern Australia* (Durham, NC: Duke University Press, 2016), 12. Compare this approach, concerned with a general mediatization of the social environment, to Agha, for whom "a mediatized social process is mediatized in only some of its moments." See Asif Agha, "Meet Mediatization," *Language and Communication* 31, no. 3 (2011): 165.

32. Paula Chakravartty, and Srirupa Roy, "Mediatized Populisms: Inter-Asian Lineages; Introduction," *International Journal of Communication* 11 (2017): 4073–92.

33. See Émile Benveniste, *Problems in General Linguistics* (Miami: University of Miami Press, 1971).

34. Stuart Hall, "Encoding and Decoding in the Television Discourse," stenciled paper presented at the Centre for Contemporary Cultural Studies, University of Birmingham, September 1, 1973, 2.

35. Dayan and Katz, *Media Events*, 5 (emphasis in the original) In a more recent interview Dayan notes "media events may also have functioned as a laboratory, where an updated language was being invented. Thus, many formal characteristics of today's news come from media events." See Johanna Maaria Sumiala, Katja Valaskivi, and Daniel Dayan, "From Media Events to Expressive Events: An Interview with Daniel Dayan," *Television and New Media* 19, no. 2 (2018): 181. This approach can also be compared with McKenzie Wark's strategy, which is closer to mine, that "considers the production of events within the media as the primary process that nevertheless gives the appearance of merely *reflecting* 'naturally occurring' moments outside all such apparatus." McKenzie Wark, *Virtual Geography: Living with Global Media Events* (Bloomington, IN: Indiana University Press, 1994), 14–15.

36. Bernard Stiegler, *Technics and Time, 2: Disorientation*, trans. Stephen Barker (Stanford, CA: Stanford University Press, 2009), 116.

37. For related but different concepts of communicability, see Veena Das, "Specificities: Official Narratives, Rumour, and the Social Production of Hate," *Social Identities* 4, no 1 (1998): 109–30; and Charles L. Briggs, "Communicability, Racial Discourse, and Disease," *Annual Review of Anthropology* 34 (2005): 269–91.

38. Dean, *Democracy*, 23.

39. See Stuart Hall, "The Problem of Ideology-Marxism without Guarantees," *Journal of Communication Inquiry* 10, no. 2 (1986): 28–44.

40. Kajri Jain, *Gods in the Bazaar: The Economies of Indian Calendar Art* (Durham, NC: Duke University Press, 2007). And if print capitalism also enabled the rise of modern social imaginaries premised on a new sense of simultaneity, my account is equally indebted to Jain's approach to time, where "the new does not necessarily make what preexists it old or obsolete, though it can make it anew; emergence can coexist with and morph the persistence and duration of objects and technologies or media as well as of forms of power and sociality." Kajri Jain, "Gods in the Time of Automobility," *Current Anthropology* 58, no. S15 (2017): S13, https://doi.org/10.1086/688696.

41. See Kajri Jain, *Gods in the Time of Democracy* (Durham, NC: Duke University Press, 2021), 18–24.

42. Stiegler, 116.

43. Amahl A. Bishara, "Watching U.S. Television from the Palestinian Street: The Media, the State, and Representational Interventions." *Cultural Anthropology* 23, no. 3 (2008): 489, https://doi.org/10.1111/j.1548-1360.2008.00016.x; see also, Amahl A. Bishara, *Back Stories: US News Production and Palestinian Politics* (Stanford, CA: Stanford University Press, 2012).

44. Bishara, "Watching U.S. Television," 493.

45. See Robert Samet, *Deadline: Populism and the Press in Venezuela* (Chicago: University of Chicago Press, 2019); and Naomi Schiller, *Channeling the State: Community Media and Popular Politics in Venezuela* (Durham, NC: Duke University Press, 2018).

46. Dominic Boyer, *The Life Informatic: Newsmaking in the Digital Era* (Ithaca, NY: Cornell University Press, 2013).

47. Zeynep Devrim Gürsel, *Image Brokers: Visualizing World News in the Age of Digital Circulation* (Oakland: University of California Press, 2016).

48. Zeynep Devrim Gürsel, "Visualizing Publics: Digital Crowd Shots and the 2015 Unity Rally in Paris." *Current Anthropology* 58, no. S15 (2017): S143, https://doi.org/10.1086/689742.

49. This point is made by Luhmann in his study of how media distinguish between self-reference and other-reference. See Niklas Luhmann, *The Reality of the Mass Media* (Stanford, CA: Stanford University Press, 2000).

50. As quoted in former *Guardian* editor Alan Rusbridger's insider account of the struggle to maintain journalistic autonomy under conditions of digitalization. See Alan Rusbridger, *Breaking News: The Remaking of Journalism and Why It Matters Now* (New York: Farrar, Straus and Giroux, 2018).

51. Pratiksha Baxi, "Introduction: Picturing Sociological Scenes—Social Life of Law in India," *Contributions to Indian Sociology* 53, no. 1 (2019): 2.

52. Peter Goodrich, "Imago Decidendi: On the Common law of Images," *Art and Law* 1, no. 1 (2017): 10–11.

53. Apart from Goodrich, "Imago Decidendi," see Cornelia Vismann, "Tele-Tribunals: Anatomy of a Medium," *Grey Room* 10 (2003): 5–21; and Lawrence Liang, "Media's Law: From Representation to Affect," *BioScope: South Asian Screen Studies* 2, no. 1 (2011): 23–40. "The Act of Media" workshop organized by the Sarai program at the Centre for the Study of Developing Societies in Delhi (January 8–10, 2016) pursued this question in depth; https://sarai.net/the-act-of-media-workshop-report-recordings/.

54. See William Mazzarella, *Censorium: Cinema and the Open Edge of Mass Publicity* (Durham, NC: Duke University Press, 2013).

55. See Veena Das, *Critical Events: An Anthropological Perspective on Contemporary India* (New Delhi: Oxford University Press, 1995). Another important line of research on the event in anthropology drawing on the methods of the "Manchester School" is represented in Don Handelman, *Models and Mirrors: Towards an Anthropology of Public Events* (Cambridge: Cambridge University Press, 1990); and Lotte Meinert and Bruce Kapferer, eds., *In the Event: Toward an Anthropology of Generic Moments* (New York: Berghahn Books, 2015).

56. João Biehl, and Peter Locke, "Deleuze and the Anthropology of Becoming," *Current Anthropology* 51, no. 3 (2010): 317, https://doi.org/10.1086/651466. Anand Pandian's work on creativity in Tamil filmmaking is an evocative example of this type of research. See Anand Pandian. *Reel World: An Anthropology of Creation* (Durham, NC: Duke University Press, 2015).

57. Yasmeen Arif, "Event as Method," in *Event and Everyday: Empiricisms and Epistemologies*, ed. Yasmeen Arif (Delhi: Orient Blackswan, 2022).

58. Foucault deploys the concept of "eventalization" to refer to what he calls "a breach of self-evidence." See Michel Foucault, "Questions of Method," in *Power: Essential Works of Foucault, 1954–1984*, vol. 3, ed. James Faubian (New York: New Press, 2000), 223–38.

59. For a systematic overview of this problematic in linguistic anthropology, see Michael Silverstein and Greg Urban, eds. *Natural Histories of Discourse* (Chicago: University of Chicago Press, 1996).

60. Sundaram, "Publicity," S298

61. Understanding of "event-ization" as coproduction activated by reciprocal causalities between the event represented and the event of representation leaves little room for sacralizing the moment of newness or ontologizing "the event," as has been done in philosophy after Alain Badiou and the Pauline turn.

62. Ravi Sundaram, "Introduction: The Horizon of Media Studies." In *No Limits: Media Studies from India*, ed. Ravi Sundaram (New Delhi: Oxford University Press, 2013), 1.

63. Ravish Kumar, "Welcome to Eventocracy, Tracked by Comedia," *Indian Express*, December 31, 2016. For a different analytical perspective on this phenomenon, see also Ravi Sundaram, "Hindu Nationalism's Crisis Machine," *HAU: Journal of Ethnographic Theory* 10, no. 3 (2020): 734–41.

64. Mary Ann Doane, "Information, Crisis, Catastrophe," in *Logics of Television: Essays in Cultural Criticism*, ed. Meaghan Morris (Bloomington: Indiana University Press, 1990), 222.

65. See Francis Cody, "Daily Wires and Daily Blossoms: Cultivating Regimes of Circulation in Tamil India's Newspaper Revolution," *Journal of Linguistic Anthropology* 19, no. 2 (2009): 286–309; and "Echoes of the Teashop in a Tamil Newspaper," *Language and Communication* 31, no. 3 (2011): 243–54.

CHAPTER ONE

1. "Attempt to Intimidate Press? Tamil Channel Booked for Remarks Made by Guest on Show," *News Minute*, June 10, 2018, https://www.thenewsminute.com/article/attempt-intimidate-press-tamil-channel-booked-remarks-made-guest-show-82796.

2. See Michael Warner, "The Mass Public and the Mass Subject," in *Habermas and the Public Sphere*, ed. Craig J. Calhoun (Cambridge, MA: MIT Press, 1992), 377–401; and "Publics and Counterpublics," *Public Culture* 14, no. 1 (2002): 49–90.

3. Herein lies Warner's critique of the forms of domination at the center of Habermas's utopian vision of the public sphere. Habermas is, in fact, cognizant of domination but sees this utopian quality as bourgeois ideology's positive potential: "If ideologies are not only manifestations of the socially necessary consciousness in its essential falsity, if there is an aspect to them that can lay a claim to truth inasmuch as it transcends the status quo in utopian fashion . . . then ideology exists at all only from this period on." Jürgen Habermas, *The Structural Transformation of the Public Sphere: An Inquiry into a Category of Bourgeois Society*, trans. Thomas Burger (Cambridge, MA: MIT Press, 1991), 88.

4. This criticism is overstated insofar as Fraser argues that "participation is not simply a matter of being able to state propositional contents that are neutral with respect to form of expression. Rather . . . participation means being able to speak 'in one's own voice,' thereby simultaneously constructing and expressing one's cultural identity through idiom and style." Nancy Fraser, "Rethinking the Public

Sphere: A Contribution to the Critique of Actually Existing Democracy," *Social Text*, no. 25/26 (1990): 68–69.

5. Warner, "Mass Public," 399.

6. Warner, "Publics and Counterpublics," 78.

7. In his later refinements of public sphere theory, Habermas argues for the importance of the "dispersing effect" of the communicative insofar as it can be uncoupled from class structures in generating popular sovereignty. See Jürgen Habermas, "Popular Sovereignty as Procedure," in *Deliberative Democracy: Essays on Reason and Politics*, ed. James Bohman and William Rehg (Cambridge, MA: MIT Press, 1997), 62.

8. See Francis Cody "Populist Publics: Print Capitalism and Crowd Violence beyond Liberal Frameworks," *Comparative Studies of South Asia, Africa and the Middle East* 35, no. 1 (2015): 50–65; "Publics and Politics," *Annual Review of Anthropology* 40 (2011): 37–52.

9. See Christophe Jaffrelot, *India's Silent Revolution: The Rise of the Lower Castes in North India* (Delhi: Permanent Black, 2003); Yogendra Yadav, "Understanding the Second Democratic Upsurge," in *Transforming India: Social and Political Dynamics of Democracy*, ed. Francine Frankel, R. Z. Hasan, and Rajiv Bhargav (Oxford: Oxford University Press, 2000), 120–45.

10. See Bernard Bate, *Protestant Textuality and the Tamil Modern: Political Oratory and the Social Imaginary in South Asia*. E. Annamalai, Francis Cody, Constantine Nakassis, and Malarvizhi Jayanth, eds. (Stanford, CA: Stanford University Press, 2021).

11. See Partha Chatterjee, *The Politics of the Governed: Reflections on Popular Politics in Most of the World* (New York: Columbia University Press, 2004); *I Am the People: Reflections on Popular Sovereignty Today* (New York: Columbia University Press, 2019). Liberalism here is not the default position of the bourgeoisie as a socioeconomic class in the Marxian sense but was rather the ideological domain most closely associated with an older paternalist and generally upper-caste state elite.

12. Mary Ann Doane, "Information, Crisis, Catastrophe," in *Logics of Television: Essays in Cultural Criticism*, ed. Meaghan Morris (Bloomington: Indiana University Press, 1990): 222–39.

13. Tiziana Terranova, *Network Culture: Cultural Politics for the Information Age* (London: Pluto, 2004), 142.

14. For example, see Tony D. Sampson, *Virality: Contagion Theory in the Age of Networks* (Minneapolis: University of Minnesota Press, 2012).

15. William Mazzarella, *Censorium: Cinema and the Open Edge of Mass Publicity* (Durham, NC: Duke University Press, 2013), 224n5.

16. Bate, *Protestant Textuality*. This period also saw the growth of a thriving Dalit press in Tamil. See J. Balasubramaniam, *Sooriyodhayam Mudhal Udhayasooriyan Varai: Dalit Itazhkal, 1869–1943* (Nagarcoil: Kalachuvadu, 2017).

17. "The Old Lady of Mount Road," *Hindu*, May 28, 2003.

18. See Rangaswami Parthasarathy, *A Hundred Years of* The Hindu: *The Epic Story of Indian Nationalism* (Madras: Kasturi and Sons, 1978); Doraisami Sadasivan, *The*

Growth of Public Opinion in the Madras Presidency, 1858–1909. (Madras: University of Madras, 1974).

19. See R. A. Padmanabhan, *Tamil Itazhkal, 1915–1966* (Nagercoil: Kalachuvadu, 2003), 13–22.

20. On P. Varadarajulu Naidu, see A. R. Venkatakchalapathy, "Munnurai," in *Cenrupōna Nātkal,* ed. A. R. Venkatakchalapathy (Nagercoil: Kalachuvadu, 2015), 11–36.

21. Padmanabhan, *Tamil Itazhkal,* 100–49.

22. See A. M. Sami, *Italālar Ātittanār* (Chennai: International Institute of Tamil Studies, 1990).

23. See Marguerite Ross Barnett, *The Politics of Cultural Nationalism in South India* (Princeton, NJ: Princeton University Press, 1976).

24. For comparison with the Hindi language press, see Paula Chakravartty, and Srirupa Roy, "Media Pluralism Redux: Towards New Frameworks of Comparative Media Studies 'Beyond the West,'" *Political Communication* 30, no. 3 (2013): 349–70; Anup Kumar, *The Making of a Small State: Populist Social Mobilisation and the Hindi Press in the Uttarakhand Movement* (Hyderabad: Orient Blackswan, 2011); Taberez Ahmed Neyazi, *Political Communication and Mobilisation: The Hindi Media in India* (Cambridge: Cambridge University Press, 2018); Sevanti Ninan, *Headlines from the Heartland: Reinventing the Hindi Public Sphere* (Los Angeles: Sage, 2007); Ursula Rao, *News as Culture: Journalistic Practices and the Remaking of Indian Leadership Traditions* (New York: Berghahn Books, 2010); and Per Ståhlberg, *Lucknow Daily: How a Hindi Newspaper Constructs Society* (Stockholm: Stockholm Studies in Social Anthropology, 2002).

25. Robin Jeffrey, *India's Newspaper Revolution: Capitalism, Politics, and the Indian-Language Press, 1977–99* (Oxford: Oxford University Press, 2000); "The Future of News: Back to the Coffeehouse," *Economist,* July 9, 2011, http://www.economist.com/node/18928416.

26. See Francis Cody, "Daily Wires and Daily Blossoms: Cultivating Regimes of Circulation in Tamil India's Newspaper Revolution," *Journal of Linguistic Anthropology* 19, no. 2 (2009): 286–309; and "Echoes of the Teashop in a Tamil Newspaper," *Language and Communication* 31, no. 3 (2011): 243–54.

27. See Partha Chatterjee. *The Nation and Its Fragments: Colonial and Postcolonial Histories* (Princeton, NJ: Princeton University Press, 1993); and Dipesh Chakrabarty, "'In the Name of Politics': Democracy and the Power of the Multitude in India." *Public Culture* 19, no. 1 (2007): 35–57.

28. See Bernard Bate, *Tamil Oratory and the Dravidian Aesthetic: Democratic Practice in South India* (New York: Columbia University Press, 2009); Lisa Mitchell, *Language, Emotion, and Politics in South India: The Making of a Mother Tongue* (Bloomington: Indiana University Press, 2009); Sumathi Ramaswamy, *Passions of the Tongue: Language Devotion in Tamil India, 1891–1970* (Berkeley: University of California Press, 1997); and Narendra Subramanian, *Ethnicity and Populist Mobilization: Political Parties, Citizens, and Democracy in South India* (New Delhi: Oxford University Press, 1999).

29. See Anupama Rao, *The Caste Question: Dalits and the Politics of Modern India* (Berkeley: University of California Press, 2009).

30. See Christophe Jaffrelot, *Modi's India: Hindu Nationalism and the Rise of Ethnic Democracy* (Princeton, NJ: Princeton University Press, 2021); Thomas Blom Hansen, *The Saffron Wave: Democracy and Hindu Nationalism in Modern India* (Princeton, NJ: Princeton University Press, 1999); Thomas Blom Hansen, *Wages of Violence: Naming and Identity in Postcolonial Bombay* (Princeton, NJ: Princeton University Press, 2001); Arvind Rajagopal, *Politics after Television: Religious Nationalism and the Reshaping of the Indian Public* (Cambridge: Cambridge University Press, 2001); Stanley Jeyaraja Tambiah. *Leveling Crowds: Ethnonationalist Conflicts and Collective Violence in South Asia* (Berkeley: University of California Press, 1996).

31. For exemplary work on crowds in anthropology, see Nusrat Sabina Chowdhury, *Paradoxes of the Popular: Crowd Politics in Bangladesh.* (Stanford, CA: Stanford University Press, 2019); William Mazzarella, "The Myth of the Multitude, or, Who's Afraid of the Crowd?.," *Critical Inquiry* 36, no. 4 (2010): 697–727; Megan Steffen, ed. *Crowds: Ethnographic Encounters* (London: Bloomsbury Academic, 2020).

32. See Chowdhury, *Paradoxes of the Popular.*

33. Gabriel Tarde, "The Public and the Crowd," in *Gabriel Tarde on Communication and Social Influence: Selected Papers,* ed. Terry N. Clark, trans. Morris Janowitz (Chicago: University of Chicago Press, 1969), 278.

34. Tarde, 278.

35. Thomas Blom Hansen, "Democracy against the Law: Reflections on India's Illiberal Democracy," in *Majoritarian State: How Hindu Nationalism Is Changing India,* ed. Angana P. Chatterji, Christophe Jaffrelot, and Thomas Blom Hansen (London: Hurst, 2019), 19–40.

36. See Alice Jacob, *Violation of Journalistic Ethics and Public Taste: A Compendium of Adjudications Rendered by the Press Council of India* (Bombay: N. M. Tripathi, 1984).

37. Anupama Katakam, "Targeting Journalists," *Frontline,* September 24, 2004, https://frontline.thehindu.com/static/html/fl2119/stories/20040924003802600.htm.

38. Sarkaria Commission of Inquiry. See compilation by Virendra Kumar, ed. *Committees and Commissions in India,* vol. 14, *1976* (New Delhi: Concept, 1993).

39. Nakkīran Gopal, *Challenge* (Chennai: Nakkheeran, 1998). The later events are detailed in the *Report of the Madras Union of Journalists* submitted to the Press Council of India.

40. See "Three Killed in *Dinakaran* Attack," *Times of India,* May 9, 2007, http://timesofindia.indiatimes.com/india/3-people-killed-in-Dinakaran-attack/articleshow/2023934.cms.

41. "All Acquitted in *Dinakaran* Attack Case," *Hindu,* December 10, 2009.

42. Tambiah, *Leveling Crowds.*

43. *Freedom of the Press/Media—Report for 2008,* compiled by Indian Social Institute, New Delhi.

44. I should note that the staff and reporters at *Dinamalar* are not necessarily Brahmins.

45. See Hugo Gorringe, "'Banal Violence'? The Everyday Underpinnings of Collective Violence," *Identities: Global Studies in Culture and Power* 13, no. 2 (2006): 237–60; *Untouchable Citizens: Dalit Movements and Democratisation in Tamil Nadu* (New Delhi: Sage, 2005).

46. See Amahl A. Bishara, "Watching U.S. Television from the Palestinian Street: The Media, the State, and Representational Interventions." *Cultural Anthropology* 23, no. 3 (2008): 489, https://doi.org/10.1111/j.1548-1360.2008.00016.x

47. This second attack was similar to the 2008 attack on the *Andhra Jyothi* newspaper office by Madiga Reservation Porata Samithi activists eventually leading to an application of the ST and SC Atrocities Act against the editor and two reporters because of their responses to the attack.

48. "AIADMK Activists Attack '*Nakkheeran* Office,'" *Hindu*, January 18, 2012.

49. What has been called a "re-feudalization" of the public sphere in Habermas, *The Structural Transformation*.

50. Habermas. "Popular Sovereignty," 62.

51. Chatterjee, *Politics of the Governed*; *I am the People*.

52. Nivedita Menon, in her introduction to *Empire and Nation*, urges us to read Chatterjee against the grain of his own tendency to assign political society to an empirical group and to treat it instead as a mode of claim making. I write in sympathy with this move. Nivedita Menon, introduction to *Empire and Nation: Selected Essays*, by Partha Chatterjee (New York: Columbia University Press, 2010), 1–22.

53. Ernesto Laclau, *On Populist Reason* (London: Verso, 2005).

54. See Francis Cody, "Wave Theory: Cash, Crowds, and Caste in Indian Elections," *American Ethnologist* 47, no. 4 (2020): 402–16.

55. William Mazzarella, "The Anthropology of Populism: Beyond the Liberal Settlement." *Annual Review of Anthropology* 48, no. 1 (2019), 49.

56. Karen Strassler, *Demanding Images: Democracy, Mediation, and the Image-Event in Indonesia* (Durham, NC: Duke University Press, 2020).

57. Laclau, *On Populist Reason*, 158. Susan Buck-Morss makes a similar observation when she notes that "the logical trick in this argument is that the collective of the 'people' that supposedly constitutes the democratic sovereignty does not exist until that sovereignty is constituted." Susan Buck-Morss, *Dreamworld and Catastrophe: The Passing of Mass Utopia in East and West* (Cambridge, MA: MIT Press, 2002), 9.

58. Quoted in Hugo Gorringe, "Party Political Panthers: Hegemonic Tamil Politics and the Dalit Challenge." *South Asia Multidisciplinary Academic Journal* 5 (2011), https://doi.org/10.4000/samaj.3224.

59. Judith Butler, *Notes toward a Performative Theory of Assembly* (Cambridge, MA: Harvard University Press, 2015).

60. Arvind Rajagopal, "Putting America in Its Place," *Public Culture* 25, no. 3 (2013): 390.

61. Important works in South India include not only the *Thirukkural*, especially verses on *araciyal* (politics, or the nature of rule) and the *Purunanuru* on king-

ship, both in Tamil, but also the late medieval and early modern *needhi* texts in Telugu analyzed in Velcheru Narayana Rao and Sanjay Subrahmanyam, "Notes on Political Thought in Medieval and Early Modern South India," *Modern Asian Studies* 43, no 1 (2009): 175–210. All of these would be in some respects incommensurable with liberal, left, and republican theory but were brought into contact with such theories early in the twentieth century by intellectuals of the anticolonial, anticaste, and Dravidian movements.

62. On technology, see Yuk Hui, *The Question Concerning Technology in China: An Essay in Cosmotechnics* (Cambridge, MA. MIT Press, 2016); on the political, see Prathama Banerjee, *Elementary Aspects of the Political: Histories from the Global South* (Durham, NC: Duke University Press, 2020).

CHAPTER TWO

1. For good arguments see Aparna Vishwanathan, "Seven Reasons Why Criminal Defamation Should Be Declared Unconstitutional," *Wire*, https://thewire.in/law/seven-reasons-why-criminal-defamation-should-be-declared-unconstitutional, and "Time to Abolish Criminal Defamation," *Hindu*, December 2, 2015.

2. Arvind Rajagopal, *Politics after Television: Religious Nationalism and the Reshaping of the Indian Public* (Cambridge: Cambridge University Press, 2001).

3. "Avalam!," *Dinamalar*, June 30, 2014.

4. "'Dinamalar' nalitazhukku ethiraaha tamizhaha mudalvar manu," *Dinamalar*, July 2, 2014.

5. William Mazzarella and Raminder Kaur, "Between Sedition and Seduction: Thinking Censorship in South Asia." In *Censorship in South Asia: Cultural Regulation from Sedition to Seduction*, ed. Raminder Kaur and William Mazzarella (Bloomington: Indiana University Press, 2009) 21.

6. Mitra Sharafi. *Law and Identity in Colonial South Asia: Parsi Legal Culture, 1772–1947* (Cambridge: Cambridge University Press, 2014), 278; Katheryn Temple, *Scandal Nation: Law and Authorship in Britain, 1750–1835* (Ithaca, NY: Cornell University Press, 2003), 198–99.

7. For an astute analysis of how public portrayal of the case began to bear on legal reasoning, see J. Barton Scott, "How to Defame a God: Public Selfhood in the Maharaj Libel Case." *South Asia: Journal of South Asian Studies* 38, no. 3 (2015): 387–402.

8. Rajeev Dhavan, "On the Law of the Press in India." *Journal of the Indian Law Institute* 26, no. 3 (1984): 295. Mazzarella and Kaur have written about the dynamic of courting publicity that challenges norms of civility and decorum in terms of the what they call the lure of "profitable provocation." Mazzarella and Kaur, "Between Sedition and Seduction," 3.

9. For an elaboration of this argument about secrets and publicity in late capitalism, see Jodi Dean, *Publicity's Secret: How Technoculture Capitalizes on Democracy* (Ithaca, NY: Cornell University Press, 2002).

10. M. Madhava Prasad, *Cine-Politics: Film Stars and Political Existence in South India* (New Delhi: Orient Blackswan, 2014).

11. Gautam Bhatia, *Offend, Shock, or Disturb: Free Speech under the Indian Constitution* (New Delhi: Oxford University Press, 2016); Lawrence Liang, "Reasonable Restrictions and Unreasonable Speech," in *Sarai Reader 4: Crisis/Media*, ed. Monica Narula, Shuddhabrata Sengupta, Ravi Sundaram, Ravi S. Vasudevan, Awadhanedra Sharan, Jeebesh Bagchi, and Geert Lovink (New Delhi: Autonomedia, 2004), 434–40.

12. See Anushka Singh, *Sedition in Liberal Democracies* (New Delhi: Oxford University Press, 2018), 203. The other perceived threat to national integrity was from Sikh activists demanding a Khalistan state.

13. Prabhu Chawla, "Tamil Nadu: Subtle Suppression," *India Today*, September 30, 1982. Like Kamaraj's law, MGR's amended section 292-A of the IPC, regarding publication and circulation of obscene material, adding the concept of "scurrilous" writing and effectively blending it with defamation.

14. This is in addition to a large number of criminal defamation cases, using section 499, that had already piled up against Veerasamy for his persistent accusations of corruption. See S. H. Venkatramani, "Shying Away," *India Today*, August 31, 1985.

15. Prabhu Chawla, "Nation Wide Protests against Anti Press Laws Has Delayed Impact on Tamil Nadu," *India Today*, October 18, 1988.

16. For a fuller discussion of political repression under MGR, see M. S. S. Pandian, *The Image Trap: M. G. Ramachandran in Film and Politics* (New Delhi: Sage, 1992).

17. S. H. Venkatramani, "M.G. Ramachandran's Kidney Ailment Remained a Well-Kept Secret," *India Today*, November 15, 1984.

18. The article was given the provocative title, "Tamil Nadu Gives Its Drivers a License to Kill," *Times of India*, August 25, 2012.

19. "Why So Many Criminal Defamation Cases from Tamil Nadu?," *Hindu*, November 30, 2015.

20. "Rising Intolerance," *Hindu*, April 25, 2003.

21. "A Crude and Unconstitutional Misadventure," *Hindu*, November 8, 2003.

22. It is a different matter that the *Hindu*, unlike *Murasoli*, slipped back into a relatively amicable relationship with the chief minister when she returned to power in 2011, although this does speak to the different temporalities at play in the relationship between spectacular breaches and everyday threats.

23. "A Crude and Unconstitutional Misadventure," *Hindu*, November 8, 2003.

24. See Sianne Ngai, *Ugly Feelings* (Cambridge, MA: Harvard University Press, 2005).

25. For an especially nuanced analysis of the gendered dangers of publicity in the Tamil film industry, see Amanda Weidman, *Brought to Life by the Voice: Playback Singing and Cultural Politics in South India* (Oakland: University of California Press, 2021).

26. Also detailed his books *Challenge* (Chennai: Nakkheeran, 1998); and *Yuththam* (Chennai: Nakkheeran, 2011).

27. Nirupama Subramanian, "Ex-convict Auto Shankar's Autobiography Takes Madras by storm," *India Today*, November 30, 1994.

28. R. Rajagopal v. State of Tamil Nadu (1994) 6 SCC 632.

29. R. Rajagopal v. J. Jayalalitha, AIR 2006 Mad 312.

30. See also "I have 211 cases against me'—Nakkeeran Gopal on His Battle with Criminal Defamation," *News Minute*, May 20, 2015, http://www.thenewsminute .com/article/i-have-211-cases-against-me-nakkeeran-gopal-his-battle-criminal -defamation.

31. R. Rajagopal v. J. Jayalalitha, AIR 2006 Mad 312.

32. "Maattukari Saappidum Maami Naan," *Nakkeeran*, January 7, 2012.

33. "Dialysis Garden Report," *Nakkeeran*, July 15, 2015, cited in petition filed by City Public Prosecutor, Chennai, against R. R. Gopal and A. Kamaraj.

34. Georges Bataille, *The Tears of Eros* (San Francisco, CA: City Lights Press, 1989), 67.

35. Claude Lefort, "The Image of the Body and Totalitarianism," in *The Political Forms of Modern Society: Bureaucracy, Democracy, Totalitarianism* (Cambridge, MA: MIT Press, 1986), 292–306.

36. Prasad, *Cine-Politics*; Rajan Krishnan, "When Kathavarayan Spoke His Mind: The Intricate Dynamics of the Formations of the Political through Film-Making Practices in Tamil Nadu," in *New Cultural Histories of India: Materiality and Practices*, ed. Partha Chatterjee, Tapati Guha-Thakurta, and Bodhisattva Kar (Delhi: Oxford University Press, 2014); Rajan Krishnan, "Rajini's Sivaji: Screen and Sovereign," *Economic and Political Weekly* 42, no. 27/28 (July 14–20, 2008): 2861–63; S. V. Srinivas, *Politics as Performance: A Social History of the Telugu Cinema* (Ranikhet: Permanent Black, 2013).

37. This formulation borrows from the theorization of brand in Constantine V. Nakassis, "Brands and Their Surfeits," *Cultural Anthropology* 28, no. 1 (2013): 111–12.

38. The is also the well-known study of lower criminal courts in the US: Malcolm M. Feeley, *The Process Is the Punishment: Handling Cases in a Lower Criminal Court* (New York: Russell Sage Foundation, 1979).

39. For example, an editor at *Dinamalar* was arrested and jailed under section 4 of the Tamil Nadu Women Harassment (prevention) Act for an allegedly defamatory article exposing a prostitution ring in the cinema industry. Similarly, the political folk singer Kovan was recently jailed for alleged sedition in response to a song parody about the chief minister that circulated widely on social media.

40. Bernard Bate, *Tamil Oratory and the Dravidian Aesthetic: Democratic Practice in South India* (New York: Columbia University Press, 2009).

41. Some exceptions can be found. Cyrus Broacha, anchor of the television spoof show *The Week That Wasn't*, was charged for making fun of Jayalalithaa, and a case of defamation was charged against the cinema star turned politician Kamal Haasan, who was accused of defaming the posthumous image of Jayalalithaa on his reality TV show, *Bigg Boss*, season 2.

CHAPTER THREE

1. *Murugan vs. Tamil Nadu*, 2015 (WP nos. 1215 and 20375), bundled a number of criminal claims against the author, who was defended by his publisher, Kalachuvadu,

the People's Union for Civil Liberties (PUCL), and the Tamil Nadu Progressive Writers and Artists Association (Tamilnādu Murppōkku Eluttālar Sangam).

2. My argument owes much to conversations with Lawrence Liang, whose work on the intersections of law and film remain a cornerstone of this approach. See Lawrence Liang, "Media's Law: From Representation to Affect," *BioScope: South Asian Screen Studies* 2, no. 1 (2011): 23–40.

3. Peter Goodrich, "Imago Decidendi: On the Common law of Images," *Art and Law* 1, no. 1 (2017): 3.

4. Justice Kaul had, in fact, already contributed to the latter discourse as a judge in Bombay in a well-known judgement where he defended the great modernist M. F. Hussein against threats from Hindu fundamentalists who objected to his paintings of goddesses. Several writers sympathetic to Murugan raised worries about the degree to which the rhetoric of the judgement in his case rested on the chief justice's own cultivated capacity to discern the merit of a piece of literature.

5. Pierre Bourdieu, "The Force of Law: Toward a Sociology of the Juridical Field," *Hastings Law Journal* 38 (1987): 820.

6. Veena Das, *Critical Events: An Anthropological Perspective on Contemporary India* (New Delhi: Oxford University Press, 1995), 109.

7. Robert M. Cover, "Foreword: Nomos and Narrative," *Harvard Law Review* 97, no. 4 (1983):4–68; Upendra Baxi, "Judicial Discourse: Dialectics of the Face and the Mask," *Journal of the Indian Law Institute* 35, no. 1/2 (1993): 1–12.

8. Kalyani Ramnath, "The Runaway Judgment: Law as Literature, Courtcraft and Constitutional Visions," *Journal of Indian Law and Society* 3 (2011): 3.

9. Bourdieu, "The Force of Law," 830.

10. Rajeev Dhavan, *Publish and Be Damned: Censorship and Intolerance in India* (New Delhi: Tulika Books, 2008), 78.

11. Jacques Derrida, "Force de loi: Le fondement mystique de l'autorité," *Cardozo Law Review* 11, no. 5/6 (1990): 920–1046.

12. R. Muthukrishnan vs R. Mallika, April 29, 2016, Rev. Appln. No.219 of 2015 in CMA.No.3235 of 2014.

13. "Justice N Kirubakaran: The Newsmaker Judge," *India Legal*, May 14, 2022, https://www.indialegallive.com/cover-story-articles/focus/justice-n-kirubakaran-the-newsmaker-judge-of-madras-high-court/.

14. S. Ramanathan, "Crime, Corruption and Chaos, Tamil Nadu's judicial badlands: Part 1—Lawyers vs Judges," *News Minute*, November 2, 2015, https://www.thenewsminute.com/article/crime-corruption-and-chaos-tamil-nadus-judicial-badlands-part-1-lawyers-vs-judges-35634.

15. Baxi, "Judicial Discourse."

16. Scholars such as Pratiksha Baxi as well as Ponni Arasu and Priya Thangarajah have demonstrated how the protection of habeas has been used to track down women in marriages of choice and queer relationships. This extensive use of habeas to detain is now increasingly questioned by the court. Pratiksha Baxi, "Habeas Corpus in the Realm of Love: Litigating Marriages of Choice in India,"

Australian Feminist Law Journal 25, no. 1 (2006): 59–78; Ponni Arasu and Priya Thangarajah, "Queer Women and Habeas Corpus in India: The Love that Blinds the Law," *Indian Journal of Gender Studies* 19, no. 3 (2012): 413–35. While most news reports claimed that Pavithra's husband had also filed a complaint against Shameel with the Vellore police, later human rights investigations show that he had, in fact, first suspected someone else of kidnapping her and that Shameel had voluntarily turned himself in for questioning.

17. Giorgio Agamben, *Homo sacer: Sovereign Power and Bare Life* (Stanford, CA: Stanford University Press, 1998), 125, emphasis in original.

18. The fact that Pavithra worked in a leather factory would have made many assume that she was Dalit regardless of whether they verified her community background.

19. Thanthi TV, *Ambur Kalavaram Uruvana Kathai* (Story of the origins of the Ambur riots). See also Human Rights Advocacy and Research Foundation, "Fact Finding: Death of Shameel Basha; Fact Finding Investigation into the Death of Shameel Basha due to Illegal Detention and Torture by Pallikonda Police Station Officials, Vellore District on 26th June 2015," July 1, 2015, http://hrf.net.in/fact -finding-investigation-into-the-death-of-shameel-basha-due-to-illegal-detention -and-torture-by-pallikonda-police/.

20. My rendering is based on a verbatim transcript reported in many papers but most fully in *Dinamalar*'s article from July 5, 2015, "Ambur Kalavaratukku Karanamana Pavithra Chennaiyil Thangi Irukka Uttaravu" (Pavithra, the cause of the Ambur Riots ordered to stay in Chennai).

21. Wendy Brown, *States of Injury: Power and Freedom in Late Modernity* (Princeton, NJ: Princeton University Press, 1995), 178.

22. Carole Pateman, *The Sexual Contract* (London: Polity, 1988).

23. Pratiksha Baxi, *Public Secrets of Law: Rape Trials in India* (New Delhi: Oxford University Press, 2014), 42.

24. When I later confronted Subramani about his headline in the *Times of India*, he admitted that the headline itself was misleading insofar as it followed the narra- tive line of making Pavithra the cause of the Ambur riots, but he defended the rest of his article and the fact that the judge's words about divorce were in the main text and did not serve as a headline as it did in other papers.

25. Veena Das and Deborah Poole, "State and Its Margins: Comparative Ethnogra- phies," in *Anthropology in the Margins of the State*, ed. Veena Das and Deborah Poole (Santa Fe, NM: School of Advanced Research, 2004), 17.

26. Justin B. Richland, "Jurisdiction: Grounding Law in Language," *Annual Review of Anthropology* 42 (2013): 214.

27. Erving Goffman, "Footing," *Semiotica* 25 no. 1/2 (1979): 1–30.

28. "Kathambam: Vivakarattukku Enge Kidaikkum?," *Thi Inthu*, July 24, 2015.

29. Dhananjay Mahapatra, "C S Karnan Moves Supreme Court for Recall of 'Illegal' Jail Order," *Times of India*, May 12, 2017, https://timesofindia.indiatimes.com /india/c-s-karnan-moves-supreme-court-for-recall-of-illegal-jail-order/article show/58635854.cms.

30. Quoted in Supreme Court of India Suo Moto Contempt Petition no. 1 of 2017, against Hon'ble Shree Justice C. S. Karanan.

31. Smita Chakraburtty, "The Curious Case of Justice Karnan," *Economic and Political Weekly* 52, no. 18 (May 2017).

32. Quoted on page 17 of the contempt petition, https://judicialreforms.org/justice -karnan-contempt-detailed-judgement/.

33. Kaleeswaram Raj, "Justice Karnan: A Strange Case," *The Week*, May 7, 2017. Like the mythical son of Surya, after whom he is named, Justice Karnan "'burns from the karma' of his harsh words," despite being recognized as "a good man." Alf Hiltebeitel, *Dharma: Its Early History in Law, Religion, and Narrative* (Oxford: Oxford University Press, 2011), 458.

34. Suraj Yengde, *Caste Matters* (New Delhi: Viking Press, 2019).

35. See Lauren Berlant, *Cruel Optimism* (Durham, NC: Duke University Press, 2011).

36. Begoña Aretxaga, "Maddening States," *Annual Review of Anthropology* 32 (2003): 405.

37. Webb Keane, *Signs of Recognition: Powers and Hazards of Representation in an Indonesian Society* (Berkeley: University of California Press, 1997).

38. Veena Das, *Life and Words: Violence and the Descent into the Ordinary* (Berkeley: University of California Press, 2007), 178.

CHAPTER FOUR

1. See Eric J. Hobsbawm, *Primitive Rebels: Studies in Archaic Forms of Social Movement in the 19th and 20th Centuries* (Manchester: Manchester University Press, 1959).

2. Dharmeratnam Sivaram (Taraki)'s eleven-part essay on "Tamil Militarism," originally published in the *Lanka Guardian*, sought to provide a history of this figuration of Tamil ethnicity, https://tamilnation.org/forum/sivaram/920501lg .htm.

3. M. S. S. Pandian, "The Moral World of 'Sandalwood' Veerappan," *Economic and Political Weekly* 34, no. 52 (December 25–31, 1999): 3660.

4. Thinking over the longer term, we can surmise that the attraction of fame through news coverage must have been powerful for the classic "public enemies" of the 1930s, like Bonnie and Clyde, just as it was for the fictional characters in Oliver Stone's film, *Natural Born Killers* (1994).

5. This was a nontechnologized world that was often ventriloquized in the print of official news organs in special columns devoted to representing "talk on the street," like *Dinamalar*'s Teas Shop Bench, or *Junior Vikatan*'s Mr. Eagle. See Francis Cody, "Echoes of the Teashop in a Tamil Newspaper," *Language and Communication* 31, no. 3 (2011): 243–54.

6. See, for example, Shahid Amin's classic study of rumors surrounding Gandhi's powers as they circulated across oral and print forms, or my earlier work on "regimes of circulation" among newspaper readers at the teashop bench in Tamil Nadu. Shahid Amin, "Gandhi as Mahatma: Gorakhpur District, Eastern UP, 1921–2," in *Selected Subaltern Studies*, ed. Edward Said and Gayatri Chakraborty Spivak (New York: Oxford University Press, 1987); Francis Cody, "Daily Wires

and Daily Blossoms: Cultivating Regimes of Circulation in Tamil India's Newspaper Revolution," *Journal of Linguistic Anthropology* 19, no. 2 (2009): 286–309.

7. Ravi Sundaram, *Pirate Modernity: Delhi's Media Urbanism* (New York: Routledge, 2009).

8. Ravi Sundaram, "Hindu Nationalism's Crisis Machine," *HAU: Journal of Ethnographic Theory* 10, no. 3 (2020): 736.

9. For a fascinating conceptualization of "heresay publics" as a critique of liberal publicity from within, see Rihan Yeh, *Passing: Two Publics in a Mexican Border City* (Chicago: University of Chicago Press, 2018).

10. Ranajit Guha, *Elementary Aspects of Peasant Insurgency* (New Delhi: Oxford University Press, 1983), 260.

11. Veena Das, *Life and Words: Violence and the Descent into the Ordinary* (Berkeley: University of California Press, 2007), 108.

12. For an account of the legend of Kattabomman that examines how this "local" hero became a nationalist figure across media forms, see Sumathi Ramaswamy, "The Nation, the Region, and the Adventures of a Tamil Hero," *Contributions to Indian Sociology* 28, no. 2 (1994): 295–322.

13. See Alice E. Marwick, "Instafame: Luxury Selfies in the Attention Economy," *Public Culture* 27, no. 1 (2015): 137–60.

14. Kajri Jain, "Gods in the Time of Automobility," *Current Anthropology* 58, no. S15 (2017): S13.

15. The police officer who was credited with having caught Veerappan describes this rumor and others in his book, Vijay Kumar, *Veerappan: Chasing the Brigand* (New Delhi: Rupa, 2017).

16. Eventually published as a book, Auto Shankar, *Auto Shankarin Marana Vākkumūlam* (Chennai: Nakheeran, 2002).

17. Shiva Subramanian and Raj Chengappa, "If I Was a Bad Man God Will Strike Me Down with a Bolt of Lightning: Veerappan," *India Today*, May 15, 1993, https://www.indiatoday.in/magazine/special-report/story/19930515-if-i-was-a-bad-man-god-will-strike-me-down-with-a-bolt-of-lightning-veerappan-811061-1993-05-15.

18. https://m.madhyamam.com/en/features/2017/feb/6/veerappan-had-strange-sixth-sense-did-amazing-u-turns (accessed July 8, 2019, no longer posted).

19. See Hobsbawm, *Primitive Rebels*.

20. See David Shulman, "On South Indian Bandits and Kings," *Indian Economic and Social History Review* 17, no. 3 (1980): 283–306.

21. Pandian, "Moral World," 3660.

22. Abraham Verghese, "The Bandit King," *Atlantic*, February 1, 2001.

23. This episode is also recounted in Gopal's book about his relationship with Veerappan. Nakkīran Gopal, *Nānum Vīrappanum!* (Chennai: Nakkheeran, 2004), 14–16.

24. When another round of kidnappings took place shortly after, this time involving naturalists in the Bandipur Tiger Reserve, Gopal did not play the role of negotiator, perhaps to allay growing mistrust. See the firsthand account in Krubakar

Senani and S. R. Ramakrishna, *Birds, Beasts and Bandits: 14 Days with Veerappan* (New Delhi: Penguin Books, 2011).

25. On these uncanny resonances across time, see M. Madhava Prasad, "Where Does the Forest Begin?," *Economic and Political Weekly* 35. No. 47 (November 18, 2000): 4138.

26. H. S. Balram, "Rumour Mill Brings Veerappan Back into Focus," *Times of India*, February 3, 2002, https://timesofindia.indiatimes.com/city/bengaluru/Rumour-mills-bring-back-Veerappan-into-focus/articleshow/134141236.cms.

27. Shulman, "On South Indian Bandits and Kings," 305.

28. See William Mazzarella, "Beautiful Balloon: The Digital Divide and the Charisma of New Media in India," *American Ethnologist* 37, no. 4 (2010): 783–804; and Assa Doron and Robin Jeffrey, *The Great Indian Phone Book* (Cambridge, MA: Harvard University Press, 2013).

29. For an important ethnography of social media and cell phone use in Tamil Nadu, see Shriram Venkatraman, *Social Media in South India* (London: University College London Press, 2017).

30. T. R. Pachamuthu, the owner of *Puthiya Thamailmurai*, does have a small political party that relatively few people are aware of called the India Jananayaka Katchi (IJK).

31. Puthiya Thalaimurai had achieved a TAM (Television Audience Measurement) Media Research rating of 29.15, and its closest competitor, Sun News, had 16.39. See N. S. Ramnath, "New Competition for Tamil Nadu TV Channels," *Forbes India*, June 5, 2012.

32. See Francis Cody, "Metamorphoses of Popular Sovereignty: Cinema, Short Circuits, and Digitalization in Tamil India," *Anthropological Quarterly* 93, no. 2 (Spring 2020): 57–88; "Millennial Turbulence: The Networking of Tamil Media Politics" *Television and New Media* 21, no. 4 (2020): 392–406.

33. Compare, for example, Rodrigo Ochigame and James Holston. "Filtering Dissent: Social Media and Land Struggles in Brazil," *New Left Review* 99 (2016):85–108.

34. danah boyd, "Social Network Sites as Networked Publics: Affordances, Dynamics, and Implications," in *Networked Self: Identity, Community, and Culture on Social Network Sites*, ed. Zizi Papacharissi (New York: Routledge, 2010): 39–58.

35. Pierre Nora, "Monster Events," *Discourse* 5, no. 1 (1983): 5–20.

36. Violence against Dalits has always been prevalent in Tamil Nadu, but has taken on new forms of publicity in recent years, especially through spectacular murders. On public hate and digitalization more generally, see Sahana Udupa, Iginio Gagliardone and Peter Hervik, eds., *Digital Hate: The Global Conjuncture of Extreme Speech* (Bloomington: Indiana University Press, 2021).

37. India had already seen the atrocious power of WhatsApp-enabled communal rumor mongering in Muzaffarnagar, Uttar Pradesh, in 2013, where the circulation of images of dead bodies was used to foment an anti-Muslim riot.

38. This narrative draws on my discussions with freelance journalist Kavitha Muralidharan, who has researched this case extensively. See also Perundevi Srinivasan, "Love Meets Death: 'Honor,' Violence, and Inter-Caste Marriages in Tamil Nadu," Chicago Tamil Forum: Poesis/Politics of Language and Place in Tamilagam, Chi-

cago, May 25–27, 2017, version 6.1.2017; and Sandhya Ravishankar, "Love, Caste and Fury in Tamil Nadu: How a Small-Time Crook Came to Symbolise Gounder Pride," *Scroll.in*, October 28, 2015, https://scroll.in/article/762879/love-caste -and-fury-in-tamil-nadu-how-a-small-time-crook-came-to-symbolise-gounder -pride.

39. I have learned much about the more general culture of vigilante surveillance of intercaste relationships from conversations with Stalin Rajangam and a fact-finding report by Intellectual Circle for Dalit Actions (ICDA). See also S. Ramanathan, "Caste-Gestapo in TN Cracking Down on Dalit Boys Falling in Love with Caste-Hindu Girls?," *News Minute*, July 6, 2015, https://www.the newsminute.com/article/caste-gestapo-tn-cracking-down-dalit-boys-falling -love-caste-hindu-girls-31893.

40. See Dhanya Rajendran, "OBC Leader Says Murder of Dalit Boy Is Not a Big Deal," *Quint*, July 14, 2015, https://www.thequint.com/news/india/obc-leader -says-murder-of-dalit-boy-is-not-a-big-deal.

41. Das, *Life and Words*, 108–34.

42. Udupa, Gagliardoen, and Hervik, *Digital Hate*.

43. See "The Star-Anchors Driving Tamil TV News Uprising," *News Minute*, June 13, 2015, https://www.thenewsminute.com/article/star-anchors-driving-tamil-tv -news-uprising.

44. Arun Janardhanan, "Gokulraj Murder Case Prime Accused Yuvaraj Surrenders," *Indian Express*, October 12, 2015, http://indianexpress.com/article/india/india -news-india/gokulraj-murder-case-prime-accused-yuvaraj-surrenders/.

45. See Sahana Udupa, "*Gaali* Cultures: The Politics of Abusive Exchange on Social Media," *New Media and Society* 8, no. 2 (2017): 187–206; "Internet Hindus: New India's Ideological Warriors." In *Handbook on Religion in Asian Cities*, ed. by Peter van der Veer. (Berkeley: University of California Press, 2015), 432–49.

46. Yuvaraj's mode of political entrepreneurship resembles that of *gau rakshaks* (cow protectors) in North India, who film and project themselves attacking Muslims or Dalits whom they suspect of eating beef in an attempt to become well known within Hindutva political circles. See Aman Sethi, "How to Become a Gau Rak- shak Celebrity," *Quint*, August 8, 2016, https://www.thequint.com/news/politics /how-to-become-a-gaurakshak-celebrity-narendra-modi-una-dalit-muslim-uttar -pradesh-muzaffarnagar.

47. See Judith Butler, *Excitable Speech: A Politics of the Performative* (New York: Routledge, 1997), 43.

CHAPTER FIVE

1. Michael Warner, "Publics and Counterpublics," *Public Culture* 14, no. 1 (2002): 68.

2. Michael Hardt and Antonio Negri, *Assembly* (New York: Oxford University Press, 2017), xiv.

3. Jeffrey S. Juris, "The New Digital Media and Activist Networking within Anti Corporate Globalization Movements," *Annals of the American Academy of Political and Social Science* 59, no. 1 (2005): 193.

4. Bernard Stiegler, "Telecracy against Democracy," *Cultural Politics* 6, no. 2 (2010): 172.

5. Rosalind C. Morris, "Theses on the new Öffentlichkeit," *Grey Room* 51 (2013): 110.

6. Rosalind C. Morris, "Populist Politics in Asian Networks: Positions for Rethinking the Question of Political Subjectivity," *Positions: East Asia Cultures Critique* 20, no. 1 (2012):52. These analyses are echoed by Vicente Rafael, who writes of "telecommunicative fantasies," and Jodi Dean, who warns of the "technological fetishism" of digital publics. Vicente L. Rafael, "The Cell Phone and the Crowd: Messianic Politics in the Contemporary Philippines," *Public Culture* 15, no. 3 (2003): 399–425; Jodi Dean, *Democracy and Other Neoliberal Fantasies: Communicative Capitalism and Left Politics* (Durham, NC: Duke University Press, 2009).

7. Morris, "Theses," 98. On the question of voice, speaking, and public politics, compare with Laura Kunreuther, *Voicing Subjects: Public Intimacy and Mediation in Kathmandu* (Berkeley: University of California Press, 2014).

8. See Ilana Gershon, "Language and the Newness of Media," *Annual Review of Anthropology* 46 (2017): 15–31; and Lisa Gitelman, *Always Already New: Media, History, and the Data of Culture* (Cambridge, MA: MIT Press, 2008).

9. The term *sousveillance* is attributed in the literature to Steven Mann and has been elaborated by Simone Browne as an important strategy in American and Canadian Black struggles against racist surveillance. See Simone Browne, *Dark Matters: On the Surveillance of Blackness* (Durham, NC: Duke University Press, 2015).

10. Eyal Weisman, *Forensic Architecture: Violence at the Threshold of Detectability* (New York: Zone Books, 2017), 11. Ravi Sundaram's work on the technological sensorium and the drive to transparency speaks to the divergent temporalities of legal evidence and popular exposure in "sting journalism," which could be said to have anticipated this moment of mass forensics. My thinking on circuits also owes much to his formulations of this problem.

11. Nusrat Sabina Chowdhury, *Paradoxes of the Popular: Crowd Politics in Bangladesh.* (Stanford, CA: Stanford University Press, 2019).

12. Mythili Sivaraman, *Haunted by Fire: Essays on Caste, Class, Exploitation, and Emancipation* (New Delhi: LeftWord Books, 2013).

13. See Raminder Kaur, *Kudankulam: The Story of an Indo-Russian Nuclear Power Plant* (Oxford: Oxford University Press, 2020); and Minnie Vaid, *The Ant in the Ear of an Elephant.* New Delhi: Rajpal and Sons, 2016).

14. For an interesting analysis of the political life of this petition in the UK, see Raminder Kaur, "The Digitalia of Everyday Life: Multi-situated Anthropology of a Virtual Letter by a 'Foreign Hand,'" *HAU: Journal of Ethnographic Theory* 9, no. 2 (2019): 299–319.

15. Ranajit Guha, *Elementary Aspects of Peasant Insurgency* (New Delhi: Oxford University Press, 1983).

16. S. Vijay Kumar, "TN Records Most Number of Protests," *Hindu*, March 27, 2017, https://www.thehindu.com/news/national/tamil-nadu/tn-records-most-number-of-protests/article17671084.ece.

17. For the best collection of analyses of the jallikattu protests, many of them concerned precisely with the question of where they fit in relation to the Dravidian-

nationalist movement if not as much with the questions of media and mediation that are the main concerns of this chapter, see S. S. Sivasankar, *Jallikattu Pōrāttam* (Chennai: Kizhakku Pathippaham, 2017).

18. Kavitha Muralidharan, "Inside the Macho, Divisive World of Tamil Nadu's Bull Taming Sport Jallikattu," *Hindustan Times*, January 13, 2017.

19. Compare with Jessica Winegar, "The Privilege of Revolution: Gender, Class, Space, and Affect in Egypt," *American Ethnologist* 39, no. 1 (2012): 67–70.

20. For an account of the protests that focuses a great deal on this aspect of spontaneous provisioning, see Swapna Sundar, *Occupy Marina!* (Chennai: Emerald, 2017).

21. For an insightful critique of Hardt and Negri that analyzes the practice of separating "good" crowds from "bad" in many strands of thought that appear otherwise unconnected, see William Mazzarella, "The Myth of the Multitude, or, Who's Afraid of the Crowd?" *Critical Inquiry* 36, no. 4 (2010): 697–727.

22. For important accounts of these events and the broader media environments in which the ethos of leaderless emergence can thrive, see Maple Razsa and Andrej Kurnik, "The Occupy Movement in Žižek's hometown: Direct Democracy and a Politics of Becoming," *American Ethnologist* 39, no. 2 (2012): 238–58; and Zeynep Tufekci, *Twitter and Teargas: The Power and Fragility of Networked Protest* (New Haven, CT: Yale University Press, 2017).

23. Rafael, "Cellphone and the Crowd," 399.

24. Kabir Tambar, "Secular Populism and the Semiotics of the Crowd in Turkey," *Public Culture* 21, no. 3 (2009): 532.

25. See Yarimar Bonilla and Jonathan Rosa, "#Ferguson: Digital Protest, Hashtag Ethnography, and the Racial Politics of Social Media in the United States," *American Ethnologist* 42, no. 1 (2015): 4–17.

26. Ernesto Laclau, *On Populist Reason* (London: Verso, 2005).

27. As reported in R. Ramasubramanian, "Jallikattu Protestors Battle Tamil Nadu Police, But for Many, Modi, Centre Are Main Target," *Wire*, January, 23, 2017, https://thewire.in/101989/suppression-of-anti-modi-sentiments-at-marina-beach-undermines-media-credibility/.

28. See Jay David Bolter and Richard Grusin, *Remediation: Understanding New Media* (Cambridge, MA: MIT Press, 2000).

29. Puthiya Thalaimurai's YouTube channel had over eight million subscribers at the time of writing.

30. I borrow these words from an analysis of early twentieth-century populism and media in the United States: Richard Bauman, "Projecting Presence: Aura and Oratory in William Jennings Bryan's Presidential Races," in *Scale: Discourse and Dimensions of Social Life*, ed. Somerson Carr and Michael Lempert (Berkeley: University of California Press, 2016), 25.

31. Amahl A. Bishara, "Watching U.S. Television from the Palestinian Street: The Media, the State, and Representational Interventions." *Cultural Anthropology* 23, no. 3 (2008): 488–530, https://doi.org/10.1111/j.1548-1360.2008.00016.x.

32. Activists I have interviewed were not aware of the book *We the Media* on the loss of corporate news monopolies with the production and circulation of information

in the age of the internet: Dan Gillmore, *We the Media: Grassroots Journalism by the People, for the People*. Newton, MA: O'Reilly Media, 2004).

33. In the words of an anthropologist who wrote a monograph-length study of the genre, "No village sound is more disturbing than the shrill cries announcing a death." Isabelle Clark-Decès, *No One Cries for the Dead: Tamil Dirges, Rowdy Songs, and Graveyard Petitions* (Berkeley: University of California Press. (2005), 21.

34. I am borrowing from Manual De Landa's language used to characterize Deleuze's idea of "double articulation," a concept borrowed from linguistics. Manuel De Landa, "Deleuze, Diagrams, and the Genesis of Form," *Amerikastudien/American Studies* 45, no. 1 (2000): 33–41.

35. Brian Massumi, *Parables for the Virtual: Movement, Affect, Sensation* (Durham, NC: Duke University Press, 2002), 87; Madhavi Menon, *Indifference to Difference: On Queer Universalism*. Minneapolis: University of Minnesota Press, 2015.

36. I write here in concordance with Mazzarella's critique of Massumi's valuation of the politics of immediation: William Mazzarella, "Affect: What Is It Good For?," *Enchantments of Modernity: Empire, Nation, Globalization*, ed. Saurabh Dube (New Delhi: Oxford University Press, 2009), 291–309.

37. The impossibility of society in village life is an argument from Bhimrao Ramji Ambedkar, "Philosophy of Hinduism," in *Dr. Babasaheb Ambedkar: Writings and Speeches*, vol. 3, ed. Vasant Moon (New Delhi: Dr. Ambedkar Foundation, 2014).

38. Tiziana Terranova, *Network Culture: Cultural Politics for the Information Age* (London: Pluto, 2004), 142

39. *Network Culture*, 142.

40. *Network Culture*, 144.

41. "The Day Tuticorin Burned," Citizens for Justice and Peace, July 16, 2018, is the most extensive and damning report of these events: https://cjp.org.in/the-day-tuticorin-burned/.

42. Karen Strassler, *Demanding Images: Democracy, Mediation, and the Image-Event in Indonesia* (Durham, NC: Duke University Press, 2020), 10.

43. Ravi Sundaram, "Publicity, Transparency, and the Circulation Engine: The Media Sting in India," *Current Anthropology* 56, no. S12 (2015): S297–S305.

EPILOGUE

1. On sovereignty as vulnerable to public uptake, see also Danilyn Rutherford, *Laughing at Leviathan: Sovereignty and Audience in West Papua* (Chicago: University of Chicago Press, 2012); and Sidharthan Maunaguru, "Vulnerable Sovereignty: Sovereign Deities and Tigers' Politics in Sri Lanka," *Current Anthropology* 61, no. 6 (2020): 686–712.

2. On the separation of a medium from the information that carries it in cybernetic theory, see Katherine Hayles, *How We Became Posthuman: Virtual Bodies in Cybernetics, Literature, and Informatics* (Chicago: University of Chicago Press, 1999). On the body as medium, see John Durham Peters, *The Marvelous Clouds*

Toward a Philosophy of Elemental Media (Chicago: University of Chicago Press, 2015).

3. Ravi Sundaram, "Hindu Nationalism's Crisis Machine," *HAU: Journal of Ethnographic Theory* 10, no. 3 (2020): 734–41.

4. Sundaram, "Hindu Nationalism's Crisis Machine," 735. A recent and well-documented example is the Delhi BJP leader Kapil Mishra's Twitter-driven recruitment drive for members of what he terms "team Hindu ecosystem." See Shambhavi Thakur and Meghnad Sahasrabhojanee, "Hate Factory: Inside Kapil Mishra's 'Hindu Ecosystem,'" *News Laundry*, February 15, 2021, https://www
.newslaundry.com/2021/02/15/we-infiltrated-the-telegram-groups-of-the-bjp
-leaders-online-network-to-see-what-they-do

5. See S. Ramanathan, "Why TN Journalists Are Fighting the Right-Wing Attack on Tamil TV Media," *New Minute*, July 23, 2020, https://www.thenewsminute.com
/article/why-tn-journalists-are-fighting-right-wing-attack-tamil-tv-media-129243.

6. "Madan Ravichandran's Explosive Insider Account of How Periyarists, Communists Impose Ideological Hegemony in Tamil Media," *#Swarajya*, July 11, 2020, https://swarajyamag.com/politics/madan-ravichandrans-explosive-insider
-account-of-how-periyarists-communists-impose-ideological-hegemony-in
-tamil-media.

7. I owe this insight to a conversation I had well before the Gunasekaran affair with A. S. Paneerselvan from the *Hindu* and R. Vijaya Sankar from *Frontline*, July 20, 2018.

8. On the "networkability" of the event, see Brian Massumi, *Parables for the Virtual: Movement, Affect, Sensation* (Durham, NC: Duke University Press, 2002), 87; and Tony D. Sampson, *Virality: Contagion Theory in the Age of Networks* (Minneapolis: University of Minnesota Press, 2012), 118.

9. William E. Connolly, "The Evangelical-Capitalist Resonance Machine." *Political Theory* 33, no. 6 (2005): 869–86.

10. William Mazzarella, *The Mana of Mass Society* (Chicago: University of Chicago Press, 2017).

11. For an influential definition of political engineering, see Austin Ranney, "'The Divine Science': Political Engineering in American Culture," *American Political Science Review* 70, no. 1 (1976): 140.

12. Kajri Jain, *Gods in the Time of Democracy* (Durham, NC: Duke University Press, 2021), 18.

13. Julia Carrie Wong and Hannah Ellis-Petersen, "Facebook Planned to Remove Fake Accounts in India—Until it Realized a BJP Politician Was Involved," *Guardian*, April 15, 2021, https://www.theguardian.com/technology/2021/apr/15
/facebook-india-bjp-fake-accounts.

14. See Swati Chaturvedi, 2016, *I Am a Troll: Inside the Secret World of the BJP's Digital Army* (New Delhi: Juggernaut Books, 2016); Rohit Chopra, *The Virtual Hindu Rashtra: Saffron Nationalism and New Media* (New Delhi: HarperCollins India, 2019); Sahana Udupa, "Internet Hindus: New India's Ideological Warriors," in *Handbook on Religion in Asian Cities*, ed. Peter van der Veer (Berkeley: University of California Press, 2015), 432–49.

15. On surplus populations, see Partha Chatterjee, "Democracy and Economic Transformation India," *Economic and Political Weekly* 43, no. 16 (April 19, 2008): 53–62; and Kalyan Sanyal, *Rethinking Capitalist Development: Primitive Accumulation, Governmentality and Post-Colonial Capitalism* (New Delhi: Routledge, 2007). For a thoughtful journalist account, see Snigdha Poonam, *Dreamers: How Young Indians Are Changing Their World* (New Delhi: Penguin Random House India, 2018).

16. N. Katherine Hayles, *Unthought: The Power of the Cognitive Nonconscious* (Chicago: University of Chicago Press, 2017); Mark B. N. Hansen, *Feed-Forward: On the Future of Twenty-First-Century Media* (Chicago: University of Chicago Press, 2015), 58; Sandeep Mertia, "Introduction: Relationalities Abound," in *Lives of Data: Essays on Computational Cultures from India*, ed. Sandeep Mertia (Amsterdam: Institute of Network Cultures, 2020), 16.

17. Hayles, *Unthought*, 19.

18. Hansen, *Feed-Forward*, 18–19.

19. By the same token, it is impossible to think the technological mediation of political power without the human mediator. "There is no vector without humans; there are no humans without vectors. On can't separate one from the other." McKenzie Wark, *Telesthesia: Communication, Culture, and Class* (Cambridge: Polity, 2012), 8.

20. For a powerful critique of the norm of "objectivity" in US journalism, see Lewis Raven Wallace, *The View from Somewhere: Undoing the Myth of Journalistic Objectivity* (Chicago: University of Chicago Press, 2019).

21. Hannah Arendt, "Truth and Politics," in *The Portable Hannah Arendt*, ed. Peter Baehr (New York: Penguin Books, 2000), 545–75. On journalism in "posttruth" societies, see Noelle Molé Liston, *The Truth Society: Science, Disinformation, and Politics in Berlusconi's Italy* (Ithaca, NY: Cornell University Press, 2021); and Natalia Roudakova, *Losing Pravda: Ethics and the Press in Post-Truth Russia* (Cambridge: Cambridge University Press, 2017).

22. The idea of "truthiness" is, of course, given to us by the inimitable Stephen Colbert.

23. Zeba Siddiqui, "Indian Journalists Accused of Sedition over Protest Reporting," Reuters, February 1, 2021, https://www.reuters.com/article/us-india-farms-protests-journalists-idUSKBN2A1lI8.

24. From Reporters Without Boarders' report in 2022, https://rsf.org/en/country/india. With an average of three or four journalists killed in connection with their work every year, India is one of the world's most dangerous countries for the media. Journalists are exposed to all kinds of physical violence, including police violence, ambushes by political activists, and deadly reprisals by criminal groups or corrupt local officials. Supporters of Hindutva, the ideology that spawned the Hindu far right, wage all-out online attacks on any views that conflict with their thinking. Terrifying coordinated campaigns of hatred and calls for murder are conducted on social media, campaigns that are often even more violent when they target women journalists, whose personal data may be posted online as an additional incitement to violence. The situation is also still very worrisome in Kashmir, where reporters are often harassed by police and paramilitaries, with some being subjected to so-called provisional detention for several years.

25. Prominent English-language examples include the *Wire*, *Scroll.in*, the *News Minute*, and in Tamil journalism, மின்னம்பலம் (*Minnambalam*).

26. Louise Amoore, *Cloud Ethics: Algorithms and the Attributes of Ourselves and Others* (Durham, NC: Duke University Press, 2020), 6.

27. Achille Mbembe, "Future Knowledges," Abiola Lecture, presented at the African Studies Association Annual Meetings in Washington, DC, December 1–3, 2016.

28. See Ilana Gershon, "Language and the Newness of Media," *Annual Review of Anthropology* 46 (2017): 15–31; and Lisa Gitelman, *Always Already New: Media, History, and the Data of Culture* (Cambridge, MA: MIT Press, 2008).

29. The concept of pharmacology here is derived from Derrida's reading of Plato's pharmakon as both poison and remedy: Jacques Derrida, *Dissemination*, trans. Barbara Johnson (Chicago: University of Chicago Press, 1981). See also Bernard Stiegler, *What Makes Life Worth Living: On Pharmacology* (London: Polity, 2013).

30. Stiegler, *What Makes Life Worth Living*, 2.

Bibliography

Agamben, Giorgio. *Homo sacer: Sovereign Power and Bare Life*. Stanford, CA: Stanford University Press, 1998.

Agha, Asif. "Meet Mediatization." *Language and Communication* 31, no. 3 (2011): 163–70.

Ambedkar, Bhimrao Ramji. "Philosophy of Hinduism." In *Dr. Babasaheb Ambedkar: Writings and Speeches*, vol. 3, edited by Vasant Moon. New Delhi: Dr. Ambedkar Foundation, 2014.

Amin, Shahid. "Gandhi as Mahatma: Gorakhpur District, Eastern UP, 1921–2." In *Selected Subaltern Studies*, edited by Edward Said and Gayatri Chakraborty Spivak. New York: Oxford University Press, 1987.

Amoore, Louise. *Cloud Ethics: Algorithms and the Attributes of Ourselves and Others*. Durham, NC: Duke University Press, 2020.

Anderson, Benedict. *Imagined Communities: Reflections on the Origin and Spread of Nationalism*. 2nd ed. London: Verso, 1991.

Arasu, Ponni, and Priya Thangarajah. "Queer Women and Habeas Corpus in India: The Love that Blinds the Law." *Indian Journal of Gender Studies* 19, no. 3 (2012): 413–35.

Arendt, Hannah. "Truth and Politics." In *The Portable Hannah Arendt*, edited by Peter Baehr, 545–75. New York: Penguin Books, 2000.

Arif, Yasmeen, ed. *Event and Everyday: Empiricisms and Epistemologies*. Delhi: Orient Blackswan, 2022.

Aretxaga, Begoña. "Maddening States." *Annual Review of Anthropology* 32 (2003): 393–410.

Balasubramaniam, J. *Sooriyodhayam Mudhal Udhayasooriyan Varai: Dalit Itazh-kal, 1869–1943*. Nagarcoil: Kalachuvadu, 2017.

Banerjee, Prathama. *Elementary Aspects of the Political: Histories from the Global South*. Durham, NC: Duke University Press, 2020.

Barnett, Marguerite Ross. *The Politics of Cultural Nationalism in South India*. Princeton, NJ: Princeton University Press, 1976.

Baskaran, S. Theodore. *The Message Bearers: The Nationalist Politics and the Entertainment Media in South India 1880–1845*. Madras: Cre-A, 1981.

Bataille, Georges. *The Tears of Eros*. San Francisco, CA: City Lights Press, 1989.

Bate, Bernard. *Protestant Textuality and the Tamil Modern: Political Oratory and the Social Imaginary on South Asia*, edited by E. Annamalai, Francis Cody, Constantine Nakassis, and Malarvizhi Jayanth. Stanford, CA: Stanford University Press, 2021.

———. *Tamil Oratory and the Dravidian Aesthetic: Democratic Practice in South India*. New York: Columbia University Press, 2009.

Baudrillard, Jean. "Toward a Critique of the Political Economy of the Sign." Translated by Carl R. Lovitt and Denise Klopsch. *SubStance* 5, no. 15 (1976): 111–16

Bauman, Richard. "Projecting Presence: Aura and Oratory in William Jennings Bryan's Presidential Races." In *Scale: Discourse and Dimensions of Social Life*, edited by Somerson Carr and Michael Lempert, 25–51. Berkeley: University of California Press, 2016.

Baxi, Pratiksha. "Habeas Corpus in the Realm of Love: Litigating Marriages of Choice in India." *Australian Feminist Law Journal* 25, no. 1 (2006): 59–78.

———. "Introduction: Picturing Sociological Scenes—Social Life of Law in India." *Contributions to Indian Sociology* 53, no. 1 (2019): 1–18.

———. *Public Secrets of Law: Rape Trials in India*. New Delhi: Oxford University Press, 2014.

Baxi, Upendra. "Judicial Discourse: Dialectics of the Face and the Mask." *Journal of the Indian Law Institute* 35, no. 1/2 (1993): 1–12.

Benveniste, Émile. *Problems in General Linguistics*. Miami: University of Miami Press, 1971.

Berlant, Lauren. *The Anatomy of National Fantasy: Hawthorne, Utopia, and Everyday Life*. Chicago: University of Chicago Press, 1991.

———. *Cruel Optimism*. Durham, NC: Duke University Press, 2011.

Bhatia, Gautam. *Offend, Shock, or Disturb: Free Speech under the Indian Constitution*. New Delhi: Oxford University Press, 2016

Biehl, João, and Peter Locke. "Deleuze and the Anthropology of Becoming." *Current Anthropology* 51, no. 3 (2010): 317–51. https://doi.org/10.1086/651466.

Bishara, Amahl. *Back Stories: US News Production and Palestinian Politics*. Stanford, CA: Stanford University Press, 2012.

——. "Watching U.S. Television from the Palestinian Street: The Media, the State, and Representational Interventions." *Cultural Anthropology* 23, no. 3 (2008): 488–530. https://doi.org/10.1111/j.1548-1360.2008.00016.x.

Bolter, Jay David, and Richard Grusin. *Remediation: Understanding New Media*. Cambridge, MA: MIT Press, 2000.

Bonilla, Yarimar, and Jonathan Rosa. "#Ferguson: Digital Protest, Hashtag Ethnography, and the Racial Politics of Social Media in the United States." *American Ethnologist* 42, no. 1 (2015): 4–17.

Bourdieu, Pierre. "The Force of Law: Toward a Sociology of the Juridical Field." *Hastings Law Journal* 38 (1986): 814–53.

boyd, danah. "Social Network Sites as Networked Publics: Affordances, Dynamics, and Implications." In *Networked Self: Identity, Community, and Culture on Social Network Sites*, edited by Zizi Papacharissi, 39–58. New York: Routledge, 2010.

Boyer, Dominic. *The Life Informatic: Newsmaking in the Digital Era*. Ithaca, NY: Cornell University Press, 2013.

Briggs, Charles L. "Communicability, Racial Discourse, and Disease." *Annual Review of Anthropology* 34 (2005): 269–91.

Brown, Wendy. *States of Injury: Power and Freedom in Late Modernity*. Princeton, NJ: Princeton University Press, 1995.

Browne, Simone. *Dark Matters: On the Surveillance of Blackness*. Durham, NC: Duke University Press, 2015.

Buck-Morss, Susan. *Dreamworld and Catastrophe: The Passing of Mass Utopia in East and West*. Cambridge, MA: MIT Press, 2002.

Butler, Judith. *Excitable Speech: A Politics of the Performative*. New York: Routledge, 1997.

——. *Notes toward a Performative Theory of Assembly*. Cambridge, MA: Harvard University Press, 2015.

Chakrabarty, Dipesh. "'In the Name of Politics': Democracy and the Power of the Multitude in India." *Public Culture* 19, no. 1 (2007): 35–57.

Chakravartty, Paula, and Srirupa Roy. "Mediatized Populisms: Inter-Asian Lineages; Introduction." *International Journal of Communication* 11 (2017): 4073–92.

——. "Media Pluralism Redux: Towards New Frameworks of Comparative Media Studies 'Beyond the West.'" *Political Communication* 30, no. 3 (2013): 349–70.

Chatterjee, Partha. "Democracy and Economic Transformation in India." *Economic and Political Weekly* 43, no. 16 (April 19, 2008): 53–62.

————. *I Am the People: Reflections on Popular Sovereignty Today*. New York: Columbia University Press, 2019.

————. *The Nation and Its Fragments: Colonial and Postcolonial Histories*. Princeton, NJ: Princeton University Press, 1993.

————. *The Politics of the Governed: Reflections on Popular Politics in Most of the World*. New York: Columbia University Press, 2004.

Chaturvedi, Swati. *I Am a Troll: Inside the Secret World of the BJP's Digital Army*. New Delhi: Juggernaut Books, 2016.

Chopra, Rohit. *The Virtual Hindu Rashtra: Saffron Nationalism and New Media*. New Delhi: HarperCollins India, 2019.

Chowdhury, Nusrat Sabina. *Paradoxes of the Popular: Crowd Politics in Bangladesh*. Stanford, CA: Stanford University Press, 2019.

Clark-Decès, Isabelle. *No One Cries for the Dead: Tamil Dirges, Rowdy Songs, and Graveyard Petitions*. Berkeley: University of California Press, 2005.

Cody, Francis. "Daily Wires and Daily Blossoms: Cultivating Regimes of Circulation in Tamil India's Newspaper Revolution." *Journal of Linguistic Anthropology* 19, no. 2 (2009): 286–309.

————. "Echoes of the Teashop in a Tamil Newspaper." *Language and Communication* 31, no. 3 (2011): 243–54.

————. "Metamorphoses of Popular Sovereignty: Cinema, Short Circuits, and Digitalization in Tamil India." *Anthropological Quarterly* 93, no. 2 (Spring 2020): 57–88.

————. "Millennial Turbulence: The Networking of Tamil Media Politics." *Television and New Media* 21, no. 4 (2020): 392–406.

————. "Populist Publics: Print Capitalism and Crowd Violence beyond Liberal Frameworks." *Comparative Studies of South Asia, Africa and the Middle East* 35, no. 1 (2015): 50–65.

————. "Publics and Politics." *Annual Review of Anthropology* 40 (2011): 37-52.

————. "Wave Theory: Cash, Crowds, and Caste in Indian Elections." *American Ethnologist* 47, no. 4 (2020): 402–16.

Connolly, William E. "The Evangelical-Capitalist Resonance Machine." *Political Theory* 33, no. 6 (2005): 869–86.

Cover, Robert M. "Foreword: Nomos and Narrative." *Harvard Law Review* 97, no. 4 (1983):4 68.

Das, Veena. *Critical Events: An Anthropological Perspective on Contemporary India*. New Delhi: Oxford University Press, 1995.

————. *Life and Words: Violence and the Descent into the Ordinary*. Berkeley: University of California Press, 2007.

———. "Specificities: Official Narratives, Rumour, and the Social Production of Hate." *Social Identities* 4, no 1 (1998): 109–30.

Das, Veena, and Deborah Poole. "State and Its Margins: Comparative Ethnographies." In *Anthropology in the Margins of the State*, edited by Veena Das and Deborah Poole, 3–33. Santa Fe, NM: School of Advanced Research, 2004.

Dayan, Daniel, and Elihu Katz. *Media Events: The Live Broadcasting of History*. Cambridge, MA: Harvard University Press, 1992.

Dean, Jodi. *Democracy and Other Neoliberal Fantasies: Communicative Capitalism and Left Politics*. Durham, NC: Duke University Press, 2009.

———. *Publicity's Secret: How Technoculture Capitalizes on Democracy*. Ithaca, NY: Cornell University Press, 2002.

Debord, Guy. *Comments on the Society of the Spectacle*. Translated by Malcolm Imrie. London: Verso, 1998.

De Landa, Manuel. "Deleuze, Diagrams, and the Genesis of Form." *Amerikastudien/American Studies* 45, no. 1 (2000): 33–41.

Derrida, Jacques. *Dissemination*. Translated by Barbara Johnson. Chicago: University of Chicago Press, 1981.

———. "Force de loi: Le fondement mystique de l'autorite." *Cardozo Law Review* 11, no. 5/6 (1990): 920–1046.

Dhavan, Rajeev. "On the Law of the Press in India." *Journal of the Indian Law Institute* 26, no. 3 (1984): 288–332.

———. *Publish and Be Damned: Censorship and Intolerance in India*. New Delhi: Tulika Books, 2008.

Doane, Mary Ann. "Information, Crisis, Catastrophe." In *Logics of Television: Essays in Cultural Criticism*, edited by Meaghan Morris, 222–39. Bloomington: Indiana University Press, 1990.

Doron, Assa, and Robin Jeffrey. *The Great Indian Phone Book*. Cambridge, MA: Harvard University Press, 2013.

Esser, Frank, and Jesper Strömbäck, eds. *Mediatization of Politics: Understanding the Transformation of Western Democracies*. New York: Springer, 2014.

Feeley, Malcolm M. *The Process Is the Punishment: Handling Cases in a Lower Criminal Court*. New York: Russell Sage Foundation, 1979.

Fisher, Daniel. *The Voice and Its Doubles: Media and Music in Northern Australia*. Durham, NC: Duke University Press, 2016.

Foucault, Michel. "Questions of Method." In *Power: Essential Works of Foucault, 1954–1984*, vol. 3, edited by James Faubian, 223–38. New York: New Press, 2000.

Fraser, Nancy. "Rethinking the Public Sphere: A Contribution to the Critique of Actually Existing Democracy." *Social Text*, no. 25/26 (1990): 56–80.

Gershon, Ilana. "Language and the Newness of Media." *Annual Review of Anthropology* 46 (2017): 15–31.

Gillmor, Dan. *We the Media: Grassroots Journalism by the People, for the People.* Newton, MA: O'Reilly Media, 2004.

Gitelman, Lisa. *Always Already New: Media, History, and the Data of Culture.* Cambridge, MA: MIT Press, 2008.

Goffman, Erving. "Footing." *Semiotica* 25, no. 1/2 (1979): 1–30.

Goodrich, Peter. "Imago Decidendi: On the Common Law of Images." *Art and Law* 1, no. 1 (2017): 1–57.

Gopal, Nakkīran. *Challenge*. Chennai: Nakkheeran, 1998.

———. *Nānum Vīrappanum!* Chennai: Nakkheeran, 2004.

———. *Yuththam.* Chennai: Nakkheeran, 2011.

Gorringe, Hugo. "'Banal Violence'? The Everyday Underpinnings of Collective Violence." *Identities: Global Studies in Culture and Power* 13, no. 2 (2006): 237–60.

———. "Party Political Panthers: Hegemonic Tamil Politics and the Dalit Challenge." *South Asia Multidisciplinary Academic Journal* 5 (2011). https://doi.org/10.4000/samaj.3224.

———. *Untouchable Citizens: Dalit Movements and Democratisation in Tamil Nadu.* New Delhi: Sage, 2005.

Guha, Ranajit. *Elementary Aspects of Peasant Insurgency.* New Delhi: Oxford University Press, 1983.

Gürsel, Zeynep Devrim. *Image Brokers: Visualizing World News in the Age of Digital Circulation.* Berkeley: University of California Press, 2016.

———. "Visualizing Publics: Digital Crowd Shots and the 2015 Unity Rally in Paris." *Current Anthropology* 58, no. S15 (2017): S135–S48. https://doi.org/10.1086/689742.

Habermas, Jürgen. "Popular Sovereignty as Procedure." In *Deliberative Democracy: Essays on Reason and Politics,* edited by James Bohman and William Rehg. Cambridge, MA: MIT Press, 1997.

———. *The Structural Transformation of the Public Sphere: An Inquiry into a Category of Bourgeois Society.* Translated by Thomas Burger. Cambridge, MA: MIT Press, 1991.

Hall, Stuart. "Encoding and Decoding in the Television Discourse." Stenciled paper presented at the Centre for Contemporary Cultural Studies, University of Birmingham, September 1, 1973.

———. "The Problem of Ideology-Marxism without Guarantees." *Journal of Communication Inquiry* 10, no. 2 (1986): 28–44.

Handelman, Don. *Models and Mirrors: Towards an Anthropology of Public Events.* Cambridge: Cambridge University Press, 1990.

Hansen, Mark B. N. *Feed-Forward: On the Future of Twenty-First-Century Media.* Chicago: University of Chicago Press, 2015.

———. "Ubiquitous Sensation or the Autonomy of the Peripheral: Towards an Atmospheric, Impersonal, and Microtemporal Media." In *Throughout: Art and Culture Emerging with Ubiquitous Computing,* edited by Ulrik Ekman, 63–88. Cambridge, MA: MIT Press, 2012.

Hansen, Thomas Blom. "Democracy against the Law: Reflections on India's Illiberal Democracy." In *Majoritarian State: How Hindu Nationalism Is Changing India,* edited by Angana P. Chatterji, Christophe Jaffrelot, and Thomas Blom Hansen, 19–40. London: Hurst, 2019.

———. *The Saffron Wave: Democracy and Hindu Nationalism in Modern India.* Princeton, NJ: Princeton University Press, 1999.

———. *Wages of Violence: Naming and Identity in Postcolonial Bombay.* Princeton, NJ: Princeton University Press, 2001.

Hardt, Michael, and Antonio Negri. *Assembly.* New York: Oxford University Press, 2017.

Hayles, N. Katherine. *How We Became Posthuman Virtual Bodies in Cybernetics, Literature, and Informatics.* Chicago: University of Chicago Press, 1999.

———. *Unthought: The Power of the Cognitive Nonconscious.* Chicago: University of Chicago Press, 2017.

Hiltebeitel, Alf. *Dharma: Its Early History in Law, Religion, and Narrative.* Oxford: Oxford University Press, 2011.

Hobsbawm, Eric J. *Primitive Rebels: Studies in Archaic Forms of Social Movement in the 19th and 20th Centuries.* Manchester: Manchester University Press, 1959.

Hui, Yuk. *The Question Concerning Technology in China: An Essay in Cosmotechnics.* Cambridge, MA. MIT Press, 2016.

Jacob, Alice. *Violation of Journalistic Ethics and Public Taste: A Compendium of Adjudications Rendered by the Press Council of India.* Bombay: N. M. Tripathi, 1984.

Jaffrelot, Christophe. *India's Silent Revolution: The Rise of the Lower Castes in North India.* Delhi: Permanent Black, 2003.

Jagoda, Patrick. *Network Aesthetics.* Chicago: University of Chicago Press, 2016.

Jain, Kajri. *Gods in the Bazaar: The Economies of Indian Calendar Art.* Durham, NC: Duke University Press, 2007.

———. "Gods in the Time of Automobility." *Current Anthropology* 58, no. S15 (2017): S13–S26. https://doi.org/10.1086/688696.

———. *Gods in the Time of Democracy.* Durham, NC: Duke University Press, 2021.

Jeffrey, Robin. *India's Newspaper Revolution: Capitalism, Politics, and the Indian Language Press, 1977–99.* Oxford: Oxford University Press, 2000.

Juris, Jeffrey S. "The New Digital Media and Activist Networking within Anti Corporate Globalization Movements." *Annals of the American Academy of Political and Social Science* 59, no. 1 (2005): 189–208.

Kaur, Raminder. "The Digitalia of Everyday Life: Multi-situated Anthropology of a Virtual Letter by a 'Foreign Hand.'" *HAU: Journal of Ethnographic Theory* 9, no. 2 (2019): 299–319.

———. *Kudankulam: The Story of an Indo-Russian Nuclear Power Plant.* Oxford: Oxford University Press, 2020.

Keane, Webb. *Signs of Recognition: Powers and Hazards of Representation in an Indonesian Society.* Berkeley: University of California Press, 1997.

Krishnan, Rajan. "Rajini's Sivaji: Screen and Sovereign." *Economic and Political Weekly* 42, no. 27/28 (July 14–20, 2007): 2861–63.

———. "When Kathavarayan Spoke His Mind: The Intricate Dynamics of the Formations of the Political through Film-Making Practices in Tamil Nadu." In *New Cultural Histories of India: Materiality and Practices*, edited by Partha Chatterjee, Tapati Guha-Thakurta, and Bodhisattva Kar, 223–45. Delhi: Oxford University Press, 2014.

Kumar, Anup. *The Making of a Small State: Populist Social Mobilisation and the Hindi Press in the Uttarakhand Movement.* Hyderabad: Orient Blackswan, 2011.

Kumar, Ravish. "Welcome to Eventocracy, Tracked by Comedia." *Indian Express.* December 31, 2016.

Kumar, Vijay. *Veerappan: Chasing the Brigand.* New Delhi: Rupa, 2017.

Kumar, Virendra, ed. *Committees and Commissions in India.* Vol. 14, *1976.* New Delhi: Concept, 1993.

Kunreuther, Laura. *Voicing Subjects: Public Intimacy and Mediation in Kathmandu.* Berkeley: University of California Press, 2014.

Laclau, Ernesto. *On Populist Reason.* London: Verso, 2005.

Lefort, Claude. "The Image of the Body and Totalitarianism." In *The Political Forms of Modern Society: Bureaucracy, Democracy, Totalitarianism*, 292–306. Cambridge, MA: MIT Press, 1986.

Liang, Lawrence. "Media's Law: From Representation to Affect." *BioScope: South Asian Screen Studies* 2, no. 1 (2011): 23–40.

———. "Reasonable Restrictions and Unreasonable Speech." In *Sarai Reader 4: Crisis/Media*, edited by Monica Narula, Shuddhabrata Sengupta, Ravi Sundaram, Ravi S. Vasudevan, Awadhanedra Sharan, Jeebesh Bagchi, and Geert Lovink, 434–40. New Delhi: Autonomedia, 2004.

Liston, Noelle Molé. *The Truth Society: Science, Disinformation, and Politics in Berlusconi's Italy.* Ithaca, NY: Cornell University Press, 2021.

Luhmann, Niklas. *The Reality of the Mass Media*. Stanford, CA: Stanford University Press, 2000.

Mankekar, Purnima. *Screening Culture, Viewing Politics: An Ethnography of Television, Womanhood, and Nation in Postcolonial India*. Durham, NC: Duke University Press, 1999.

Marwick, Alice E. "Instafame: Luxury Selfies in the Attention Economy," *Public Culture* 27, no. 1 (2015): 137–60.

Massumi, Brian. *Parables for the Virtual: Movement, Affect, Sensation*. Durham, NC: Duke University Press, 2002.

Maunaguru, Sidharthan. "Vulnerable Sovereignty: Sovereign Deities and Tigers' Politics in Sri Lanka," *Current Anthropology* 61, no. 6 (2020): 686–712.

Mazzarella, William. "Affect: What Is It Good For?" In *Enchantments of Modernity: Empire, Nation, Globalization*, edited by Saurabh Dube, 291–309. New Delhi: Oxford University Press, 2009.

———. "The Anthropology of Populism: Beyond the Liberal Settlement." *Annual Review of Anthropology* 48, no. 1 (2019): 45–60.

———. "Beautiful Balloon: The Digital Divide and the Charisma of New Media in India." *American Ethnologist* 37, no. 4 (2010): 783–804.

———. *Censorium: Cinema and the Open Edge of Mass Publicity*. Durham, NC: Duke University Press, 2013.

———. "Culture, Globalization, Mediation." *Annual Review of Anthropology* 33, no. 1 (2004): 345–67.

———. *The Mana of Mass Society*. Chicago: University of Chicago Press, 2017.

———. "The Myth of the Multitude, or, Who's Afraid of the Crowd?" *Critical Inquiry* 36, no. 4 (2010): 697–727.

Mazzarella, William, and Raminder Kaur. "Between Sedition and Seduction: Thinking Censorship in South Asia." In *Censorship in South Asia: Cultural Regulation from Sedition to Seduction*, edited by Raminder Kaur and William Mazzarella. Bloomington: Indiana University Press, 2009.

Mbembe, Achille. "Future Knowledges." Abiola Lecture, presented at the African Studies Association Annual Meetings in Washington, DC, December 1–3, 2016.

McCormack, Derek P. "Elemental Infrastructures for Atmospheric Media: On Stratospheric Variations, Value and the Commons." *Environment and Planning D: Society and Space* 35, no. 3 (2017): 418–37.

Mehta, Nalin. *Behind a Billion Screens: What Television Tells Us about Modern India*. New Delhi: HarperCollins India, 2015.

Meinert, Lotte, and Bruce Kapferer, eds. *In the Event: Toward an Anthropology of Generic Moments*. New York: Berghahn Books, 2015.

Menon, Madhavi. *Indifference to Difference: On Queer Universalism*. Minneapolis: University of Minnesota Press, 2015.

Menon, Nivedita. Introduction to *Empire and Nation: Selected Essays*, by Partha Chatterjee, 1–22. New York: Columbia University Press, 2010.

Mertia, Sandeep. "Introduction: Relationalities Abound." In *Lives of Data: Essays on Computational Cultures from India*, edited by Sandeep Mertia. Amsterdam: Institute of Network Cultures, 2020.

Mitchell, Lisa. *Language, Emotion, and Politics in South India: The Making of a Mother Tongue*. Bloomington: Indiana University Press, 2009.

Morris, Rosalind C. "Populist Politics in Asian Networks: Positions for Rethinking the Question of Political Subjectivity." *Positions: East Asia Cultures Critique* 20, no. 1 (2012): 37–65.

———. "Theses on the New Öffentlichkeit." *Grey Room* 51 (2013): 94–111.

Moulier-Boutang, Yann. *Cognitive Capitalism*. London: Polity, 2011.

Nakassis, Constantine V. "Brands and Their Surfeits." *Cultural Anthropology*, 28, no. 1 (2013): 111–26.

Neyazi, Taberez Ahmed. *Political Communication and Mobilisation: The Hindi Media in India*. Cambridge: Cambridge University Press, 2018.

Ngai, Sianne. *Ugly Feelings*. Cambridge, MA: Harvard University Press, 2005.

Ninan, Sevanti. *Headlines from the Heartland: Reinventing the Hindi Public Sphere*. Los Angeles: Sage, 2007.

Nora, Pierre. "Monster Events." *Discourse* 5, no. 1 (1983): 5–20.

Ochigame, Rodrigo, and James Holston. "Filtering Dissent: Social Media and Land Struggles in Brazil." *New Left Review* 99 (2016): 85–108.

Padmanabhan, R. A. *Tamil Itazhkal, 1915–1966*. Nagercoil: Kalachuvadu, 2003.

Pandian, Anand. *Reel World: An Anthropology of Creation*. Durham, NC: Duke University Press, 2015.

Pandian, M. S. S. *The Image Trap: M.G. Ramachandran in Film and Politics*. New Delhi: Sage, 1992.

———. "The Moral World of 'Sandalwood' Veerappan." *Economic and Political Weekly* 34, no. 52 (December 25–31, 1999): 3659–60

Panneerselvan, A. S. "My Days at Sun TV." In *21st Century Journalism in India*, edited by Nalini Rajan. New Delhi: Sage Publications, 2007.

Parthasarathy, Rangaswami. *A Hundred Years of* The Hindu: *The Epic Story of Indian Nationalism*. Madras: Kasturi and Sons, 1978.

Pateman, Carole. *The Sexual Contract*. London: Polity, 1988.

Peters, John Durham. *The Marvelous Clouds: Toward a Philosophy of Elemental Media*. Chicago: University of Chicago Press, 2015.

Poonam, Snigdha. *Dreamers: How Young Indians Are Changing Their World*. New Delhi: Penguin Random House India, 2018.

Postman, Neil. "The Humanism of Media Ecology." *Proceedings of the Media Ecology Association* 1, no. 1 (2000): 10–16.

Prasad, M. Madhava. *Cine-Politics: Film Stars and Political Existence in South India*. Hyderabad: Orient Blackswan, 2014.

———. "Where Does the Forest Begin?" *Economic and Political Weekly* 35, no. 47 (November 18, 2000): 4138–40.

Rafael, Vicente L. "The Cell Phone and the Crowd: Messianic Politics in the Contemporary Philippines." *Public Culture* 15, no. 3 (2003): 399–425.

Rajagopal, Arvind. *Politics after Television: Religious Nationalism and the Reshaping of the Indian Public*. Cambridge: Cambridge University Press, 2001.

———. "Putting America in Its Place." *Public Culture* 25, no. 3 (2013): 387–99.

Ramaswamy, Sumathi. "The Nation, the Region, and the Adventures of a Tamil Hero." *Contributions to Indian Sociology* 28, no. 2 (1994): 295–322.

———. *Passions of the Tongue: Language Devotion in Tamil India, 1891–1970*. Berkeley: University of California Press, 1997.

Ramnath, Kalyani. "The Runaway Judgment: Law as Literature, Courtcraft and Constitutional Visions." *Journal of Indian Law and Society* 3 (2011): 1–28.

Ranney, Austin. "'The Divine Science': Political Engineering in American Culture." *American Political Science Review* 70, no. 1 (1976): 140–48.

Rao, Anupama. *The Caste Question: Dalits and the Politics of Modern India*. Berkeley: University of California Press, 2009.

Rao, Ursula. *News as Culture: Journalistic Practices and the Remaking of Indian Leadership Traditions*. New York: Berghahn Books, 2010.

Rao, Velcheru Narayana, and Sanjay Subrahmanyam. "Notes on Political Thought in Medieval and Early Modern South India." *Modern Asian Studies* 43, no. 1 (2009): 175–210.

Razsa, Maple, and Andrej Kurnik. "The Occupy Movement in Žižek's Hometown: Direct Democracy and a Politics of Becoming." *American Ethnologist* 39, no. 2 (2012): 238–58.

Richland, Justin B. "Jurisdiction: Grounding Law in Language." *Annual Review of Anthropology* 42 (2013): 209–26.

Roudakova, Natalia. *Losing Pravda: Ethics and the Press in Post-Truth Russia*. Cambridge: Cambridge University Press, 2017.

Rusbridger, Alan. *Breaking News: The Remaking of Journalism and Why It Matters Now*. New York: Farrar, Straus and Giroux, 2018.

Rutherford, Danilyn. *Laughing at Leviathan: Sovereignty and Audience in West Papua.* Chicago: University of Chicago Press, 2012.

Sadasivan, Doraisami. *The Growth of Public Opinion in the Madras Presidency, 1858–1909.* Madras: University of Madras, 1974.

Samet, Robert. *Deadline: Populism and the Press in Venezuela.* Chicago: University of Chicago Press, 2019.

Sami, A. M. *Italālar Ātittanār.* Chennai: International Institute of Tamil Studies, 1990.

Sampson, Tony D. *Virality: Contagion Theory in the Age of Networks.* Minneapolis: University of Minnesota Press, 2012.

Sanyal, Kalyan. *Rethinking Capitalist Development: Primitive Accumulation, Governmentality and Post-Colonial Capitalism.* New Delhi: Routledge, 2007.

Schiller, Naomi. *Channeling the State: Community Media and Popular Politics in Venezuela.* Durham, NC: Duke University Press, 2018.

Schudson, Michael. *The Power of News.* Cambridge, MA: Harvard University Press, 1995.

Scott, J. Barton. "How to Defame a God: Public Selfhood in the Maharaj Libel Case." *South Asia: Journal of South Asian Studies* 38, no. 3 (2015): 387–402.

Senani, Krubakar, and S. R. Ramakrishna. *Birds, Beasts and Bandits: 14 Days with Veerappan.* New Delhi: Penguin Books, 2011.

Shankar, Auto. *Auto Shankarin Marana Vākkumūlam.* Chennai: Nakheeran, 2002.

Sharafi, Mitra. *Law and Identity in Colonial South Asia: Parsi Legal Culture, 1772–1947.* Cambridge: Cambridge University Press, 2014.

Shulman, David. "On South Indian Bandits and Kings." *Indian Economic and Social History Review* 17, no. 3 (1980): 283–306.

Silverstein, Michael, and Greg Urban, eds. *Natural Histories of Discourse.* Chicago: University of Chicago Press, 1996.

Singh, Anushka. *Sedition in Liberal Democracies.* New Delhi: Oxford University Press, 2018.

Sivaraman, Mythili. *Haunted by Fire: Essays on Caste, Class, Exploitation, and Emancipation.* New Delhi: LeftWord Books, 2013.

Sivasankar, S. S. *Jallikattu Pōrāttam.* Chennai: Kizhakku Patippaham, 2017.

Srinivas, S. V. *Politics as Performance: A Social History of the Telugu Cinema.* Ranikhet: Permanent Black, 2013.

Srinivasan, Perundevi. "Love Meets Death: 'Honor,' Violence, and Inter-Caste Marriages in Tamil Nadu." Chicago Tamil Forum: Poesis/Politics of Language and Place in Tamilagam, Chicago, May 25–27, 2017. Version 6.1.2017.

Ståhlberg, Per. *Lucknow Daily: How a Hindi Newspaper Constructs Society.* Stockholm: Stockholm Studies in Social Anthropology, 2002.

Steffen, Megan, ed. *Crowds: Ethnographic Encounters*. London: Bloomsbury Academic, 2020.

Stiegler, Bernard. *Technics and Time, 1: The Fault of Epimetheus*. Translated by Richard Beardsworth and George Collins. Stanford, CA: Stanford University Press, 1998.

———. *Technics and Time, 2: Disorientation*. Translated by Stephen Barker. Stanford, CA: Stanford University Press, 2009.

———. "Telecracy against Democracy." *Cultural Politics* 6, no. 2 (2010): 171–80.

———. *What Makes Life Worth Living: On Pharmacology*. London: Polity, 2013.

Strassler, Karen. *Demanding Images: Democracy, Mediation, and the Image-Event in Indonesia*. Durham, NC: Duke University Press, 2020.

Subramanian, Narendra. *Ethnicity and Populist Mobilization: Political Parties, Citizens, and Democracy in South India*. New Delhi: Oxford University Press, 1999.

Sumiala, Johanna Maaria, Katja Valaskivi, and Daniel Dayan. "From Media Events to Expressive Events: An Interview with Daniel Dayan." *Television and New Media* 19, no. 2 (2018): 177–87.

Sundar, Swapna. *Occupy Marina!* Chennai: Emerald, 2017.

Sundaram, Ravi. "Hindu Nationalism's Crisis Machine." *HAU: Journal of Ethnographic Theory* 10, no. 3 (2020): 734–41.

———. "Introduction: The Horizon of Media Studies." In *No Limits: Media Studies from India*, edited by Ravi Sundaram, 1–18. New Delhi: Oxford University Press, 2013.

———. *Pirate Modernity: Delhi's Media Urbanism*. New York: Routledge, 2009.

———. "Publicity, Transparency, and the Circulation Engine: The Media Sting in India." *Current Anthropology* 56, no. S12 (2015): S297–S305.

Sundaramoorthy, E., and M. R. Arasu, eds. *Tiravita Iyakka Italkal*. Chennai: International Institute of Tamil Studies, 2008.

Tambar, Kabir. "Secular Populism and the Semiotics of the Crowd in Turkey." *Public Culture* 21, no. 3 (2009): 517–37.

Tambiah, Stanley Jeyaraja. *Leveling Crowds: Ethnonationalist Conflicts and Collective Violence in South Asia*. Berkeley: University of California Press, 1996.

Tarde, Gabriel. "The Public and the Crowd." In *Gabriel Tarde on Communication and Social Influence: Selected Papers*, edited by Terry N. Clark, translated by Morris Janowitz, 277–94. Chicago: University of Chicago Press, 1969.

Temple, Katheryn. *Scandal Nation: Law and Authorship in Britain, 1750–1835*. Ithaca, NY: Cornell University Press, 2003.

Terranova, Tiziana. *Network Culture: Cultural Politics for the Information Age*. London: Pluto, 2004.

Thakurta, Paranjoy Guha. "What Future for the Media in India? Reliance Takeover of Network18." *Economic and Political Weekly* 49, no. 25 (2014): 12–14.

Tiwary, Ishita. "Unsettling News: Newstrack and the Video Event," *Culture Machine* 19 (2020). https://culturemachine.net/vol-19-media-populism/unsettling-news-newstrack-and-the-video-event-ishita-tiwary/.

Tufekci, Zeynep. *Twitter and Teargas: The Power and Fragility of Networked Protest*. New Haven, CT: Yale University Press, 2017.

Udupa, Sahana. "*Gaali* Cultures: The Politics of Abusive Exchange on Social Media." *New Media and Society* 8, no. 2 (2017): 187–206.

———. "Internet Hindus: New India's Ideological Warriors." In *Handbook on Religion in Asian Cities*, edited by Peter van der Veer, 432–49. Berkeley: University of California Press, 2015.

Udupa, Sahana, Iginio Gagliardone, and Peter Hervik, eds. *Digital Hate: The Global Conjuncture of Extreme Speech*. Bloomington: Indiana University Press, 2021.

Vaid, Minnie. *The Ant in the Ear of an Elephant*. New Delhi: Rajpal and Sons, 2016.

Venkatakchalapathy, A. R. "Munnurai." In *Cenrupōna Nātkal*, edited by A. R. Venkatakchalapathy, 11–36. Nagercoil: Kalachuvadu, 2015.

Venkatraman, Shriram. *Social Media in South India*. London: University College London Press, 2017.

Virilio, Paul. *The Lost Dimension*. Translated by Daniel Moshenberg. Los Angeles: Semiotext(e), 1991.

Vismann, Cornelia. "Tele-Tribunals: Anatomy of a Medium." *Grey Room* 10 (2003): 5–21.

Wallace, Lewis Raven. *The View from Somewhere: Undoing the Myth of Journalistic Objectivity*. Chicago: University of Chicago Press, 2019.

Wark, McKenzie. *Telesthesia: Communication, Culture, and Class*. London: Polity, 2012.

———. *Virtual Geography: Living with Global Media Events*. Bloomington, IN: Indiana University Press, 1994.

Warner, Michael. "The Mass Public and the Mass Subject." In *Habermas and the Public Sphere*, edited by Craig J. Calhoun, 377–401. Cambridge, MA: MIT Press, 1992.

———. "Publics and Counterpublics." *Public Culture* 14, no. 1 (2002): 49–90.

Weidman, Amanda. *Brought to Life by the Voice: Playback Singing and Cultural Politics in South India*. Oakland: University of California Press, 2021.

Weisman, Eyal. *Forensic Architecture: Violence at the Threshold of Detectability*. New York: Zone Books, 2017.

Winegar, Jessica. "The Privilege of Revolution: Gender, Class, Space, and Affect in Egypt." *American Ethnologist* 39, no. 1 (2012): 67–70.

Yadav, Yogendra. "Understanding the Second Democratic Upsurge." In *Transforming India: Social and Political Dynamics of Democracy*, edited by Francine Frankel, R. Z. Hasan, and Rajiv Bhargav, 120–45. Oxford: Oxford University Press, 2000.

Yeh, Rihan. *Passing: Two Publics in a Mexican Border City*. Chicago: University of Chicago Press, 2018.

Yengde, Suraj. *Caste Matters*. New Delhi: Viking Press, 2019.

Zuboff, Shoshana. *The Age of Surveillance Capitalism: The Fight for a Human Future at the New Frontier of Power*. New York: Public Affairs, 2018.

Index

Page numbers in italics refer to figures.